consists of the worship of local deities, often malevolent, who control illness and accident, and therefore serve a significant, pragmatic function in village society.

Morris E. Opler's essay examines the ways in which religious practices link individuals to culture and culture to individuals by means of particularization and generalization. John J. Gumperz sees religious drama in North India as a means of communication among a diverse population. Alan R. Beals shows how social conflict and secular interaction take place under the auspices of religious ceremony in a South Indian region.

Priests and shamans are seen by Gerald D. Berreman as exemplifying two main divisions in the religion of the Pahari of the Himalayas. Pauline Mahar Kolenda finds that sweepers (untouchables) interpret scriptural theory to suit their needs rather than in a more literal, universal way. Both Michael M. Ames and Nur Yalman give structural analyses of Sinhalese Buddhism: Ames describes the role of magical-animism in the system, while Yalman looks for underlying motifs in its healing rituals.

The last paper is by Edward B. Harper, editor of the volume and associate professor of anthropology at the University of Washington. He deals with two of the major aspects of Hindu religious practice—the concepts of purity and pollution—and concludes the book with an examination of the relation of religious practice and belief to social structure.

Written by some of America's most eminent scholars of South Asian civilization, the papers in this book were first presented at a conference on Religion in South Asia at the University of California. Edited and with much new material added, they were published in a special supplementary issue of the *Journal of Asian Studies*, and now they have been collected in this book so that students and scholars as well as readers interested in religion and Asian culture may have access to them.

RELIGION IN SOUTH ASIA

RELIGION IN SOUTH ASIA

Edited by EDWARD B. HARPER

UNIVERSITY OF WASHINGTON PRESS SEATTLE 1964

Library of Congress Catalog Card Number 64-23197
Printed in the United States of America

Contents

RELIGION IN SOUTH ASIA

Editor's Preface

THE papers which constitute this volume originated from the Conference on Religion in South Asia, held on the University of California campus in Berkeley in August 1961. The idea of such a conference was suggested to me by McKim Marriott and Richard L. Park, and the generous financial support of the Committee on South Asia of the Association for Asian Studies, Inc., and the Center for South Asian Studies of the Institute of International Studies of the University of California made this five-day conference possible.

It was run informally, with the papers distributed to participants in advance. Approximately half of our working time was spent in discussing the papers, the other half in discussing general methods and problems relating to religion in South Asia. Most of the papers have subsequently been rewritten and generally reflect the authors' views at a time later than August 1961. This reworking helps to account for the eighteen-month delay between the conference and the submission of this manuscript to the Press. The conference participants included: Michael Ames, Alan R. Beals, Gerald D. Berreman, John Gumperz, Edward B. Harper, Edward J. Jay, Pauline Mahar Kolenda, William McCormack, J. Michael Mahar, David G. Mandelbaum, Gertrude Woodruff Marlowe, McKim Marriott, Vidya Ninas Misra, Karl Potter, William Rowe, J. F. Staal, Burton Stein, and Nur Yalman.

I am particularly indebted to Dorothy Spencer, Richard L. Park, McKim Marriott, Gertrude Woodruff Marlowe, and Pauline Mahar Kolenda for their substantial help, patience, and encouragement in the formulation and organization of this conference.

A comment on how the name "Conference on Religion in South Asia" was chosen should help illuminate some of the problems we encountered. Such a trivial matter as a name formed a subject of considerable moment. At an early stage of organization, the title "Conference on Hinduism" was tried out. This had the obvious disadvantage of implying a more or less exclusive concern with the theological and philosophical aspects of a religious system rather than with all possible facets. Most of the conference participants had worked as anthropologists in rural parts of South Asia and had focused at least part of their attention upon the nonphilosophic traditions of its inhabitants, such as supernatural theories of disease causation, shamanism, "'mother-goddess" complexes, or animal sacrifice to local deities. To include as Hinduism these aspects of religion would be to ignore the boundaries drawn around the religious system by many of its intellectual leaders, scholars who conceive of Hinduism as a philosophical tradition and an accompanying social system from which they exclude such phenomena as spirit possession and evil eye.

The term "Popular Hinduism," used in some of the older literature, had an opposite disadvantage—it implied not only that the concern of the seminar was exclusive of the "Great Tradition," but also that the Sanskritic and philosophical traditions were "unpopular." In short, using either "Hinduism" or "Popular Hinduism" alone tends to create a false dichotomy.

Even the term "Hinduism" itself posed an obstacle by obscuring similarities between Hinduism and other religious systems which form part of the complex civilization of South Asia. Not only is the religion of many tribalists similar to that of those more properly called Hindus, but the literature abounds with references to a common belief and action system participated in by Hindu and non-Hindu personnel alike within the dominant civilization. Specifically, in many local regions of South Asia there appear to be levels of a religious system common not only to Hindus of differing sects and castes, but also to non-Hindus such as Muslims, Jains, Buddhists, and Christians, not to mention "semi-Hindus" such as Sikhs and Lingayats, when two or more of these are found in geographical association with one another. For this reason, we wanted to include seminar participants who had studied the religious system and social structure of non-Hindu and non-tribal peoples on the South Asian subcontinent. Our difficulty in obtaining conference participants who had done field work among such peoples reflects a large void in our knowledge about the general subject of religion in South Asia.

The final title, "Religion in South Asia," was selected as reflecting the subject matter of the conference we envisaged and yet as being sufficiently broad to allow us to focus upon the wide range of phenomena appropriate to an exploratory seminar.

Edward B. Harper
University of Washington
February, 1963

Introduction: Process and Structure in South Asian Religion

DAVID G. MANDELBAUM

THE studies in this volume explore some of the main aspects of Hinduism in India and of Buddhism in Ceylon. Because each article is based on the author's field observations, it deals with the realities of religion as well as with its ideology, and with actual religious behavior no less than with its hopes and beliefs. These papers are not intended to give a systematic coverage of the two religions; each is rather a systematic analysis of a certain part of the religion as practiced. The emphasis is on structure and process more than on description and content. The gods are not catalogued nor are the main ceremonies enumerated; rather, the meaning of deities and of ritual in the lives of the practitioners is examined.

Both Hinduism and Buddhism reach deeply, pervasively, into the life of the individual and the makeup of society. Both provide their faithful with the kinds of answers and services which a world religion, each in its own phrasing, affords everywhere. In his religion, the individual can find a plan for his life, from the daily ritual of worship, through the annual cycle of ceremonies, to the ritual observances of the life cycle. It can provide goal and purpose to settle discomforting doubt and drift; it can offer prop and protection where one's own strength fails; it can be a source of certainty and reassurance when one's own wisdom is lacking. In so doing, religion—including the whole set of belief, roles, and action in relation to the supernatural—also imparts a rationale for society and a means of bolstering social cohesion.

Although a major religion can proffer all these boons for individual and society, it does not always do so. The services of religion are not equally necessary to all personalities, for all stages of life, or for all temporal circumstances. A religious occasion may set the scene for disruption and strife; religious postulates can be the source of anxiety as well as of solace. But whatever dysphoric effects religion may have in India and Ceylon, religious devotion is strong among most of the people, and religious practice is a constant part of the village environment.

Religion, in the anthropologist's view, takes in the whole of a people's belief and practice toward the supernatural, that is toward their concepts of all that is beyond man's own power and mundane knowledge. This broad view has not commonly been taken in studies of Hinduism and Buddhism. There is often a selective tendency in that literature not entirely unlike that which is so firmly asserted by one of the characters, a disputatious parson, in Fielding's novel *Tom Jones*. The parson says, "When I mention religion I mean the Christian religion; and not only the Christian religion, but the Protestant religion; and not only the Protestant religion, but the Church of England." Frequently studies of religion in South Asia focus on

Dr. Mandelbaum is Professor of Anthropology at the University of California, Berkeley.

scriptural texts with very little mention of the reality and totality of religious activity. In the papers of this volume, a broad range of religious ideas and acts are included, from the transcendent ethics of scripture to the propitiation of bothersome spirits.

Under the aegis of religion, people serve many purposes. The processes by which some of these main purposes are accomplished form the center of interest in three of the papers. Opler takes up the way in which religious practices help link person to culture and culture to person. Beals shows how secular social interaction is fostered under the mantle of religious ceremony. Gumperz examines religion as an agency of communication, as a metalanguage.

Five of the papers are more concerned with structure than with process, though each deals with structure in a way that clarifies process as well. Berreman lays out the two main divisions of religion among the Pahari of the Himalayas, the priest representing the one, the shaman the other. Kolenda examines the relation between scriptural concept and actual interpretation as known to sweepers in a village of Uttar Pradesh. Both Ames and Yalman present structural analyses of Sinhalese Buddhism: Ames gives a more descriptive analysis, showing the principal parts of the system; Yalman gives a more thematic analysis, of how certain motifs are used. Harper also focuses on a theme, a regnant motif of Hinduism, the idea of purity and pollution. It is so powerful and pervasive an idea that in analyzing it, Harper also deals with the structure of belief and the relation of theme to social structure.

Each of these analyses is presented only as it applies to the people of a specific locality, a single village, a region, or at largest, the main culture area of Ceylon. But because these papers, read together, illumine more than the practices of a particular place or of a particular aspect of religion in South Asia, this introduction attempts to indicate how the results of these several studies may be linked and extended more broadly.

Of the papers which illustrate process, Morris Opler's shows how an individual's personal concerns are generalized and related to the grand truths postulated by his culture and conversely, how the grand doctrine of the religion is made particular to his own concerns so that he may use it as model. Thus he is not alone; his troubles and fears are assuaged by being shared, his choices laid out for him with the highest sanction. A mother's anxiety for the welfare of her son, Opler notes, is generalized in the rite which safeguards all sons, and a mother evidently feels the better for merging her own concern into the common ritual.

The complementary process, of particularization, is illustrated by Opler from a Shiah Muslim ceremony he observed in a village of North India. In the celebration of the rite, an elder recited a poem on the martyrdom of Husain and then appealed to his emotionally moved listeners to take the lesson of Husain to heart in their own conduct. This grand event of Shiah doctrine is thus regularly presented as a vivid exhortation for personal conduct, namely to stand ready to sacrifice all for the right, never to yield to the evil enemy. The power of such exhortation has sometimes aroused men to violence against whatever enemies come to hand; but while the ritual may generate strife among groups, it usually binds closer the band of believers because each member finds in it a mutually shared bridge between his own cares and the grander, safer, nobler verities. Both Muslim and Hindu rites are cited by Opler to illustrate common religious processes. Elsewhere in the book, Islam and the several great religions and sects of South Asia other than Hinduism and Buddhism are little mentioned, but the processes which are discussed are found widely throughout the area, among peoples of the several faiths.

Alan Beals presents an example of how religion provides the auspices for social interchange. A principal element of society in South Asia is the village community. A village exists as a locale in space and as a unit of administration; its inhabitants interact daily as neighbors or kinsmen and often all in the village enjoy (or suffer) a common reputation, but the chief occasion when all the villagers act in concert for one common purpose is during certain religious ceremonies. In the part of South India studied by Beals, one such occasion is the interlocal festival performed by the members of a village in honor of a local deity and for the benefit of visitors from other villages. Villagers of virtually all castes and sects in the community participate together in performing the rite and this joint action helps demonstrate and so bolsters the solidarity of the community.

All in it benefit from the favorable reputation which a village gains from a well-staged festival—even though other villagers tend to grant approval only grudgingly. Guests affirm their own village communality through the wrestling bouts which are a feature of these festivals. Each wrestler is a member of a team and each team represents its village. A whole village can feel triumphant when its team triumphs and all can assure each other that their village will do better next time in case it loses. It is mainly the younger men who are concerned with wrestling, but their interests, as well as those of their elders, are linked into the religious celebration. In the course of the festival, an individual expects to find recreation, adventure, opportunity for attaining distinction. The activities also include the renewal of kinship bonds when each family of the host village entertains its relatives, especially the affinal relatives, from other villages. But the emphasis of this festival is as much on the solidarity of kith as on that of kin. Differences of caste rank are not emphasized; they are little evident in the rites, or in the wrestling matches, or in the dramatic presentations.

Beals finds that despite the many expectations concerning the individual and social benefits to be derived, festivals are often the scenes of bloody conflicts. Villages which hold such festivals are themselves typified by the presence of conflict. Beals concludes that despite the contradictory nature of the evidence, the interlocal festival does contribute to social solidarity in indirect fashion by providing avenues for the regulation or control of existing conflicts.

Religion is generally a benign context for behavior in South Asia and a principal stimulus for voluntary cooperation. A religionist, a sacred performance, or holy symbols of one sect are usually given respect, or at least not openly scorned, by those of other faiths. To be sure, not everything supernatural is benign. Malevolent spirits are feared; there is uneasiness about the evil eye; many a bloody riot has boiled up in the wake of a religious procession. But apart from circumstances of stress, religious roles and acts are given the benefit of any doubt, and there is very little doubt about religion itself.

That is one reason why religion facilitates communication. John Gumperz examines the function of religious symbols in mass communication and the role of the religious communicator in the dissemination of new ideas. Gumperz says that in the study of religion the subcontinent may be viewed as a single large field of social action. There is a code of religious symbols which is well understood across lines of caste, denomination, and region. The role of religious communicator is free from many of the restrictions that the caste structure imposes on interaction across group boundaries. Thus religious performance can provide an audience for a secular message which is couched in the mutually understood religious symbols. An example of this mutuality is the mention, in Alan Beals' paper, that the village festival in one predominantly Hindu village is given in honor of a Muslim saint.

There really is a common cultural base for society in India, even though there has been more rhapsody than evidence offered in proof of it. That unity comes in no small part from a shared religious outlook. It is a way of viewing the whole realm of the supernatural as having a certain structure, including certain main categories. Two of these categories appear in Berreman's distinction between the typical functions of the priest and those of the shaman.

The Pahari are hillmen living on the northernmost fringe of the culture area of Hinduism and their religious patterns differ somewhat, mainly in being attenuated, from those of the Hindu villagers on the plains below them. Yet in maintaining both priests and shamans, and in assigning separate functions to each, the Pahari of the far north of India are quite like peoples of the far south whom I have studied and they share this feature with many, perhaps most, villagers of the subcontinent.

Very widely in India, priests and shamans have different but complementary characteristics. Although the roles of these religious specialists may partially overlap in any particular case, each functionary has a total role pattern which is quite distinct from that of the other. Perhaps the most general distinction is that which Berreman formulates well for the Pahari: priests deal with the maintenance of the whole social and religious system and with the long-range welfare of their clients; shamans deal with the exigencies of daily life, with the immediate and worldly welfare of their clients. Priests perform the rites required for the continuation of society and for the eternal fate of the soul; shamans are consulted to diagnose the cause of an ailment, to tell why a family has had misfortunes, and usually to prescribe what must be done to find a cure for the illness or a solution to the troubles.

Associated with each of these functions is a series of characteristics. Most dramatic is the fact that the shaman becomes possessed by a supernatural being at the proper occasions and then the voice of the spirit answers the questions asked by his clients. No spirit enters or speaks through the priests who conduct the rituals at temples and at domestic shrines. Shamans are usually drawn from the lower levels of a local social hierarchy, rarely from those higher groups who have the right to act as priests to the scriptural deities. Although Beals mentioned a Brahmin who acted as a shaman, this is quite rare in most parts of India.

A priest is a religious technician who fills a specific office; usually he is a member of a jati (an hereditary, endogamous caste group) of priests. In contrast, a shaman's role is more achieved than ascribed, more dependent on the individual's own capacities. Typically the Brahmins of a locality will not perform priestly services for the lowest castes and these people seek such services from a non-Brahmin jati, preferably one whose customary practices are more pure than their own or, alternatively, their priests may be drawn from a particular lineage of their own jati.

A shaman should make himself ritually pure at the time of his seance, but otherwise neither he nor his jati fellows need be particularly rigorous in avoiding pollution. Members of a jati whose hereditary occupation is that of priesthood must be more meticulous about ritual purity than those for whom they provide priestly services. A priest must try to keep himself and his kin relatively pure at all times and if he does become ritually defiled, must cleanse himself quickly. Those whose hereditary jati calling is that of priest usually are given some esteem as a group. Any prestige won by a successful shaman does not extend to his family and jati. Temple priests tend to have a stable, continuous clientele, and family priests commonly have long-term jajmani relations with their clients. A shaman's clients consult him only when they have special need, pay him for each consultation, and feel free to shop around for shamanistic services.

We must note that while priests are given more general respect than are shamans, among Brahmins whose traditional calling is that of scholar and priest, those who are scholars are considered superior to those who are priests. A priest, no matter how ritually meticulous he may be, must still deal with others and so risk pollution. Not so a Brahmin scholar.

Among the Pahari, the traditional priests are conservatives while shamans can and do innovate, though only within a narrow range of religious practice. For all the prestige which is given to the priest, the shaman often has more personal influence, above all because he gives more dramatic and convincing proof of his supernatural connections and does so before the eyes of his clients.

There is a further difference, and one of fundamental importance, in the kinds of supernaturals with whom each specialist deals—the Brahmin priest with the ultimate, transcendent gods, the shaman with the proximate, local deities. The priest serves the long-range functions of the universalistic gods. These gods do not usually possess shamans. The specific functions of the shaman are those attributed to the supernaturals who are his familiar spirits. Shamans normally pay formal respect to the high gods in their devotions, but they do not have much to do with them.

The shrine of a local deity may be cared for by a man who is also leader in whatever ritual is done for that spirit. This caretaker-ritualist is also called a priest in the English literature on the subject, but it is important to distinguish between the priests of the high gods, who are mainly of Brahmin jatis and whose services are believed necessary for the maintenance of the world and society, and the priests of the local godlings, usually of the lower jatis, whose services help propitiate a particular spirit. The priest and the shaman for a local deity may be the same person, but more often different individuals perform the two roles. The local deity is regarded as subordinate to the high gods but with great, even if restricted, powers of its own. It usually has attributes—such as a taste for blood sacrifice—not condoned by the higher ethics nor by their Brahmin interpreters.

The priests who serve the high gods look to the upholding of soul and society (perhaps better, *atma* and *dharma*) through the worship of those gods whose power and prescience are universal and on whom the universe depends. These gods are not primarily thought to be much concerned with curing a particular illness or righting any one mortal's mischance; worship of them in daily ritual, in calendric ceremonies, and in life-cycle observance is usually for more general and abstract purposes. It is the local deity who is apt to cause personal misfortune and who, through the mediation of the shaman, can also correct it.

This distinction is made clear in Edward Harper's paper. Harper observes that the high gods, among the people he studied in northwestern Mysore, are almost never strongly malevolent. Their benevolent powers, however, are for keeping the world in order or for bestowing supernal merit rather than for protecting against disease or granting specific boons. The latter are in the keeping of the lesser deities, but the pragmatic good they can grant is tempered by their inclination to malevolence toward men if they should be inadvertently defiled or otherwise displeased.

The complexes of belief and behavior associated with each type of deity have been called the Great Tradition and the Little Tradition. There is a real difference between the two, but these terms can be misleading. In the first place, both complexes are used practically everywhere in village India. The Great Tradition is great in the sense that most villagers acknowledge that the scriptural gods are paramount and that their worship is on a higher, purer plane than is that of the local deities. Moreover, the Great Tradition has been developed over many centuries through continual effort by sophisticated religious specialists. It is couched in the pan-Indian sacred language, Sanskrit, and commands the awe which attaches to sacred texts, whether in the written word or, as in India, long transmitted through rote memory.

Yet local deities are also worshipped, though in different forms and under different names, throughout the subcontinent. Even in the great centers of Sanskrit learning, people perform rituals to local deities for local purposes. There are various subtypes of local deities, such as ghosts, disease controllers, village guardians; they are not exalted in scripture and are little mentioned in the sacred literature. Their names, forms, and rituals vary from place to place according to the regional vernacular, but their functions seem to be quite constant. They are the supernaturals who can cause and cure an illness; they can do mischief or rectify it; they do not enjoin on their worshippers any high degree of ascetic purity, but they are quick to anger and retaliation if their environs are defiled or their prerogatives slighted, even accidentally.

The one aspect of religion might more aptly be called the transcendental complex and the other the pragmatic complex. One is ultimate, supernal, derived from Sanskrit texts; the other is proximate, local, validated by vernacular tales. Whatever terms are chosen, the important fact is that both are used as part of the whole setting of religion in India, each is employed for generally differing (though frequently overlapping) purposes within the frame of religion and each is popularly considered to be complementary to the other.[1]

	Transcendental Complex	*Pragmatic Complex*
Religious Functions	long term welfare system maintenance ultimate goals	personal or local exigencies individual welfare proximate means
Forms	universal gods Sanskritic texts cyclical rites preponderant	local deities vernacular folklore cyclical rites; *ad hoc* rites important
Practitioners	priests as ritual technicians	shamans who become possessed (also caretaker-ritualists)
	office hereditary in jati	achieved role
	high caste-rank	usually lower caste-rank
	clients in jajmani or other stable arrangement	clients not in bound relationship
	prestige adheres to calling and jati	individual prestige
	exemplars of ritual purity	demonstrators of supernatural presence

[1] This listing of the main features of each complex is a preliminary sorting out. As noted above, there is always some overlap in certain particulars in any one locality.

In traditional village life, as in Pahari tradition, there is no antagonism between the two usages and little or no friction between their respective practitioners. The Brahmin priest does not forbid the propitiation of the local spirits, nor does the shaman's indwelling voice decry the worship of the Sanskritic gods or deny their stringent requirements for ritual purity. The two are complementary, each serving important but differing religious purposes.

Both are observed at all levels of the social hierarchy and both contribute to the total religious practice of the village community. The transcendental complex is in the keeping of the higher castes since their men alone were trained in the study of Sanskrit scripture and in the performance of the more complex rites. The version of the literate tradition followed in any one place cannot include all the practices approved in any sacred scripture; there is always a selection of scriptural precepts as guides for conduct. The precepts which are selected are most rigorously carried out by the higher castes in a locality but the basic principles, as of purity and pollution, are honored, insofar as they are known and can be practiced, at the very bottom of the social hierarchy.

The pragmatic complex is more in the keeping of religious specialists drawn from the lower jatis, but people of the highest caste rank, especially women, will make offerings at the local shrines, consult shamans, and may even participate in some way in the festivals of the local deities. Hence there is no sharp social division in religious practice; the higher groups do not follow the literate tradition only and the lower jatis only the vernacular complex. There is rather a separation of religious specialists by caste level and a greater intensity of worship of the universalistic, system-maintaining gods by the higher jatis (who do manage the social systems) and of the pragmatic deities by the lower.

Frequently enough, a local deity or rite becomes translated into a scriptural type and conversely a Sanskritic god or ceremony may become transposed into a local setting. These processes have been identified as universalization and parochialization by McKim Marriott, and are mentioned in Kolenda's and in Harper's papers. Such transpositions seem not to blur the functional distinctions, that local deities attend chiefly to local, personal exigencies and universal gods are considered to be mainly concerned with the larger, ultimate problems. The separation of religious function has been opposed by those movements which claimed sole rights to worship, whether in *bhakti* devotion to a high god or for a monotheistic religion. Historically however, the separation of function has prevailed in India.

Why has there been this division of function? It may be the Indian answer to certain of the basic questions which confront followers of all religions. These are the polarities to which Nur Yalman's paper refers, between self and society, immediate and eternal, illness and health. In India the gods charged with the cosmic verities are not expected to attend to a baby's colic or a lost cow. Yet both baby and cow must be cared for, since they are part of the grand design. The Indian answer is through specialization of function and hierarchical arrangement among supernaturals, as among men.

The grand design given in theological concepts is not the actual practice of village religion. Pauline Kolenda's paper shows how the two are reconciled in the lowest social rank of a village in western Uttar Pradesh. The Hindu concept of Karma postulates that one's fate in this life is a direct result of one's conduct in previous lives. Acceptance of this doctrine should preclude any striving to change one's fate or social position. And yet village life is full of strenuous attempts to improve one's physical health and social status. Kolenda's review of some anthropological studies shows that while high-caste persons usually know and accept the idea of Karma, there are some in the lower ranks who either do not know of it or reject it if they do.

The Sweepers studied by Kolenda, however, knew about Karma in a general way, did not really reject it, but interpreted it to suit their requirements from religion, which are those of "preventing or relieving misfortunes in this world" rather than of attaining salvation in some distant eternity. While Brahmins say that Untouchables are such because of individual failings in a previous existence, the Sweepers explain it as an unfortunate accident of group history. Illness and death, they believe, are fated, but one can die before his fated time, especially through the anger of a local spirit, and so efforts can be made to avert or remedy such a blow if it should come. Preventive acts are also necessary; hence mothers perform many kinds of ritual to preserve the health of their children. For many villagers, the idea of Karma is only an ultimate explanation and part of the belief system of the high gods. It is not to be taken as the first answer to a pressing problem of practical life. Such solutions are more in the province of the pragmatic, local deities.

We come now to the three longest papers in the volume by Ames, Yalman, and Harper. Although different in approach, they are substantial and remarkable contributions which, together with the other contributions, open the way to a clearer understanding of religion in India and Ceylon, and beyond that to the nature of religion as an attribute of man.

Michael Ames gives us an outline description and structural analysis of the total religious system of the Sinhalese of Ceylon. The totality includes both Buddhism and "magical-animism." He sets forth the principal parts of that system, describes the ideas which infuse it, and indicates some of the problems entailed in its practice. The religion is that of the Theravada Buddhists who constitute nearly two-thirds of the population of the island, and whose language is Sinhalese.

Sinhalese Buddhism is, in certain fundamental respects, quite analogous to the Hinduism we have been discussing. Since it has roots in early Indian religion, we should scarcely expect it to be completely distinct. But it also differs from Hinduism, not only in its forms and texts, but also in structure; and yet these structural differences can equally be seen as different degrees of elaboration on common religious postulates.

To take one functional similarity, the Sinhalese, like the Indian villagers of Kolenda's example, are not fatalists—they do not resign themselves to illness and misfortune. When ill, they vigorously try every method of cure and alleviation known to them, whether magical rite or Western medicine. This is so even though they all subscribe wholeheartedly to the Buddhist precept of Nirvanaya, the other-worldly ideal of the ultimate good being release from this world and to the related concept of Karmaya (the Karma discussed in Kolenda's paper) the impersonal, automatic, inevitable law of the cosmos which decrees that a person's present fate is the result of his deeds in a past incarnation. He cannot alter the consequences of the facts of life after life. But, as Ames says, a Sinhalese can do his utmost to test whether a misfortune is really the result of a bad celestial account, a mere organic disorder, or magical intrusion. If it is the last, he can remedy the condition by appeal to those supernaturals whose realm is the causing and curing of physical illness.

Here we find a central similarity between religion in Ceylon and in India. Among Sinhalese Buddhists, as with the Pahari and other Indian Hindus, there is a dichotomy of religious function, or as Ames puts it, of value orientations. The universal godhead, Buddha, commands the ultimate, most general goals, as do the universal gods of Hinduism. The Sinhalese approach the Buddha for the sake of their eternal good, which in Buddhism (as in Hindu theology) is salvation through release from the cycle of rebirths in this world. But for immediate, proximate, and local favors, the Sinhalese use a different set of supernaturals, whose powers are more specialized and restricted, whose jurisdiction is more parochial, whose status is far subordinate to the Buddha. Each religious division is further subdivided; it happens that the names and forms of some of the high gods of Hinduism refer, in Sinhalese religion, to deities of the parochial roster, charged with pragmatic functions, and deferent to the Supreme One.

Nur Yalman's contribution analyzes the healing rituals of the pragmatic side of Sinhalese religion and in doing so describes the several types of "worldly" supernaturals. They too are arranged in a hierarchy of worth, and the ranking within this division follows the same principle by which the transcendent division is ranked above the pragmatic. The higher of the healing deities are those whose powers are more general, more protective and prophylactic, while the lower supernaturals have only the more narrow capabilities of making and mending mischief. As in Hinduism, the lesser supernaturals rather than the supreme divinity enter shamans in possession.

The similarity extends to the basic relationship between the two complexes. They are used in a complementary way in Ceylon as in India. The deities, doctrines, and practitioners of the one are not considered to be antagonistic to the other. Each has its proper sphere; there is no question that the universal functions are the more important, but there is also no question—in the traditional culture—that people should try to get pragmatic help from the parochial supernaturals.

Astrology, in India as in Ceylon, provides a much-used bridge between the two complexes. It postulates a cosmic process that is impersonal, abstract, transcendent, immutable. At the same time, it offers means by which each person can adapt to the universal movement so as to advance his welfare. By properly timing his acts, he can link his own fate into the grand mechanism in a propitious way.

From both Yalman's and Ames' accounts, Sinhalese religion appears more rationalized, more closely integrated, more socially unified than is Hinduism. To some extent, this is because of the vast disparity of the populations and areas involved. In respect to size, a more equable comparison would be with one of the Hindu sects of a particular region. Sinhalese Buddhists number about six million, Hindus in India are about 370 million or of the order of the combined populations of all of Africa and all of South America. Generalizing about this vast and differentiated bulk of humanity is hazardous, and yet is not impossible because there is the underpinning of shared religious symbols and values which we have noted in discussing Gumperz' paper.

Sinhalese religion is more rationalized in that the categories are neater and are kept more distinct. Thus external pollution is very important in the pragmatic, healing rites and not in Buddhist observance. In Hinduism, pollution is important to both categories. The tighter integration of Sinhalese religion is reflected in the close physical proximity of the shrines of the two complexes (Buddhist temples frequently have shrines of the lesser deities on their grounds) with unquestioned functional separation. One kind of shrine is never used for a religious purpose appropriate to the other. In Hinduism there is less physical contiguity, but more overlap in function, so that a particular boon may be requested of a high god and of a local spirit.

The greater social coherence in Ceylon lies in the fact that everyone in the society can seek benefits equally from each complex, according to his individual need. In Hinduism, those of high rank participate less in the parochial rites while members of the lowest jatas could not enter the precincts sacred to the great gods. Ames tells us that all Sinhalese are familiar with and fully subscribe to the basic precepts of theology, while in India, as Pauline Kolenda found, there are those who know little and others who care less about the theological postulates. The leaders and exemplars of the universal complex among the Sinhalese are monks who obey a stipulated code of conduct. The Hindu exemplars and guides have no such single and detailed code; they vary much more by jati and sect in specifics of behavior and ritual. Similarly, the Buddhist salvation ideal and the path to it are laid down in a single, pervasive doctrine. Among Hindus, religious specialists in the service of the same god in the same locality may advocate different ways to salvation, some through ritual, others through devotion, still others through the meditation which is the Hindu root of Theravada doctrine.

Sinhalese Buddhism places an enormous burden on the individual, in a most egocentric way, by making each person responsible daily and through all eternity for his acts and for his infinitesimally slow progress to the one great good. But the religion simultaneously eases the burden by allowing for some meritorious action here and now and by providing a "vast proliferation" of magical ritual which can be used for specific hurts. The fact of the availability of these practices tacitly assures men that mere mortal flesh is worth doing something for and that there is something which can effectively be done for it.

Ames points out that a crucial problem, a fundamental paradox, of Sinhalese religion is that the central, legitimating ideal of the whole faith is unattainable, cannot be fully realized in this life. But this may present more of a problem to an analysis than to the Sinhalese. The ideal gives direction to religious practice; it confirms that there is a goal which is loftier and larger than any commonplace worldly goal. The fact that the goal is not attainable is far from a handicap; indeed a great religion can scarcely brook an attainable goal or a realizable dominant ideal. If it did, it would become merely part of the local, pragmatic religious complex. What is required of a viable paramount ideal is that it not be practical, that it be useful for guiding action and not for prescribing behavior. In the latter-day universalist doctrine of Marxism, the unattainable ideal of the withering away of the state has not in the slightest impeded the spread of the doctrine. Nor have Buddhists rejected their faith over many centuries because they could not see their way clear to attaining Nirvanaya.

A problem which confronts followers of redemptive religions, Ames notes, is that these religions offer salvation from the world and yet practice and practitioners must remain very much a part of the world. In Theravada Buddhism and in Hinduism, a similar solution to this problem is provided. The theology of the universal complex defines the polarity of life and death in such a way as to impugn both, while the practice of the pragmatic complex affirms both. The two complexes are used as complementary agencies, each appropriate in its own context. This arrangement apparently fulfills religious needs so well that other solutions offered by other religions have not historically had much appeal, either in India or Ceylon.

As the two complexes within Sinhalese religion complement each other, so do the two papers on that religion fit together. Ames' treatment places Buddhist concept in the foreground; Yalman's focuses on pragmatic rituals. Yalman describes specific rites in detail; Ames gives an abstracted survey of the whole religion. Ames dwells more on the kind of evidence derived from informants versed in scripture, Yalman more on the religious behavior of villagers.

The respective methodological procedures are also complementary. Ames presents a descriptive analysis, outlining the several parts of the system of Sinhalese religion, showing the differences among the parts and how they fit together. Yalman's is a thematic analysis, demonstrating how certain simple concepts underlie the great elaboration of ritual. Both authors address themselves finally to broad questions of theory. Ames poses the dilemma of all redemptive religions. Yalman discusses myth and ritual as means of dealing with the polar oppositions inherent in human life, oppositions felt by devotees of any religion.

The final paper in the volume, by Edward Harper, deals with a theme that is used in religious belief and behavior among the peoples of both India and Ceylon. It is the idea of ritual purity and pollution which pervades much personal and social action. Harper's substantial analysis greatly advances our understanding of this underlying principle. So fundamental a concept, used in so many different contexts, by so many peoples, is bound to be complex and expressed in myriad forms. Yet the theme itself is not complicated even though the specific ways in which it is applied are. Harper's data are mainly from the Havik Brahmins of northwestern Mysore, but his explanation enlightens our study of all Indian culture, so that we can begin to formulate the kind of pan-Indian statement which is given in the following comments.

There is also much concern with pollution among the Sinhalese, and while their concepts can be seen as special phrasings of the theme used by Hindus, that comparison deserves a separate discussion. For our present introductory and generalizing purposes, we sketch answers to three broad questions about the purity-pollution concept as it is found among most peoples of India. The questions are: What is it used for? What does it consist of? How is it applied?

What is purity-pollution used for? Many kinds of interaction are regulated according to these standards. In the first instance, these criteria are used to regulate the relation of man to supernatural. This is first because people think of it primarily as a religious matter, as purity or pollution in ritual behavior. They are also put forward as the prime rationale for social interaction between castes. Further, a person's behavior in respect to his own bodily functions is shaped by considerations of purity and pollution, particularly concerning what, how, and with whom he eats.

In religious observance, a worshipper may approach supernaturals only if he is in a state of purity. The high gods will certainly not respond favorably to one who comes before them in anything less than a pure state while the local deities can be terrible in their retribution against one who defiles them, even if only inadvertently.[2]

[2] This is another general distinction between the supernaturals of the ultimate and those of the

In most social relations, the relative state of purity-pollution of the participants sets limits on the kind of interaction they may have with each other. Those who eat together at the same time and place, of the same food, must be in quite equal states of purity. A person may eat only such food as has been prepared by someone who is at least as pure as he is. For this reason as well as for many others, husband and wife must come from families of about equal status in ritual purity.

Not all interaction is closely controlled by criteria of purity-pollution. In dramatic performances, as Gumperz' paper mentions, in wrestling, as Beals notes, in the context of work, of government, of commerce, people of different degrees of pollution may interact closely (wrestling is one of the closer activities) without much concern for calibrating social distance. But when the same men enter into other contexts, of home and of worship, then the social distances demanded by criteria of purity are more applicable. The strictness of observance varies a great deal; the Brahmins described by Harper are very purity-conscious. The people in the area studied by Beals are much less concerned with purity and pollution, but even there the general rules are known and, especially between the highest and lowest groups, applied. Every person's state of purity-pollution depends not only on his own conduct but also on the conduct ascribed to his jati, his caste. Therefore a person's relations with anyone of a different jati follow considerations of relative purity. And these considerations bear on his own personal activities. If a man has done something involving ritual contagion, he must purify himself before he can properly carry on with activities which require him to be relatively pure, as worshipping or eating with his peers.

What do purity and pollution consist of? Pollution is the more active, positive quality; purity is mainly the cleansing of and isolation from polluting experiences. What then pollutes? Contact through the senses with a polluting object or activity. Such an object has generally to do with bodily emissions and with death, of either man or animal. Defecation pollutes a person as does contact with feces. Spittle pollutes the spitter if it comes on him after it has left his mouth. Menstruation pollutes a woman so greatly that she is a potent source of ritual contamination until her flow is over and she has properly purified herself. Childbirth is the greatest of all bodily emissions and entails deep pollution and long purification. A death in a family is the most serious source of pollution, preventing the relatives of the deceased (up to twenty-one generations removed in Havik Brahmin theory) from engaging in normal work and worship until a period of isolation has passed and ritual purification has been undergone.

There are different kinds of pollution. Some kinds of defilement are individual; other kinds are corporate. Defecation pollutes only the person. A man's death makes his whole circle of kin impure. Some kinds are temporary; others are permanent. Every person is temporarily defiled every day when he performs his bodily functions. A ritual wash, perhaps also a brief sacred recitation, erases that defilement. But those whose traditional jati occupation is sweeping away and cleaning up nightsoil or handling dead animals or the products of carcasses (as leatherworkers) are permanently defiled. They are corporately and permanently less pure than those

proximate complex. Officiants of the high gods are expected to keep themselves in a more intense and continual state of purity than is required for the servants of the local supernaturals, but the high gods are also less perturbed by a breach of purity in their vicinity.

whose traditional calling requires no such defiling contacts. It does not matter if a particular individual or indeed any individual of a jati whose traditional occupation is leatherworking actually works with leather. The fact that his ancestors once did is enough to impose permanent and corporate barriers to his close interaction with people of purer jati tradition.

Their social disability does not lead those of the lowest jatis to reject the purity-pollution criteria. They may not be able to carry out stringent purity observances because they cannot afford the time and money to do so—though as Harper notes, the lowest jati is sometimes more meticulous about some aspects of purification than are some of the middle jatis—but they too put themselves in a purer state before beginning to worship. A shaman, Harper observes, becomes possessed only after he is ritually purified and those of the lowest jatis also require purification of their people after menstruation, childbirth, and death.

To remove ritual impurities, flowing water is a basic solvent. Most purification involves washing or bathing. The recitation of sacred verse or holy names is also a common ingredient of purification. The deeper kinds of defilement require a sequence of ritual procedures, first isolation, then performance of ritual acts, finally symbolic reintegration into society. Places are purified by the external application of cowdung and water, for the cow has special properties for purity possessed by no other living creature. Persons who are deeply defiled because of personal acts may be purified by drinking a mixture of the products of the cow.

There are different degrees of pollution intensity. Objects, men, gods have different potentials for defilement, both for transmitting it and for being defiled. Thus different foods are ranked according to the different degrees of ritual and social disability which eating them entails. A Havik Brahmin should eat only vegetarian food; the act of eating in itself brings on a mild, temporary, individual disability which is easily expunged. But if he should eat of the most potently defiling food of all, the flesh of the cow, that would involve him in such serious pollution that no cleansing ritual would be sufficiently great to purge him of his defilement, thus necessitating his being declared no longer a member of his former society.

Those of other jatis of the same locality, less pure in custom and lower in rank than the Havik Brahmins, customarily eat certain kinds of non-vegetarian food. The type of food in a jati's traditional diet forms an important criterion by which its members are socially ranked. The Havik Brahmins are one of those jatis whose food observances are so involuted that they will not even eat any vegetables whose color resembles that of meat. But food taboos of some kind are also observed at the lowest echelons of a local caste order. Those very low-ranking people who will eat carrion beef (commonly they claim the carcasses of the cows and bullocks which die a natural death) nevertheless exclude other kinds of food, say rats, from their diet.

Food offerings for the supernaturals are similarly differentiated. The universal gods usually receive only vegetarian foods whereas the worship of local deities often requires meat offerings. Havik Brahmins believe that the lowest forms of local spirits are innately impure, like Untouchables. But innate purity or pollution is always relative to the ritual state of the one who is exposed. What defiles a being of one status will not similarly defile a being of another status. Thus the milk of a cow which has recently calved can defile a god, but not a Brahmin. Again when illustrating a concept he labels "respect pollution," Harper points out that the cow is so much higher a creature than the purest man that even her dung can be used by him for purification. Conversely, a Havik Brahmin sees Untouchables as so deeply and permanently defiled that even the purest of them cannot help transmitting pollution to a Havik Brahmin. Again, the same principle is used by those of the lower jatis, usually with fewer taboos and lesser exclusions. They too feel themselves polluted by certain experiences; some Untouchables object to having people of any other jati, including Brahmins, too close to their hearths and homes.

An individual's state of purity is always evanescent, temporary, non-communicable, achieved through deliberate, voluntary effort. Pollution is adhesive, contagious, often involuntary.

Whenever the wholeness of an organism is changed, then there is danger of pollution. Performing the bodily functions, menstruation, shaving, cutting the hair and fingernails, eating—all these change the previous natural state of the person.

Objects and substances too are more easily defiled when their previous wholeness is disrupted. Thus Havik Brahmins can use uncooked food no matter who has handled it. They must not use any cooked or processed foodstuff prepared by someone less pure than they are. Harper makes the significant observation that as long as a fruit or nut is whole, it is not subject to ritual defilement, but once a coconut is broken or a plantain cut, a Havik cannot accept it from a member of another caste. The principle of pollution vulnerability from impaired wholeness applies throughout India, through an infinite number of local interpretations and detailed rules.

The purity aura of the pristine state can be seen in a number of the topics discussed by Harper. For example, a naked child can handle a sacred image without defiling it, as she could not do when clothed. Another instance is that of whole undiluted milk being pure, but if so much as a drop of water dilutes it, the previous quality of purity is gone. Transitional stages of all kinds are potentially polluting; an eclipse is a kind of transition of the heavenly bodies and so brings special danger of pollution of men. But the most potent sources of pollution rise from altered states of being of living creatures, particularly people. Childbirth and death, being the most drastic alterations, entail the most potent pollution.

How are the standards of pollution and purity actually applied in social situations? As everywhere, there is scope for variation and room for interpretation. Not all Havik Brahmins, for example, are equally strict about purity. In popular and in scriptural theory, the jatis whose customs involve the most defiling practices are lowest in the social scale and must be kept at the greatest social distance from those of purer habit. This is also the Havik Brahmin's theory. They are the dominant secular group in their region as well as the purest, and they assign rank to the other caste groups. They should do so on the basis of the practices of each jati, but the *de facto* relations are not the same as the rationale *de jure*. To take but one example, the jati of Lingayats (originally a sect) should be ranked very low because their doctrine deliberately rejects menstrual and childbirth seclusion and mourner's isolation. But in other respects, the Lingayats are quite stringent. They are strict vegetarians; they are devout in observing many ritual avoidances and act as priests for other jatis. In some villages, they are the dominant jati and perform many of the functions performed by Havik Brahmins in their villages. Because they are so high according to certain of the ritual and secular criteria, Havik Brahmins treat them as near equals, address them with terms of respect, and in the case of some of the Haviks interact with them quite closely. Here, as elsewhere in India, the actual relations among people of different caste levels are a result of the interplay of the strict criteria of purity and the mitigating criteria of secular power and context.

As social relations change, so do the religious concepts associated with them become modified. And shifts in religious belief and practice lead to shifts in social relations. Certain trends of change are noted in these papers. Among the Havik Brahmins, for example, Harper records a number of changes. Thus some men have been doing away with the services of a barber for shaving and have been executing this polluting task upon themselves for years. Childbirth pollution is not as stringently observed as it was once, and in caste relations the Untouchables of the area are showing new vigor in trying to improve their status.

Yet it is clear that among the Havik Brahmins, as among the other peoples discussed in these papers, the force of religion is still powerful and the traditional forms continue to have great appeal. Gumperz concludes his paper by pointing out that the new media of communication in India transmit traditional themes of religion. It is not hard to see the continuity of the religious tradition because it appears in the cinema as well as in village drama, in the Sinhalese ritual "for the consecration of a new hut for the Rural Development Society" as well as in the interlocal festivals.

But this very continuity may cloak a fundamental change in the structure of religion. Because traditional deities and myths are in such prominence, we may overlook the fact that they are used in non-traditional ways. A good example of this is given by Berreman in discussing those Brahmins among the Pahari who have set themselves up as agents of a purer, more scriptural Hinduism than the hillmen have hitherto followed. Those Pahari villagers who have had some education and experience with plains people have provided the demand for changed religious practice. The new types of Brahmin claim to lead the way to a better observance of the ancient religious tradition, but in one main respect they are leading away from the tradition of both hills and plains. Berreman quite rightly calls them "atraditional" Brahmins; they deny the traditional complementary relation of the transcendental and pragmatic complexes. They attempt to discredit shamans entirely and criticize those Brahmin priests who tolerate shamans. In their competitive zeal, they even disparage each other, something traditional priests do not do. In effect, they are trying to eliminate one of the two main divisions of the traditional religion.

The same kind of shift is noted by Ames in Ceylon among the "modern Buddhist enthusiasts" who are from the more Westernized sections. They hold up the Buddhist ideal of Nirvanaya as a state which is quite attainable and soon, not utterly distant and aeons away as the traditional belief had it. Hence they also believe that the paraphernalia of magical healing rites and all the other ways of seeking mundane comfort are superfluous. They, too, tend to reject the pragmatic side and disclaim the coexistence of the two complexes in Sinhalese religion.

These are changes of a more fundamental sort than modifications of taboos or curtailment of rites. They are basic because a system of action—and religion is always a system of action as well as of belief—cannot function well in a complex society and culture without some broad division of the kind which occurs in other institutional systems between staff and line, between policy-makers and executives, between theorists and practitioners. In contemporary Buddhism and Hinduism, one of the two divisions is losing ground. The high gods are not threatened with displacement by the Planning Commission or any other human agency. But the proximate deities and practices are jeopardized by modern medicine and technology. Yet even in its own sphere, modern medicine does not cope too well with the kinds of illness for which pragmatic rites are often used, chronic ailments, psychosomatic disorders, vague but discomforting complaints.

It is hardly likely that the traditional pragmatic rites will soon be abandoned. Their opponents, though influential, are still relatively few, and are removed from village life. Whatever may replace these rites is still in short supply. In any event, the Indian tendency to assimilate rather than to reject, to assign complementary rather than competitive functions to cultural institutions is in evidence for both complexes. In the villages, the pragmatic rites of religion and the services of modern medicine and technology are being employed in complementary fashion. The transcendent complex too is subject to new thought. Under the guidance of such leaders as Professor—now also President—Radhakrishnan, the more learned people are coming to see that in the ancient scriptures there are inspiration and long-range guidance for the new society. Thus the new structures of religion and society being wrought in India are coming about through the application of the traditional process of establishing complementary relations.

Magical-animism and Buddhism: A Structural Analysis of the Sinhalese Religious System

MICHAEL M. AMES

THIS paper is intended to present in outline form a structural analysis of the total religious system of the Sinhalese of Ceylon.

The Sinhalese, excluding those few who are Hindu, Christian, or Muslim, are Theravada Buddhists who also indulge in a rich array of magical-animistic and other "non-Buddhist" practices. Descriptive accounts of these various practices are readily available in the literature. But until now no one has examined the various beliefs and rituals to see whether and how they are related to one another, to what extent they combine to form an integrated system of "Sinhalese religion," and how this system actually functions. I will attempt such an examination by focusing on the primary religious ideals, their practical implementation, and the problems involved in this implementation. Perhaps the most crucial problem facing Sinhalese religion is that the central ideal, salvation, which legitimates all religious action, is itself practically unattainable. This fact must have far-reaching implications for the total religious system.

Materials for this study were gathered between January 1959 and December 1960.[1] Eight months were spent surveying historical records and studying Buddhist theology in London and in visiting important religious centers in Ceylon. Fourteen months were spent observing religion as practiced by Sinhalese-speaking people in a southern district of Ceylon, especially in and around Gokanna town and Rohanagama village (pseudonyms) where I did most of my field work (Ames, 1962a).

The following discussion gives prominence to the Buddhist point of view rather than to the village religion that interests most anthropologists. Let me explain why. Sinhalese religion *is* Buddhist-dominated rather than specific to any village because the monkhood, which is nation-wide rather than village-centered, is the dominant status group in the religious system. In religious matters all other groups defer to

---

The author is Assistant Professor of Anthropology at McMaster University.

[1] Research was sponsored by a grant from the Social Science Research Council. Writing of the paper extended over a number of months and several grants. The Department of Social Relations, Harvard University, awarded a stipend from the Donald Fagg Memorial Fund to cover the months from June to September, 1961, when the first draft of this paper was written and submitted to the Berkeley seminar. Revisions were made while I was a research fellow at the University of Chicago under a grant from the Committees for the Comparative Study of New Nations and for Southern Asian Studies.

In writing I have benefited immeasurably from the comments and criticisms of numerous people who, nevertheless, have no responsibility for the shortcomings of the present paper nor the opinions it expresses. I especially wish to acknowledge debts of gratitude to D. K. de Alwis, Cora DuBois, Clifford Geertz, Arnold L. Green, Talcott Parsons, and Nur Yalman whose detailed comments at various stages led to important modifications of, and additions to, the manuscript.

monks who set the standard of legitimacy for all religious ideas held by the Sinhalese. An accurate description of Sinhalese religion must therefore show this bias in favor of Buddhism, even though certain "non-Buddhist" institutions are also important. For this reason, I did not concentrate on any particular village but instead chose an area large enough to include most of the significant features of Sinhalese religious life.

In the first instance, therefore, this is a study of the Buddhist-dominated religion of the southern Sinhalese and reflects the views of my informants rather than of scholarly books. This outline, which includes only aspects of the religion which I believe to be of primary importance, is sufficiently abstract so that it most probably has relevance for Sinhalese religion everywhere on the island.

In this paper I shall first discuss the central religious beliefs of the Sinhalese. These concern the ideal of an other-worldly salvation (*nirvānaya*)[2] and the related concepts of *ķarmaya,* rebirth, merit, and demerit. Together they define the goals of the religious life; but their implementation poses certain structural problems. Religious institutions and rituals are concerned with these problems, with how the ideas are actually "put into practice." In other words, I am concerned with how the ideal of a radical, other-worldly salvation is actually institutionalized in concrete patterns of organization and ritual. How does a religion that advocates complete renunciation of the world come to terms with that world? How do people in the world come to terms with this other-worldly ideal? What are the functions of the non-Buddhist institutions—magical-animism, monastic landlordism, state patronage—that are always so closely associated with Buddhism? Do they merely represent a corruption of pure Buddhism as many observers have claimed, or do they actually facilitate Buddhist pursuits?

Complete answers to all these questions obviously cannot be given in this one paper, but I attempt to cover the more important points and to discuss their major implications. This may also possibly stimulate anthropologists to look at their village Hinduism a little differently. So far as I know, this paper represents the first attempt since Weber to subject a total religious system of greater India to a systematic sociological analysis.

Religious Beliefs

Foremost in the realm of ideas, Sinhalese classify everything as either of the world (*lauķiķa*) or not of the world (*loķottara*). *Lauķiķa,* the worldly, refers to things that are mundane, secular, profane. *Loķottara,* the other-worldly, refers to things that are supra-mundane, holy, sacred.

Other-worldly oriented things, ideas, and institutions concern what the Sinhalese call *āgama,* "soteriology," "salvation religion." Buddhism, Hinduism, Islam, Judaism,

---

[2] Colloquial Sinhalese rather than Pali or Sanskrit terms are used throughout this essay. This reflects a greater consistency in linguistic usage than actually exists, for Sinhalese may use colloquial or literary Sinhalese, Pali, or Sanskrit terms depending on their social status and the contexts in which they speak. All Buddhist scriptures are in Pali (only recently have they been translated into colloquial Sinhalese) and monks recite Pali stanzas on ceremonial occasions. Teachers and pandits frequently use "high" or literary Sinhalese and Sanskrit in their discourses; villagers prefer the more earthy colloquial Sinhalese, although even they are familiar with, and sometimes use, more erudite terms. But to introduce such vagaries in this paper would only confuse the reader. The following arbitrary orthographic conventions have therefore been adopted. Spellings are according to de Zoysa (1948–49) and transcription into English approximately according to Geiger (1938). Except for *gihi* (laity), the singular forms of word are given; where necessary. they are pluralized by adding the English "s."

Christianity are all *āgama*. All other things, even if indirectly related to *āgama,* are nevertheless essentially profane in value.

Buddhism or any soteriology as a social institution, as a "church" (*sāsanaya*), is also certainly a part of the world, and in this sense is secular. But it differs from caste, kinship, economics, government, medicine, or magic in one very special way: it is *oriented towards* other-worldly or ultimate concerns. The distinction Sinhalese make between *lokottara* and *laukika* is therefore essentially in orientations of action—"values, value-orientations"—rather than in types of concrete actions.

It is manifest intent or official purpose (*adahasa;* Pali, *cetanā*) of an action, and not simply the action itself, that determines whether it is classified as *lokottara* or *laukika.* The attitude adds sacredness to the act. What Sinhalese mean by a *lokottara cetanā* is very close to what Durkheim (1915) meant by the term "sacred." It is a moral force superimposed upon objects and actions. It is a *value* that has to do with what is ultimately meaningful, or divine. The relation between sacredness and the symbols used to represent it is as arbitrary as the relation between meaning and sound in language. Sacredness is a special *meaning* given to specific objects. No thing is inherently sacred nor is it necessarily always sacred for all people or all societies. In one context, for example, Sinhalese spirits have sacred value; but in a different context the same spirits are considered and treated as wholly profane. The last Buddha, Gotama, sanctified the Bodhi tree; the next Buddha, Maitri, will sanctify the Banyan tree.

The concept of *lokottara* and what it implies constitute the fundamental religious beliefs of the Sinhalese—the focus or "goal orientation" of their religious system. They consider salvation to be the purpose of their religious life. *Nirvānaya* is the ultimate ideal and value. Buddha, his teachings (*dharmaya*), and the monkhood (*saṅghayā*)—the "triple gem" of Buddhism—are "sacred symbols." Merit-making (*pinkama*) and meditating (*bhāvanaya*) are "sacred rituals." They are all regarded with a special kind of respect and importance; they are venerated (*vandinavā*). All other religious institutions, all other rituals, facilitate in one way or another these central beliefs (even though most of these other systems do not themselves receive veneration).

Why do Sinhalese want salvation? Because life is full of suffering (*duka*). It is *duka,* not sin, that is the primary evil of the world. Suffering is not due to an original sin, but to certain psychological defilements (*kleśa*) every person carries within himself.

Objectively considered, the Sinhalese do not of course suffer very much. They enjoy one of the highest standards of living in all Asia. But they believe they suffer, and that is what is really important. It is simply a matter of definition again: life *is* suffering. If you stand, your legs get tired: that is *duka.* So you sit down, but then your backside gets tired: that is *duka.* You eat, but then you get hungry again: that is *duka.* You will get sick: that is *duka.* You have parents and friends, but eventually they will sicken and die, and that too is *duka.* Even you must die and that is *duka.* But then you will be reborn and go through the same cycle over and over again: *that* is *duka.*

The only redemption from this constantly recurring suffering is for the individual to eradicate his own mental defilements. It is a thoroughly individualistic, or egocentric, religious creed. The mind, the psyche, is the beginning and the end.

There are usually said to be ten of these mental defilements or *kleśa:* greed (*loba*), hate (*dosa*), delusion (*moha*), conceit (*māna*), speculative views (*diṭa*), sceptical doubt (*vicikicjāva*), mental torpor (*thina*), haughtiness (*uddhata*), shamelessness (*ahira*), and lack of moral dread (*anōtapaya*). The first three—greed, anger, delusion—are considered the most important and are cited the most frequently.

These defilements are the motives that cause people to act: desire to live, to be rich, to enjoy; hate and envy of others; ignorance of the proper way to live. These passions bind one to life, and life is suffering. It is a constant round of birth (*sansāraya*), sickness, decay, and death.

This salvation ideal is usually summarized by the literati in the teachings of the Four Noble Truths: (1) all life is suffering (*duka*); (2) suffering arises through ignorant craving or attachment (*loba*); (3) this suffering can be eliminated through cessation of craving (*nirodha*); (4) cessation is achieved through following the Noble Eightfold Path. This path—right view, right intention, right speech, and so on—is meant to purify the individual of all defiling thoughts and actions, to work on his mind, to improve his spiritual condition. It forms the basis for all Buddhist rituals from the most popular to the most sophisticated.

There are several other religious concepts closely related to the ideal of *nirvānaya,* which refer to the "mechanics," the "how," of religious action. *Karmaya* is the law of volitional, ethical, or premeditated action: good leads to good and bad to bad. It is completely impersonal, automatic, and inevitable like the law of gravity; it has always existed and always will exist.

Pina (merit) and *pava* (demerit) are symbolic ways of measuring these actions. When a person does something good (*kusala karma*), he is said to be "accumulating" merit (*pina*), which only means he is accumulating good reactions (*karma vipāka*) in the future. Merit is not a substance, but a pedagogical device Buddhists use to express or to explain more abstract principles and to evaluate concrete actions in terms of those principles (see Ames, 1962b). *Pina* is a synonym for virtue or holiness.

Sansāraya, the round of rebirth, is the field in which *karmaya* and merit operate. The reaction may occur in this or in some future life. Life itself, in fact, is a long chain of interconnected events or *karmic* actions: cause and its fruit, and the fruit leading to further cause. Birth, puberty, marriage, death are nothing more than recurring links in the chain, which goes on for thousands or millions of years.

Improving chances for a better rebirth by accumulating merit will lead only so far. To attain salvation one must escape rebirth altogether; he must transcend even the desire to perform good actions. The devotee must make a complete and fundamental break with the past. Not only must he try to escape suffering; he must also learn to renounce pleasure, the desire to live, to enjoy. This is because any desire, good or bad, leads to rebirth, and rebirth leads to suffering. Rebirth *is* suffering. One first learns to cultivate good actions and then to renounce action altogether.

This argument can best be illustrated by a famous and frequently cited myth. It concerns Buddha's duel with his arch antagonist, the Evil One or God of Death. He is to Buddha as the Devil is to Christ. *Māraya* is also associated with *Kāma Deviyā,* the god of lust, of pleasure, of life. Life and death, pleasure and pain, the bait and the hook, are the same. *Kāma Deviyā* and *Māraya* are one: the opposite of Buddha.

This is the story. Gotama, the future Buddha, one day resolves to meditate beneath a certain Bōdhi tree until he finds enlightenment. But *Kāma-Māta,* the dual personality of life and death, challenges the Buddha in an attempt to break his meditative calm. He first assumes the form of *Kāma Deviyā* and employs the supreme distraction by sending three beautiful goddesses with their retinues to dance about the sage, to caress him, and to provoke desire and temptation. But they fail to arouse this remarkable sage.

Kāma Deviyā then changes his tactics; he becomes *Māraya,* the Evil One. He sends hordes of demons, hurls wind and rain, sand and flaming rocks, live coals and boiling mud at the seated Gotama. But the sage betrays no feeling for self-preservation; he does not flinch, does not stir. The demonic hordes and their weapons are repelled by his virtuous serenity. Immune to pleasure, he is also dead to fear. He has extinguished all his passion, attained Buddha-hood, reached enlightenment. He has escaped the bond of life, the bait of *Kāmaya* and *Māraya's* hook.

The moral of this story is that to attain salvation, as Buddha had done, one must escape not only from suffering and death, but also from the desire to live and from the pleasure of living. One who defeats desire (*Kāmaya*) also transcends death (*Māraya*); one renounces the pleasures of life and attains salvation. Buddha had attained supreme wisdom; he had transcended the world, forsaken it altogether for the other-worldly.

There are several points to keep in mind about this theological argument of the Sinhalese Buddhists. First, its basic principles are known to everyone, including even the humble villager (see Ames, 1962b). Second, it is believed that nothing but one's own efforts will bring about final salvation. There is no recourse to a deity or savior, no prayer, no religious grace, no sacrament, no predestination, and in fact not even an enduring soul. The individual, as the saying goes, must wander through life after life "lonely as the rhinoceros" until he achieves his goal by his own efforts.

Third, it is important to understand that in Sinhalese Buddhism there is only *one* way to salvation. All other salvation religions offer devotees several choices—usually between good works and mystical pursuits. Hindus refer to the way of mysticism or meditation (*jñāna yoga*), the way of ritual (*ḳarma yoga*), and the way of loving devotion (*bhaḳti yoga*). But all Sinhalese Buddhists maintain that the only way to obtain redemption is through systematic meditation (*bhāvanaya*), the equivalent of the Hindu *jñāna yoga.* The individual must eradicate mental defilements through a long process of mental self-purification. He must become *satpuruṣa,* a self-perfected individual. It is true that Buddhism opened salvation to all regardless of caste or sex. But its actual attainment has always been restricted to a few at any one time; it is the path for the strong in mind.

This is a radical conception of salvation. It demands extreme virtuosity, individual achievement, and absolute renunciation of the world. The social consequences of these beliefs are therefore equally radical. For the ordinary Buddhist, salvation is considered very difficult because it demands arduous meditation; it is very distant because the necessary practice takes thousands and thousands of rebirths.[3] It is perhaps paradoxical that although *nirvānaya* is the ultimate goal of the religious life, no Sinhalese is believed to have attained this goal for hundreds of years and few anticipate doing

---

[3] I must point out here, however, that not all Sinhalese believe salvation so distant or difficult to attain. Some argue with vigor that it can be reached in this life itself, and some claim that many have attained salvation since Malliyadeva. But these tend to be the arguments of Buddhist enthusiasts who live in the urbanized and suburbanized areas around Colombo, the "westernized" parts of Ceylon. It is especially their attitude regarding the immediacy of salvation that distinguishes them from the more traditionally minded people who await the coming of Maitri (see Ames, 1963).

so for many centuries to come. Salvation for the Sinhalese is out of this world in more than one respect.

It is widely believed, for example, that the last Sinhalese to attain *nirvānaya* was the "saint" (*arahat*) Malliyadeva. People are never certain when he lived; some estimate from three hundred to fifteen hundred years ago; the Pali commentaries and chronicles say (see Adikaram, 1953:66–67) he lived during the second century B.C.

It is also believed that knowledge of Buddhism is gradually disappearing from the world and that no one will be able to attain salvation until the appearance of the next Buddha, Maitri, who will re-discover the Truth and expound it to all. No one knows exactly when Maitri is due to appear, only that he will not come for a very long time. Nevertheless, most people conclude their meritorious rites with the wish (*cetanā*), "May I with this merit be reborn in Maitri's time and attain salvation after hearing his sermons."

In the area around Gokanna town and Rohanagama village where I worked, there were perhaps two hundred village temples containing about six hundred monks. In the same area, there was only one forest hermitage containing eight monks. There are about six thousand temples on the whole island; the number of better-known hermitages can be counted on two hands. No doubt some monks do practice meditation while residing in village temples; but the universal opinion is that if you *really* want to go about it in a serious way, then you must renounce not only the world but also the monkhood and retire to the seclusion of a small hermitage. In Ceylon it is felt that the monkhood also tends to be very much a part of the world—a polite way of saying that it is sometimes scandalously corrupt. A hermitage is physically cut off from the world; it possesses no property, no sexually attractive novices, no obligations to perform ritual services for the laity. There a monk has little else except meditation to occupy his mind. As the skeptical-minded Sinhalese would say, under those conditions how could anyone help being virtuous!

Even though most Sinhalese consider salvation beyond reach for many lives to come, they still value this ideal. The *nirvānaya* concept is not a thin veneer; it permeates daily life in countless ways. The most highly venerated person in Sinhalese society is the one who leaves behind his family and retires to a forest to spend his remaining days in solitary meditation. He is striving for his own salvation, and that is precisely why he is respected.

Or take for example the *Vessantara Jātaka,* the story of Buddha in a previous life. It is known by every Sinhalese, depicted in temple paintings, and recounted in temple sermons. King Vessantara decided to renounce his kingdom to concentrate on religious practices. He retired to the forest with his family. When a Brahmin beggar, sent by the gods to test Vessantara's virtue, came to him and asked for his beloved wife and children, Vessantara immediately gave them to the beggar. Now, the Sinhalese do not castigate Vessantara for this; he is, rather, revered for having achieved the supreme level of non-attachment: he could *even* renounce his family ties. Only two births after this great achievement, Vessantara was born as Siddharttha, the man who became Gotama Buddha.

Siddharttha, like his former self Vessantara, also deserted his wife and child. Tiring of palace pleasures while still young (he was the son of a wealthy lord or king), Siddharttha left them behind to search for religious wisdom. After various trials and tribulations, he found enlightenment and became known as the "Awakened One"

(Buddha). But then one day his wife, or ex-wife, brought their son along to meet his father. She told the boy that he had not received his paternal inheritance, something all fathers should bestow upon their sons before leaving the world. "Go ask your father for your inheritance," she told the boy. He did just that. In reply, Gotama Buddha offered his son the alms bowl and robe of a mendicant. "This is your inheritance, my son." Needless to say, the boy eventually joined his father's order as a monk. Sinhalese do not complain that Gotama deprived his son of his royal inheritance. Quite the contrary, they extoll Gotama for bestowing the greatest inheritance of all, the truth about salvation.

The ritual of meditation that hermit monks perform in their secluded forest hermitages directly emulates this world renunciation, the ascetic ideal of the noble sage. The ordinary merit-making rituals, by constantly playing on the same symbolic themes (see Ames, 1962b), reaffirm the same ascetic ideal. Even magic rituals, which Sinhalese claim have nothing to do with their Buddhism, refer again and again to the power and glory of Buddha.

There is no question that the ascetic, other-worldly salvation ideal is highly venerated by the Sinhalese. In this respect they are devoutly Buddhist. But on the other hand, and here is the paradox again, there is also no doubt that very few Sinhalese actually practice the ideal they venerate. I have already cited evidence for that. Now what are the implications of this paradox?

This is the problem Sinhalese face. According to their world view, they are faced with thousands of rebirths in a world full of *duka* or suffering. They believe that *nirvānaya* is the only true redemption from this evil. But this redemption is far beyond immediate reach. Then how, meanwhile, are they to deal with endless suffering and rebirth? How does the religious system attack this problem?

Religious Organization: Outline of the Religious System

Religious institutions and rituals show how ideals valued by the religion are implemented. In this respect, the various ecclesiastical structures "express" or "reflect" the important religious beliefs and the dilemmas they pose. These structures are guided by the ideal of *nirvānaya,* but they are also dominated by the immediate concern with rebirth and with combatting *duka* here and now. Because of the evaluative supremacy of the world-negating *nirvānaya* ideal, relations with the world are always strained. But because of the concern with rebirth and comfort, relations with the world are also necessary and important.

To understand this ambiguous relationship between belief and practice, it will be useful to return again to the concept of *lokottara,* the sacred or other-worldly. Not only is it used to differentiate the sacred or holy from the profane, but it also differentiates between different kinds of ecclesiastical structures. First, concrete religious institutions are divided into those that are especially sacred or primarily oriented to other-worldly concerns and those that handle the worldly aspects of religion. In effect, this distinction serves to guard against sacred institutions becoming overly concerned with the profane world; they can remain aloof while other institutions do the "dirty work." Second, the especially sacred institutions are further subdivided into ascending levels or degrees of sacredness. This provides a criterion for evaluating the moral relevance of religious actions, and helps again to set off the highly sacred from too much involvement in the world. Taken all together these institutions and their corresponding rituals constitute the religious or ecclesiastical organization, the practical application of the ideal.

I begin with the first kind of differentiation, between sacred and non-sacred religious sub-systems. A complex religious system, like a polity or economy, is composed of interconnected units or "sub-systems." Each unit performs special functions for the total system (see Parsons and Smelser, 1956:8–25). It is a Durkheimian division of labor. The role of the idea of sacredness is to differentiate these religious sub-systems into two main categories: those that possess definite sacred value and those that do not. The "goal" of religion is to realize the sacred ideals it upholds; those institutions and rituals directly concerned with this realization are also sacred. In Sinhalese religion those institutions are a part of what is normally called Buddhism. But because the salvation ideal with which Buddhism is concerned is so other-worldly, Buddhism itself, the first religious sub-system, is largely set apart from ordinary affairs of the world. There are therefore other religious sub-systems that more directly contend with the world; but it is their very worldliness that denies them full legitimacy in terms of Buddhist values. Two of these sub-systems, the temple estate and the state, are at best only quasi-sacred. Many Buddhists refuse to accord them even that much respect. They are usually said to be "not really" a part of "pure" Buddhism, even though they provide the economic facilities (temple lands) and political patronage that Sinhalese consider essential for Buddhism. Magical-animism, the propitiation of spirits, the fourth sub-system, the Sinhalese consider absolutely profane (*laukika*) and altogether separate from Buddhism. (Spirits themselves may not be profane but when invoked they become part of a profane, or magical rite.) But however Sinhalese evaluate them, these four sub-systems are both functionally interdependent and analytically distinct parts of the general Sinhalese religious system.

I will now briefly delineate the internal structure of each sub-system, suggest some of their more important inter-relations, and mention in passing some of the structural problems each must contend with.

The Structure of Buddhism

Within Buddhism there are three main axes of differentiation: sex, vocations, and ritual. (For a more extended discussion of this topic, see Ames, 1962b.) Sex is the broadest division. Only males take on monastic robes; today there is no formally organized sisterhood in Ceylon (although there are individual women calling themselves *therī* or "nuns"). Furthermore, men are considered (at least by themselves!) to be intellectually superior and more sophisticated than women; hence, in general and "in theory," they are considered more adept at salvation striving and are accorded higher religious status.

The primary differentiation in vocations is between a celibate, monastic-dwelling monkhood (*saṅghayā*)[4] and a laity (*gihi*). Each may be further subdivided: hermit monks (*tāpasayas,* or *aranyavāsiyās*) and village monks (*bhikkus,* or *gamavāsiyās*) on the one hand; lay devotees (*upāsakayās*) and ordinary householders (*gihi*) on the other. Structurally they form a pyramid with householders at the base and hermit monks

[4] There are few studies specifically of Sinhalese monasticism (Bareau, 1957; Hocart, 1931; Yalman, 1962b). But there are many general surveys of Buddhism. The most competent are Copleston (1908), Hardy (1860), and Rahula (1956); others are Dickson (1886), Gogerly (1908), Liyanage (1958), and Upham (1829). For the history of Buddhism in Ceylon see references cited in Ames, 1963.

at the apex. They represent different life styles or levels of Buddhist specialization.

Approximately corresponding to these vocations are a series of interdictions or precepts also graded hierarchically: five for the householder, eight for lay apostle, ten for monastic novice, two hundred and twenty-seven for ordained monk, and four extra special precepts (which subsume those for the ordained monk) for a virtuoso hermit monk. These precepts serve to define the duties of each vocation. (See Figure I.) The greater the number an individual observes, the more he cuts himself off

FIGURE I—BUDDHIST VOCATIONS AND RITUALS

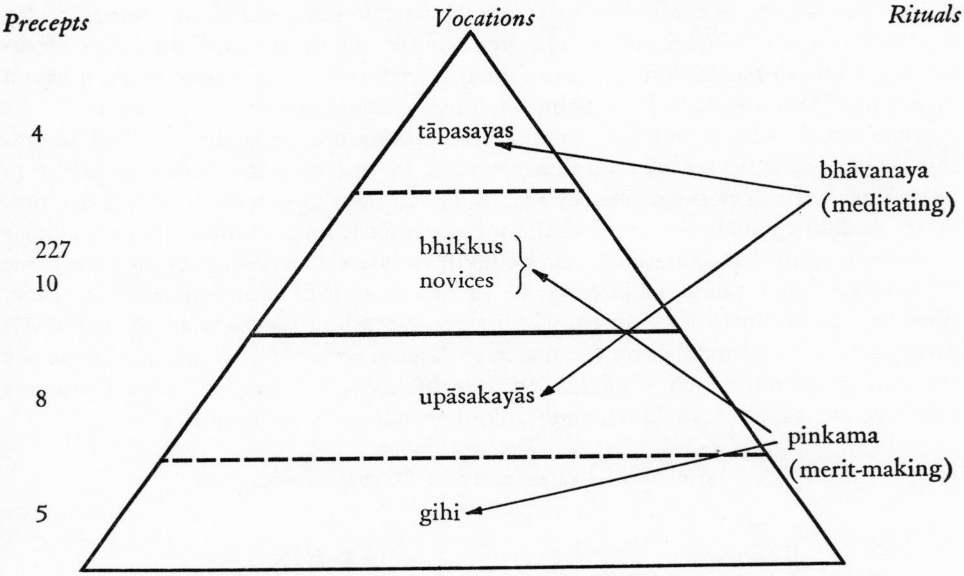

from the world. Buddhism is a thoroughly particularistic structure with multiple standards of behavior, a separate standard for each stratum in the system. Every Buddhist, whatever his level of spiritual development, "specializes" in practicing a certain number of precepts. After mastering one level, he moves on to the next higher one, either during the same life or by means of rebirth. For example, once a householder becomes old, he may become a pious lay devotee; but most householders assume that they will be monks only in some other life. The implication of this particularistic, hierarchically organized structure is that the ascetic ideal is the one all respect but not the one all attempt to emulate. Virtuoso ascetics specialize in emulating the ideal; others attain it only vicariously by venerating the ascetics.

Vocational separation is important, but Buddhism is not merely a system of monks versus householders; ritual differentiation to a certain extent crosscuts this division and helps to reunite it. Picture vocations as the horizontal strata in the system, rituals as the vertical links. Vocation, or "office," refers to a way of life, a particular role in the religious system. A role incumbent performs many tasks and participates in various rituals depending on personal ability and inclination. Rituals are based on this personal ability, or "religious virtuosity"; hence they are not necessarily confined to incumbents of any one role.

As I have said, there are two main Buddhist ritual systems: merit-making is the primary concern of ordinary householders and ordinary monks (usually village *bhikkus*); meditating, ideally at least, is the concern of hermit monks and lay devotees. In the merit-making rituals, householders give alms to monks; monks study the scriptures and give sermons to householders. Village monks (but not the hermits) in addition perform at funerals and provide other ritual services for the laity. The reward for these actions is the accumulation of merit leading to a better rebirth (*sugatiya*). The *bhāvanaya* meditating ritual system is the preoccupation of the religious virtuosos who are more concerned about striving for salvation than about earning a happy rebirth. Merit-making is the basis of "popular" or "folk" Buddhism, the "religion of the masses." Meditating is the basis of "sophisticated" or "Great Tradition" Buddhism, the religion especially of hermit monks and sometimes of lay devotees. (Note that magical-animism does not play a part in this distinction.) Merit-making leads to meditation, for through successive rebirths one may be born into a state where he is capable of practicing the more arduous meditating rituals.

Both ritual systems, like the pyramid of vocations, are internally stratified according to ascending levels of specialization. But in this case the hierarchy refers to increasing levels of performance, of mental or religious virtuosity. The primary task of *all* Buddhist rituals is to perfect the mind, either through action (merit-making) or thought control (meditation). Altogether there are six levels of performance, three within each ritual system, all integrated with one another like rungs on a ladder. First, Sinhalese divide merit-making rites into three ascending task levels: giving (*dan*), precepts (*sīla*), and meditation (*bhāvanaya*). The same word *bhāvanaya* refers to the meditating system, which is subdivided into the tasks of developing higher precepts (*sīla*), concentration (*samādhi*), and wisdom (*paññā*). (See Figure II.)

Figure II—Hierarchy of Ritual Tasks

Ritual	*Task Levels*
Bhāvanaya	—paññā (wisdom)
(meditating ritual)	—samādhi (concentration)
	—sīla (higher precepts)
Pinkama	—bhāvanaya (meditation)
(merit-making ritual)	—sīla (precepts)
	—dan (giving)

Each task is integrated with the next higher one because practice of the higher one presupposes mastery of those preceding. Alms giving (*dan dīma*) is the first, and in this respect the most important, duty for all Buddhists. They must first practice renunciation by giving objects to others. Giving leads naturally to the observance of other virtues or precepts and to the beginning practice of meditation. Each individual concentrates on whatever task in either ritual system for which he considers himself prepared. Here again we find the particularism that runs throughout Buddhism. Men are not born equal, but highly differentiated according to their individual past actions. The multiple tasks associated with every ritual, like the multiple standards associated with vocations, reflect this basic inequality. The universal standard applied to all Buddhists is that they should develop according to their individual potentials. There are bad monks and virtuous householders; each concentrates on those ritual tasks suitable to his abilities.

There are several aspects of the structure of Buddhism that I want to emphasize. First, the social importance of the division between monks and laity is that a large body of men, in accordance with their own ethics, are not economically self-sufficient. (There is about one monk for every three hundred and fifty laymen.) Monks are supposed to devote full time to religious pursuits and abstain from remunerative employment. (Today some receive salaries as teachers, but this is a hotly disputed privilege.) Furthermore, again because of monastic precepts, monks do not have authority to enforce ecclesiastical laws nor the power to regulate their affairs with the laity (see Green, 1961). Both for economic facilities and social control, therefore, monks must depend on people and institutions outside the monkhood—on landed estates and alms gifted them, and on patronage and supervision extended by the state or lay trustees.

Equally important, however, is the differentiation within the monkhood. There are hermit *tāpasaya* monks who practice the ascetic ideal and village monks who perpetuate in their temples, colleges, and ceremonies the teachings about this ideal. But when salvation is distant and knowledge of Buddhism slowly declining, the main task according to the Sinhalese is not so much to practice a difficult doctrine (with uncertain success) as it is to protect this doctrine from extinction. *Tāpasaya* monks are highly venerated but they have no practical value. People claim that if all monks disappeared into forests, Buddhism would die. Who would be left to expound the doctrine to the laity? There are only a few hermit monks but many village ones, and this is precisely the way it should be during the present age of moral decline, the *Kali Yuga*. It is the scholarly monk of the village temple and monastic college, and not the lonely hermit monk, who has practical value for the religious system. It is he who must be supported, his pursuits that must be facilitated. He is the guardian of Truth, which must be preserved even if not practiced by most people.

The next point concerns the ritual hierarchy. Again it is merit-making rather than meditating that has practical significance for the religious system. *Pinkama,* or merit-making, is the core of folk, popular, or worldly Buddhism. Monks are supported through alms-giving by the laity, who in return receive sermons. These meritorious practices lead to happy and higher rebirths for both. But *pinkama* Buddhism is linked up to the higher, more sophisticated, more virtuoso level of Buddhism: through meritorious rebirth one attains sophistication; through sophisticated meditation one attains release from all rebirth.

Perhaps it is now clear how the organization of Buddhist ritual and vocation is an attempt to resolve the paradox between a valued salvation ideal and the difficulty of its attainment. Even though *nirvānaya* is a long way off, people can still work towards it little by little by performing good deeds. Happy rebirths act as incentives to strive harder; they are also temporary respites, "holidays" one takes from his religious journey to relax, rest up, before working again to earn more merit by practicing more virtues.

The soteriological functions of village monks and *pinkama* rituals are therefore to bridge the gap between a distant salvation and the desire to achieve it. *Pinkama* is a mechanism by which an individual can raise himself up to a high enough spiritual level so he can then begin salvation striving in a serious way. Monks encourage meritorious behavior and preserve the doctrines until people are able to practice them.

There is now, however, another paradox to deal with. Merit-making, which is meant as a means to another end (salvation), becomes in practice for many people a goal in itself. Monks become so involved in the business of perpetuating the doctrine that they never get around to practicing it; they too are concerned with achieving a propitious rebirth. But here is the problem: *nirvānaya* means the end to all rebirth; merit-making leads to further rebirth. Too much concern paid to the fruits of merit therefore may actually be a denial of salvation. The gap between aspiration and achievement has appeared again, only in a slightly different form.

This is the real paradox in Sinhalese Buddhism and the one that has never been fully resolved. Performing good deeds is the first step to salvation; but salvation itself demands renunciation of all deeds both bad and good. The individual must rise above volitions of all kinds and become completely non-attached, lacking in all desires like Gotama beneath the Bōdhi tree. Dedicated salvation striving demands a complete and absolute break with all that preceded it. This is symbolized by the lonely hermit monk who renounces his attachment not only to the world but to fellow monks as well. So radical is this break that few people have ever managed to achieve it. The religious goal towards which most people are actively striving in the present life is only a happy rebirth. Even though they *intend* to go further, most Sinhalese Buddhists today have never gone beyond the first stage of their religious journey.

Other religious institutions have shifted to facilitate this secondary pursuit rather than the ultimate goal of salvation. Estate and state systems are elaborate attempts to support not the hermit monk—who in any case needs only alms and a simple forest shelter—but village monks, their temples and colleges, merit-making rituals, magic cults, and their specialists. Concerning the problem of suffering and evil, people try more to combat it temporarily rather than to transcend it entirely. Immediate consolation (*sänasilla*), not absolute redemption (*nirvānaya*), is the goal most people actually seek. The expectation of a happy rebirth is certainly important in this context. But it only alleviates *duḳa;* it does not eradicate it. Recourse to magic is another consolation. Even though they do not affect *ḳarmaya,* the magic cults provide concrete techniques for handling sickness and misfortune here and now and consequently help to make the best of a bad world.

Many others before me have emphasized this world-affirming nature of Theravada Buddhists. But they offer it as evidence for one of two contradictory propositions: either that the Buddhist ideal is not world-negating after all, or, if it is, then people are Buddhists "in name only" and are not influenced by that ideal.

But I claim it is precisely because the *nirvānaya* ideal is distant, difficult, and world-negating that merit-making and magic are important, that village monks and temple estates are considered necessary. Even in the absence of its achievement, the ideal continues to dominate these concrete and worldly patterns of religious action. It still specifies which actions have meaning. The whole religious system is concerned with the very problems this ideal has created.

I shall next turn to the other sub-systems of the religion and show in more detail how they are related to Buddhism. Magical-animism poses a special problem because it holds a very ambiguous status in the total system, and its relations to Buddhism have never been adequately treated in the literature.

My main proposition regarding Sinhalese spirit cults is that their status in the religious system is directly dependent on the nature of the salvation ideal. Change that ideal and the value placed on these cults would also change. Here is an example. In *bhakti* Hinduism and in Christianity, devotion to God is a direct means to salvation. Consequently, invoking the divinity for worldly boons is also considered a sacred or at least quasi-sacred action. It is part of the salvation effort. In Sinhalese Buddhism, no god but only individual meditation brings salvation. Therefore Sinhalese define their spirit propitiation, almost identical in practice to Hindu cults, as being wholly profane, "magical." Sinhalese gods have been divested of a salvation function and therefore they are demoted in status. The Buddhist ideal is so other-worldly, so world-negating, that its sanctification of things in the world is strictly limited to a minimum of institutions (those that lead directly out of the world). *Bhakti* Hinduism, the way of devotion *in* the world, sanctifies many more ordinary practices than a Sinhalese Buddhist would ever dream of using.

Magical-animism: Structure of Magic Ritual

In magical rituals, as in Buddhism, ritual types are a primary axis of differentiation. But whereas Buddhist ritual is graded hierarchically according to virtuosity or psychological purity—the degree of skill and virtue each level entails—magic ritual is graded according to levels of purity of objects. There are three major magic ritual systems, usually designated as demonism, astrology or grahism, and Hinduism (Wirz, 1954; Gooneratne, 1865–66), distinguishable on this basis: impure offerings are presented to goblins (*yakās*) and ghosts (*prētayās*); pure and impure offerings are presented to planetary deities (*graha deviyās*); pure offerings are presented to gods or deities (*deviyās*). Separate ritual systems and separate ritual specialists are centered around each of these three types of offerings or prestations (Yalman, 1962a; Ames, 1962c). Figure III summarizes this structural arrangement. I refer to all these systems as "magical-animistic" because all are concerned with propitiating and manipulating various spirits for profane (*laukika*) ends.

There are first the exorcist rites. An exorcist or magician (*yakädurā*) presents impure offerings (*dola*) to the goblins and ghosts to drive them away from the patient (*āturayā*). Exorcism typically takes the form of a goblin dance (*yakuma, yakun-naṭanavā*) in which the lesser spirits are propitiated and exorcised. (See Wirz, 1954: 18–104. Also Ames, 1962d; Callaway, 1829; Pertold, 1930; Seligman, 1908.)

The second magical ritual system is concerned with astrology and planetary deities that represent astral powers. An exorcist or magician (in this case called a *bali-ädurā*) presents pure-impure offerings (*baliya, balibili, pūjāva* and *dola*) to planetary deities to offset bad astrological influences affecting the patient. The typical rite is again a dance (called *bali yāga, graha yāga, graha śāntiya*) in which offerings are given to images of the planetary deities (Wirz, 1954:105–132; also de Silva, 1911). In this case the word for offering and the one for image are identical (*bali*). In some cases, the more pure *pūjāva* offering is given the planetary gods and the more polluting *dola* to their demonic aids, the *rakusās*. But in either case, the offering (*baliya, balibili, pūjā/dola*) is less polluting than *dola* offered to goblins (*yakās*) and less pure than *pūjāva* offered gods and deities (*deviyās*). Persons may also wear charmed amulets in order to repel them. Most other astrological practices, like casting and reading horoscopes, could also be included under this category.

The third system is concerned with the higher spirits, the deities or gods (*deviyās*) and godlings (*dēvatās*). A priest (*kapurāla*) presents offerings (*pūjāva* or *aḍukkuva*) to the deities to obtain their blessings (*āsīrvāda*) and assistance (*pihiṭa*) for the patient.

The typical rite here is not a dance but an offering (*dēva pūjāva*) presented to the deity at his special shrine or temple (*dēvālaya*) (Bell, 1916–17; Meerwarth-Levina, 1915–16). There are also village games and dances dedicated to the deities, especially to village guardians (*gamadēvatās*) and to regional and national gods (Le Mesurier, 1884; Obeyesekere, 1958; Wirz, 1954:132–179; Yalman, 1962d); and there are agricultural rites (Bell, 1889; Ivers, 1880).

FIGURE III—TYPES OF PRESTATIONS AND THE STRUCTURE OF MAGIC

Types of prestations	Typical ritual	Specialist (intermediary)	Spirits directly concerned
1. *dola* (impure)	*yakuma* (exorcist rite)	*yakädurā*	*yakās & prētayās*
2. *balibili*	*bali-yāga* (planetary rite)	*bali-ädurā*	*graha deviyās*
3. *pūjāva* (pure)	*dēva pūjāva* (deity offering)	*kapurāla*	*deviyās*

In each of the above three ritual types, a prestation is made to the spirits; in each case this prestation is denoted by a different term (*dola, balibili, pūjāva*) signifying different degrees of purity of the objects presented.

Pūjāva is a respectful term and may even be used in a Buddhist context: offerings to Buddha, which are extremely pure, are called *Buddha pūjāvas*. But when applied to *deviyās, pūjāva* also implies that a bargain has been made. The purpose of the offering is suggested by *oppu kirīma,* a part of the *dēva pūjāva* act. It means "to give" or "to prove, demonstrate, confirm"; also "title, deed." *Dēva pūjāva* is a demonstration of good faith, the fulfillment of a vow to the gods. The intent is to honor (*namaskāra*) and to please or flatter (*satuṭu*), as well as to invoke (*yadinavā*), the deity. No such attempt is made to influence the Buddha for he no longer exists in any form. Buddha offerings are simply means for instilling devotion and pure thoughts in the minds of those who offer.

The word *dola,* which denotes offerings to lesser spirits, carries a different connotation. It, like *pūjāva* and *dan,* also denotes "offering, giving"; but it means as well "craving" and is related to *dolanavā,* "to desire, to become fat," *dolamana,* "longing," and *dolō,* "desire." There are two kinds of *dola,* one of vegetable or mineral composition (*pidēniya*), another of burnt, fried, or roasted meat (*puluṭu*). Meat is a polluting substance; *puluṭu* is derived from *pilissunā* (burnt), and is similar to *puludu* (box, eager, miser). Here again the Buddhist theme is repeated: desirable objects, polluting objects, and greed or miserliness are all associated with one another.

In each ritual system a specialist mediates between the patient and the spirits; whether he is a *yakädurā, bali-ädurā,* or *kapurāla,* he is little more than an advocate who speaks for his client. He holds no sacramental power over the patient nor, in many cases, does he have any special control over the spirit. (An exception to the latter is the "shaman" in the more rural areas, and especially in the Kandyan regions, who doubles as a *kapurāla* and a *yakädurā* and who becomes possessed by tutelary deities; another exception is the medium in the low country who does little else but act as a mouthpiece for some deity.)

This is the overall structural outline of magical-animism. Each of the three major categories may be further subdivided in various ways. Each major spirit within each category has special rituals dedicated to himself alone. Deities have their own temples with peculiar ritual traditions. Ritual also varies according to the patient's wealth, the nature of his misfortune, and the experience of the specialist whom he hires. But now it is necessary to state several important qualifications regarding this general picture.

Those specialists who deal with lesser spirits must also in the course of the ritual pay obeisance to higher spirits. In Sinhalese theory all ghosts are controlled by goblins, and goblins by gods (see Obeyesekere, 1962). Consequently, although a *yakädurā* specializes in giving *dola* to *yakās,* he must also present *pūjāvas* to *deviyās* in order to enlist their cooperation. They see that the *yakās* keep their part of the bargain with the magician in accordance with the Buddha's command (*Budu anin*) given centuries ago. The reverse is not true. A *kapurāla* who propitiates *deviyās* does not need the help of lesser, polluting, spirits so he makes them no offerings.

The second qualification of the general outline concerns the role of Buddha in magic rituals. Practically all magic rites begin with the magician's or priest's expressing veneration (*vandanā*) for Lord Buddha. The merit earned from this virtuous act is then offered the deities (merit serves to extend their stay in the heavens), or used to frighten the goblins and ghosts. This does not mean that Sinhalese confuse Buddhism with magical-animism, only that in practice they frequently fuse them. But it is this practical fusion or "syncretism" that has led to so much confusion in the minds of observers. Either Buddhism is thought to be contaminated by magic, or magic to be an essential part of Buddhism. Another but similar point of view is that Buddhism forms the literati, sophisticate, Great Tradition part of religion while the magic cults represent the folk, village, Little Tradition of religion: Buddhism the veneer, spirit cults the "animistic substratum." None of these views is correct, some are dangerously misleading, and all have ignored the important distinctions Sinhalese make in these matters.

"Magical" Aspects of Buddhism

In ritual and myth Buddha is treated as the "god above the gods" (*dēvātidēva*) or "god of gods" (*dēvadēvayā*): there is power to his virtue (*sīlaguna*) and to his teachings (*dharma balē*); certain of his teachings (*pirita*) may be recited by monks to exorcise goblins, to bring prosperity, and to charm water (*pirit pän*) that is used for healing and protection; Buddha relics (*dhātuvas*) emanate electrifying power (*Budu rēs*); godlings bestow boons upon those who venerate Buddhist symbols; special psychic powers (*idi balē*) may be obtained through Buddhist meditation; the Buddha is venerated at the beginning, and occasionally at the end, of every magic ritual. One possible explanation for these phenomena is that they represent a parochialization, popularization, or even corruption of higher Buddhist principles: abstract theological ideas are translated into magical superstitions; a Great Tradition fuses with little traditions. My explanation is different.

Rather than representing a popularization of higher ideals, these actions are part of a much more significant process of "meaning raising" by which individuals are raised to a higher level of spiritual sophistication. The householder may first be attracted by the magical potency of a relic; but then because of the myths and rituals associated with relic veneration, he gradually comes to grasp its soteriological significance. By venerating Buddha before magic ritual, the participants symbolize their acceptance of Buddha's superiority over magic, *not* their indulgence in magical superstitions (for examples, see Leach, 1962; Yalman, 1962a).

Buddhist ritual, even though possessing magical potency, *is not magic*. Buddhist ritual is sacred; magic ritual is profane. The healing power of *pirita* is secondary; its primary purpose is the mental and spiritual development of the individual. Healing *is* the primary purpose of magic, on the other hand, and it elevates one spiritually only because of this healing power.

Buddhist ritual is not magic because it *does not compete* with magic. It is not a matter of debate among Sinhalese; Buddhism and magical-animism are wholly distinct. It is an accepted fact that things Buddhist are supreme, more efficacious, more wondrous. And it is because of this exalted position that although magically potent, things Buddhist cannot be resorted to constantly for mundane reasons. They are too sacred to perform the same functions as magic. This is demonstrated by the fact that certain Buddhist rituals *can* be used to exorcise goblins but seldom are; magic, in contrast, *never* substitutes for Buddhist rites.

Because of the exalted nature of things Buddhist, they serve both to legitimate magic and to restrict it. Certain of Buddha's teachings (*pirita*) and relics are all-powerful and the deities partake of this power because the Buddha has sanctioned their activities. He granted them permission (*varan*) to pester man for offerings provided that they desisted once those offerings were made. Buddhist ritual also helps to restrain or limit magic by setting a standard. The deities are controllable because they need the merit only man can give; nefarious goblins can be subdued by the power of Buddha's virtue.

The relation between Buddha and the spirits is illustrated by the spatial arrangement of shrines and temples. With one or two exceptions, shrines for planetary deities, goblins, and ghosts are temporary and wholly excluded from Buddhist temple (*vihāraya*) compounds. These lesser spirits are polluting and dangerous; therefore no one wishes to keep them around in permanent locations. But the *dēvālayās* shrines to deities (*deviyās*) are frequently found in conjunction with Buddhist temples and shrines. Most Buddhist temples have deity temples or shrines within their compounds; most deity temples (*dēvālayās*) contain Buddhist shrines or at least insignia. The relationship between Buddhist and deity shrines is of a very special kind. They never substitute for one another nor are they ever confused with each other. On Buddhist compounds, deity temples are either in an entirely separate, smaller building, or the deities have small shrines on the right and left sides of the Buddha in his temple. Buddhist symbols associated with deity temples and shrines are invariably placed either above the deity images within, or in a special shrine without. In all cases, if Buddhist and deity symbols are not physically separated, then the latter are spatially subordinated to the former.

The typical pattern of worship is first to visit the Buddhist temple to venerate the Buddha and his symbols (monks, relic chamber, *bōdhi* tree), then to go to the deity temple and invoke the gods. Part of the merit earned from venerating the Buddha is bestowed upon the gods in return for their blessings.

Although this may appear to some people (cf., Ariyapala, 1956; Wirz, 1954) as a degradation of "pure" Buddhism, monks tend to give a contrary explanation. I summarize the words of one:

People are going to propitiate the deities anyway, no matter what we say. Besides, Buddha never said they should not; he never said it was a demerit. Therefore, if we keep shrines in our temple compounds, whatever their reason for coming, people will at least come—and learn to venerate Buddha while invoking the deities. The deities always respect the Buddha; so it is only natural they would like to help those who come to the Buddhist temple.

Buddhism is not the only religion to dangle carrots before the horse, in this case the peasant. All religious systems have comparable "meaning-raising" devices; the more hierarchically structured the system, the more elaborate these will be. Catholics distinguish between *sacraments*—"the official channels of grace to the souls of men," and *sacramentals*—rites used to produce grace indirectly by encouraging devotion and good thoughts (Ripley, 1960:201, 207, 377). Baptism and holy communion are sacraments; making the sign of the cross, genuflection, veneration of relics, and images are sacramentals. Sinhalese religion is different in form but not in principle. It has no sacraments, no concept of grace—in Catholic terminology all Buddhist rites are really sacramentals. But the relations between sacred Buddhist rites and profane spirit cults are essentially comparable to those between Catholic sacraments and sacramentals, both of which are sacred. (See Ames, 1962d; also Leach, 1962)

Placing deity shrines within the courtyards of Buddhist temples does not vulgarize or parochialize; instead, it serves to bring magic under the control of the monks and the spirits under the suzerainty of Buddha. Invoking deities within *vihāraya* precincts is not entirely unlike the use of saints in the Roman Catholic religion or, to extend the analogy, the reinterpretation of pagan Mexican gods as Catholic saints. When anthropologists talk about the "syncretism" between Mesoamerican paganism and Catholic Christianity (Madsen, 1957; Thompson, 1954), one is frequently given the impression that the stubborn Mexican peasant has slyly outwitted the Catholic priest. Saints are said to be really little more than old gods in new disguise. The peasants are only "nominal" Christians. This is the whitewash theory of syncretism: the high religion forms only a thin veneer covering a rich jungle of pagan cults. But I am rather sceptical. Knowledge of how the Sinhalese system works leads me to suspect that someone has actually outwitted the anthropologist!

The Science of Magic

What is the distinction Sinhalese themselves make between Buddhism and the spirit cults?

First, by their term "magic" (*māyama, vijjāva*), Sinhalese usually mean something I have not discussed at all: "illusion," "hocus pocus," "jugglery." They call magic things that only appear to be true, like circus tricks, pulling rabbits out of hats, or sleight of hand trickery.

The magical-animistic cults, they say, are a science (*vidyāva*). Propitiation of the different spirits forms a part of the "science of spirits" (*bhuta* or *yakṣabhuta vidyāva*), which, like Western and native medicine, contains practical methods for dealing with disease and misfortune.

Buddhism may also utilize a scientific method. Buddha "tested" different techniques until he discovered the one true way to salvation. But in addition, he was a holy person who expounded a system of ethics, which, along with charismatic leadership, constitute an *āgama,* a soteriology. *Āgama* is a faith, followed from birth and practiced throughout every life. A science (*vidyāva*) is different: it has no holy founder, no system of ethics, no community of followers. It is applied only when the need arises and is otherwise ignored. It is non-*āgamic*.

Buddhism, or *Buńdāgama,* is concerned with the workings of the law of *ķarmaya,* with individual destiny. *Vidyāva* has nothing to do with *ķarmaya,* but with events brought about by other "natural laws" (*niyamayas*). Altogether, there are five of these laws or forces. One is *ķarmaya,* which is concerned with ethical actions: good actions lead to good results, bad actions to bad results. The other laws govern different aspects of the world and they are not the concern of Buddhism. These five laws refer to the "atmospheric" (*utu niyamaya*), "biological" (*bīja*), "physical" (*dharma*), "psychological" (*citta*), and "ethical" (*ķarma*) events in the universe.

Compare for example the Buddhist and magical ideas about purity and pollution. They reflect this division of labor between Buddhism and the "science of spirits."

Buddhism is concerned with purity of a psychological nature— the eradication of mentally defiling attitudes (*ķleśa*). This is a purity akin to virtue or morality. Pollution in a Buddhist context—that condition negatively affecting one's store of actions (*ķarmaya*) and balance of merit—is denoted by the presence in the individual's thoughts of greed, anger, delusion, conceit, or any of the other defiling attitudes. This is pollution in the sense of "sin" or demerit; *ķleśa* is in fact a synonym for *pava* (demerit or bad actions).

Magical-animism, the propitiation of spirits, is concerned with polluted (*ķiluṭu*) entities external to the psyche—none of which directly affect one's *ķarmaya*—such as blood, meat, fried foods, oil cakes, excrement, poison, possession by a goblin. Much of magic ritual is devoted to "purifying" an individual who has somehow come into contact with one or more of these polluted objects and thereby been made sick (see Yalman, 1962c).

If one has accumulated bad *ķarmaya,* then he must face the consequences. Nothing can be done except reap what was sown. And yet the Sinhalese does not resign himself to sickness and misfortune; he is not a "fatalist." Quite the contrary, he tries every conceivable method of curing or alleviation. Does this mean he is trying to contradict the law of *ķarmaya?* Not exactly; a successful cure is a demonstration that one's accumulated *ķarmaya* is not bad or that the misfortune was not due to it. Failure to be cured, on the other hand, suggests that the particular misfortune may be due to earlier sins and if so then there is no hope at all. This gives one explanation for the vast proliferation of magic ritual, most of which is devoted entirely to curing and therapy: the only way to determine whether misfortune is due to *ķarmaya* is to seek a cure. The successful cure specifies the cause: if medicine cures, then sickness was caused by an organic disorder; if magic ritual, then spirit possession (the particular ritual cure identifies the class of spirit who "caused" the trouble). If there is no success with any remedy, it must then be due to the inexorable workings of *ķarmaya.* The case of an elderly woman of Rohanagama village will illustrate the point:

She has been paralyzed from the waist down for several years. Her husband said that they have tried every possible cure. She has visited leading Western-trained physicians in

Colombo, but they could not cure her; the husband then sought out eminent *āyurvediya* physicians but their medicines did not help either. He brought monks in to chant *pirita,* priests to invoke the gods, and magicians to charm—yet his wife remains incapacitated. Following every ceremony or visit to a physician, she recovers slightly only to suffer a relapse. The husband said he does not know what he can do next. It must be her *karmaya* to suffer so much, it must be her *karmaya* that prevents a cure. Then he added that it is probably his as well for he suffers along with her; both of them are paying for previous misdeeds.

At one level Buddhism and the profane "sciences" (*bhuta vidyāva, āyurvediya*) are complementary: Buddhism is concerned with the law of *karmaya* and the sciences with other natural laws. At another level, they appear to contradict one another because both Buddhism and the sciences aim to remove suffering and misfortune. But the paradox is resolved at yet a third level, for although both appear to be providing different means to the same end, the end also differs. Each offers a different kind of release or panacea for a different kind of misfortune. *Vidyāva,* at least the portion that I designate *bhuta vidyāva* or magical-animism, attempts to provide consolation or "worldly relief" (*laukika sampata*) from what we in the West would call temporary misfortunes or "neurotic anxieties." The fact that Sinhalese consistently maintain magical-animism is not *āgama,* not *lokottara,* is a direct expression, it seems to me, of this temporary value they place upon it. It is precisely because it is not sacred, is not Buddhist, is not connected with *karmaya,* that it cannot do more than affect mundane events. Buddhism, on the other hand, offers a final or transcendental release (*lokottara sampata*) from evil itself, from what some theologians now call "existential anxieties."[5]

Although the two realms of Buddhism and magical-animism are completely separate and distinct in Sinhalese theory, they are complementary in function. This is why Sinhalese fuse them in practice. For example, although magical pollution is different from Buddhist pollution, it is nevertheless related to the latter in this manner: it may encourage mentally defiling attitudes, or at least hinder the individual's attempts to cultivate mental purity. The spirit cults that attempt to handle problems related to magical pollution are consequently facilitating Buddhist pursuits as well. Magic removes psychological and somatic obstacles so that a Buddhist may continue to perform his sacred duties; it controls mental disturbances so that one is emotionally freed to cultivate mental purity. Magic also symbolically reaffirms the sacred by expressing its own subordination to Buddhism. Many Sinhalese believe that spirits will respond more readily to invocations from virtuous rather than from wayward Buddhists. Spirits themselves symbolize the rewards and punishments of rebirth. A goblin (*yakā*) is one who was born into that circumstance through misdeeds; a god is enjoying the pleasures of past merit.

A diagram (Figure IV) may help to illustrate this facilitating or transitional function of magical-animism. A more detailed treatment of magical therapy and an attempt to show its correspondence to the socialization process will be discussed elsewhere (Ames, 1962d) so it need not be discussed here.

---

[5] Anxiety of fate and death, of emptiness and loss of meaning, of guilt and condemnation. "In all three forms anxiety is existential in the sense that it belongs to existence as such and not to an abnormal state of mind as in neurotic (and psychotic) anxiety" (Tillich, 1952:41).

Figure IV—Suggested Relationship Between Magical-Animism and Buddhism

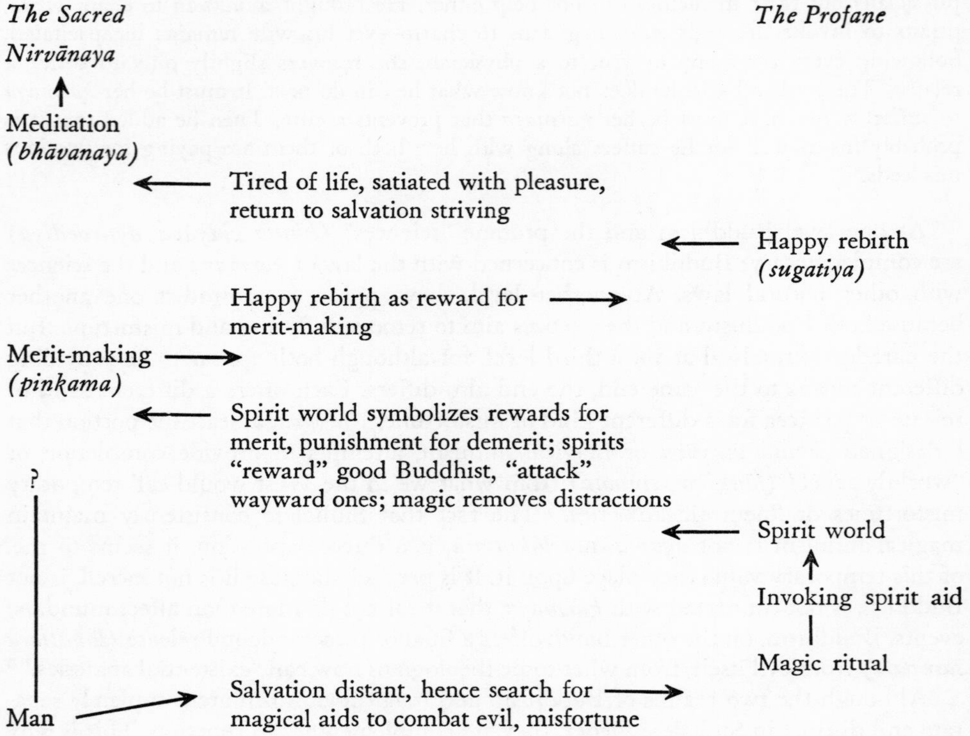

Magical-animism and Buddhism

We are now able to consider the actual position of magical-animism in relation to Buddhism, for the two do not form polar opposites along a single continuum. There is no simple dichotomy here between Great and Little Traditions, sophisticate and folk religions, urbanite and villager. Consider these two facts about Sinhalese religious participation.

First, Buddhism itself is divided into sophisticate and popular, or literati and folk, levels of participation. Those few individuals who concentrate on the ascetic ideal of *bhāvanaya* are less concerned with the more mundane merit-making; those involved in *pinkama* are not yet capable of meditation.

Second, in actual practice all Buddhists, whatever their status within the Buddhist hierarchy, tend to participate in spirit propitiation. Merit-making Buddhism is the popular or folk "religion of the masses"; spirit propitiation is something totally different and not confined to the masses at all. In effect, therefore, Buddhism and magical-animism do not lie on one continuum but on two intersecting ones.

Let me cite several examples of this dual participation. A monk is primarily concerned with his sacred duties—studying the scriptures, observing precepts, practicing meditation. While thus preoccupied, he abstains from magic healing rituals. But if he is suddenly possessed by a goblin, attacked by sorcery, or otherwise made ill, he must resort to magical exorcism, charms, or medicines just like any layman. When a young monk in my village was possessed by a goblin (*yakā*) he disrobed and underwent an exorcist rite (*yakuma*) as a layman. Once cured, he returned to monastic life. When those monks who live in secluded hermitages become mentally or physically ill, they normally return to village temples to obtain cures. In his normal life, a monk is supposed to observe two hundred and twenty-seven precepts; but it is said that for a mentally deranged monk there are no monastic rules at all. He may even drink the blood of a cock bird if it effects a cure. After all, what is the good of Buddhism, which is based on mental culture, for someone who is mentally deranged?

Lay devotees are also constantly dabbling in magic to ward off misfortunes and to obtain worldly boons. A layman thinks nothing of spending a full moon day in solemn meditation, then the following day being exorcised of a spirit. These are not contradictory actions but complementary ones.

This is the point in question. The popular form of Buddhism is not to be confused with magical-animism. Popular and sophisticated Buddhism are based on two different types of Buddhist ritual, merit-making and meditating respectively. Both types are sacred and highly systematized; they differ in that merit-making is for the masses and meditating for the few religiously sophisticated virtuosos. Magical-animism is a different matter altogether. It is not part of the Great-Little Tradition dichotomies. It is profane or non-meritorious, relatively unsystematized (in Weber's sense of "non-rationalized"), and stands outside these two Buddhist categories. It caters to both types of Buddhists.

The primary division in Sinhalese religion is therefore not between big and little traditions at all, but between *lokottara* and *laukika* value orientations or volitions (*cetanā*). Two important religious sub-systems have combined to solve this dual problem of human life—happiness in it and salvation from it. Spirit cults, oriented to worldly (*laukika*) concerns, deal with the misfortunes of daily life; Buddhism is concerned with personal destiny, with what is beyond (*lokottara*) the ordinary. It is the ultimate solution to evil, while magical-animism is only a temporary one. And the Sinhalese, both literate and non-literate, both urbanite and villager, both sophisticate and folk, participate in both sub-systems.

It is in *lokottara* concerns alone (i.e., Buddhism) that beliefs and practices are divided into sophisticated or Great (meditating) and popular or Little (merit-making) traditions. Too much concern with artificial dichotomies and the desire to classify everything according to one or another polar opposite serve only to obscure this real and fundamental division of labor that exists within a complex religious system.

There is a final point regarding magical-animism to be considered. All spirit cults, all magic rituals, are used either to alleviate misfortunes brought about by sickness, sorcery, etc., or to augment fortunes—success in an exam, election, business enterprise. They are concerned with suffering and happiness in the present life. But what if these magic cults are highly successful? Would they not then "seduce" people away from higher pursuits? Just as seeking a happy rebirth may become an end in itself rather than a means to something higher, may not recourse to magic also become an end in itself? If suffering can be alleviated by magic, who would need to worry about Buddha and his teachings—at least until he faced death and rebirth?

Literati Buddhists are quite aware of and frequently talk about the seductiveness of magic. There are also several institutionalized means, apparently devised by the literati, for coping with the problem.

There is first a mechanism built into the magic ritual systems themselves that serves to define their inferior status, their inadequacy, their transitoriness. Every magic rite, every cluster of magical symbols, every set of incantations constantly reaffirms the supremacy, the suzerainty, of Buddha *even* in magical affairs. The characteristic "homage to Buddha" (*vandanā*) performed by every magical specialist before he begins his rite is one example. All curing techniques had their origins during the time of Buddha. These mythical origins are recited during the rites. All spirits obey the laws of Buddha (*Budu anin*) and fear the power of his teachings (*dharma balē*).

There is another means, the "magical" aspect of Buddhism. Whether deity shrines are located on Buddhist temple compounds or Buddhist temples are associated with deity temples and shrines, monks are normally in residence in either case. As Buddha is suzerain of all supernaturals, so monks become suzerains of the deity cults. Monks themselves dabble in magic, become experts in the casting of spells and horoscopes. It is even claimed and widely believed that several centuries ago a famous monk called Rahula collected all the Hindu texts Sinhalese magicians used and rewrote them according to Buddhist standards. Instead of homage to Siva he wrote in homage to Buddha. According to one myth, Buddha visited Ceylon and converted the gods. They then proceeded to convert the people. According to another myth the monk Rahula "converted" all the spells and charms. They, in turn, "converted" the magicians!

There is a third device. The restraint with which official Buddhism regards magical-animism is an effective way of divesting these cults of any moral value. In the Buddhist view they are *laukika,* profane, ordinary. Not only can they not affect rebirth; neither can they influence in a positive way one's prestige in society. A successful magician may be feared for his power; but he is not therefore respected for his morality. In fact, he may even be suspected *because* of his power. A successful Buddhist, on the other hand, one who has gained spiritual powers (*idi;* levitation, etc.) through meditation, is not only respected, but absolutely worshipped.

These are institutional means for defining and limiting the seductive powers of magical-animism. How successful they are in practice and to what extent they do influence individual motivation are far more difficult to determine. There is always a certain amount of ambiguity and tension present in the relations between Buddhism and the spirit cults (as there is between religion and magic everywhere). This at least suggests that the restraining devices may not be as successful as some Buddhists might wish.

Temple Estate and State Systems

The third and fourth sub-systems are discussed together in more restricted fashion for two reasons. First, both are vastly complicated systems rent with ambiguities still scarcely understood by anyone. Second, during the past few hundred years of colonial rule, both have reacted and changed, and are still reacting, in ways that are also not clearly understood. They appear to be much less stable than Buddhism or even magical-animism. I will therefore limit myself to giving an idealized picture of how the two systems operated in traditional times (especially in the Kandyan Kingdom that preceded British rule in 1815), refer to some of the basic principles involved, and suggest what are the more important strains inherent in the relations of these systems to Buddhism and magical-animism.

As it was suggested earlier, both the estate and state were directed more towards facilitating secondary rather than primary religious goals. The dominating concern of the Sinhalese was not to attain salvation but to perpetuate Buddhism until salvation again becomes attainable. The religious function of the temple estate system was therefore, through the granting of landed estates and other goods, to provide temples and their incumbents with the facilities to teach and preserve the doctrine. This was the economic aspect of religion. The political aspect was handled by the state system. The principle here was that the King, or the leading political authority of the region, would protect religious interests and patronize religious practices especially *pinkamas* and spirit cults.

Temple estates have a long history in Ceylon (see Rahula, 1956:141–152) and are usually referred to as Buddhist Temporalities (Ceylon Government, 1938) or "monastic landlordism" (Weber, 1958:257), although the system is by no means restricted to Buddhist institutions. From early times both Buddhist temples (*vihārayas*) and "Hindu" deity temples (*dēvālayas*) were granted vast estates (*vihāragamas* and *dēvālegamas*) for their maintenance. Requirements for the temples, for the incumbent Buddhist monks (*bhikkus*) and *deviyā* priests (*kapurālas*), and for Buddhist and magic rituals were apportioned among peasants who lived on these estates as service tenants.[6] Both the state and private individuals made grants to temples; bequests ranged in size from small buildings or plots of land to large areas with their associated villages; and these bequests were usually considered meritorious because they were acts of giving (*dan dīma*).

This system of temple estates performed two main functions, one economic and the other political, two sides of the same coin. On the one hand, temple estates sustained the ceremonial life of the temples (Wijeyewardene, *et. al.*, 1956:60–62); on the other hand, they served to bolster the control of the king over his subjects (Wijeyewardene, *et. al.*, 1956:6–7):

> The Kings generally regarded Dewale lands as their own property, granted for the support of the religion but available for the Kings to deal with as they pleased. It has been said that Dewale establishments were maintained for a political purpose and that the grants were made not only to enable the performance of certain ceremonies but also to maintain a number of lay chiefs in a position suitable to their rank and influence. In relation to Vihare lands, however, the King's powers to deal with them were restrained by the sacred character which attached to them as well as by the terms of the grants by which they were dedicated to the Vihare. [However] Priests [*bhikkus*] were not vested with any control over the lands which were administered for them by lay individuals under the supervision of the King who had absolute authority over the priests and the laity. The selection and appointment of chiefs and priests of temples was a prerogative of the King.

The detailed operation of the estate system can best be understood by viewing it in its wider context, for in addition to its specifically religious function, this system was linked with three other social institutions—caste (*jātiya*), the service tenure system

[6] For brief discussions see Codrington, 1938; Pieris, 1956:73–77; Ryan, 1953:25–57. Excellent detailed information is provided in the reports of various commissions appointed by the British Colonial régime to investigate temporalities. See Crawford, 1910; Dickson, 1870; Layard, *et al.*, 1876; Sessional Papers, 1904; Wijeyewardene, *et. al.*, 1956:6–9, 25–26.

(*rājakāriya*), and secular estates (*nindagamas*). All four together formed a general societal economic complex of which the temple estate system was but one component and the one most directly related to religion (Wijeyewardene, *et. al.,* 1956:1–6).

Title to all lands nominally resided in the Crown, subject to dispensations. Grants of land made by the king, or by any other authority under his orders, to private individuals or royal officers (*nindagamas*), to Buddhist temples, and to deity temples, were combined with a feudal tenure by service (*rājakāriya,* "king's duty"). Grantees—individuals, *vihārayas, dēvālayas*—of such lands or estates (*gamas*) became the overlords or proprietors, and those who cultivated the lands their tenants. *Nindagama* overlords, instead of the king, were entitled to the services, real and in kind, performed by the tenants; the overlords were in turn liable to perform services to the Crown (temple estates were not subject to royal tax). Some lands were heritable by the tenant; others were leased on a tenancy-at-will basis. The basic principle of economic exchange underlying this granting of estates was that wages were paid in land and rent was paid in labor.

Liability to perform service was an obligation attached to the land itself; each parcel of land was in turn generally allotted to the caste group that traditionally performed the service in question. Consequently, washermen, potters, tom-tom beaters, goldsmiths, metal and stone workers, and the castes that supplied menials, laborers, cultivators, and traders each held tenancy rights to different parts of the total estate. The general rule was that the more fertile the piece of land or the larger its extent, the more honorable the services required for it, and consequently the higher the status of its tenants.

Although the British eventually legislated against *rājakāriya* on *nindagamas,* and caste is no longer sanctioned by the state, temple estates still carry service tenure obligations. Even though in recent years there are more and more legal and other complications involved in enforcing these obligations, many temples continue to receive labor and ceremonial performances from service castes (i.e., washermen, drummers).

In summary, the estate system performed an economic function for temples by providing labor, land, and material goods; for the king the same system, in conjunction with *nindagama,* performed a political function by providing a network of fiefdoms. The functions of the state system were the reverse of these. The state supplied political and legal protection to religious status groups (monks and spirit priests) who, in return, "supplied" labor power in the form of domesticated and pacified peasants.

This is how the state system was supposed to work. The state, in traditional times as represented by a patrimonial monarch, ideally a *cakkavatti* or universal emperor, was a part of the religious system in the sense that the king was dedicated to upholding the faith and protecting religious institutions, above all Buddhist ones (Davy, 1821:142, 158–164; Pieris, 1956:9–13; Rahula, 1956:67–77). This was the political aspect of religion. In return for this support, monks (*bhikkus*) and priests (both Hindu *brahmins* and Sinhalese *kapurālas*) sanctified the king on ceremonial occasions and, through their religious and educational activities, served to domesticate and pacify the masses. Insofar as the laity were bound in religious loyalty or through economic obligations to monks and other religious specialists, they were also likely to be obedient to the king who supported the specialists. At least judging from various records including the monkish chronicle *The Mahāvamsa* (Geiger, 1950, 1953), that was the fiction both monks and kings tried to promote. More than in a literal sense the king defended the faith while the faith legitimated the king (Green, 1961).

On several occasions in Sinhalese history, a special Ministry of Religion was established (Rahula, 1956:72, Chapters, VIII, IX); and more than occasionally, even down to modern times, heads of state (formerly kings, now prime ministers) ceremonially "donated" their realms to the Buddhist monkhood (Rahula, 1956:75; Geiger, 1960:204). This act was to symbolize the subordination, in a value sense at least, of the interests of the state to those of religion. Religious ideals were always, so far as one can tell, granted supremacy in the value system, and the ideal of the state was to support and to facilitate religious pursuits. In addition to political protection the king also provided the legal force behind ecclesiastical laws; he could arbitrate in monastic disputes and was expected to guard against disobedience and corruption within the monkhood. These are the duties and prerogatives of the state that were at least reflected by inscriptions and written records from earliest times.

In practice, in contrast to the ideal, the relations between religion and state were probably of a far more tenuous and ambiguous nature. What little evidence there is indicates that state and religious officials were constantly competing with one another for positions of power and that the duties of one towards the other were not always agreed upon (Green, 1961). The debate continues today.

The operation of the estate and state systems gives rise to certain obvious problems. A tragedy all religions must face, no matter how much they advocate salvation from the world, is that they become time and time again very intimately involved *in* the world. The estate and state systems over the centuries have periodically fallen into states of scandalous corruption, only to reform, to revive, and to fall again (see Rahula, 1956). Rahula argues that the wealthier the temple estates became through gifts of merit, the more people were motivated to plunder and exploit these properties. The temple incumbents, monks and spirit priests, needed protection against plunder by outsiders and from corruption within. Religious specialists have no formal hierarchies or mechanisms of control of their own; consequently they were dependent on the king to maintain law and order. But the temple incumbents also had to guard against exploitation by the king or against his neglect. This poses a dilemma especially for the monks who had vowed to withdraw from the world. Once temporalities were recognized as a necessity for the perpetuation of the religion, the monks considered it their duty to perpetuate temporalities (Rahula, 1956:168 passim). As a consequence, monks came back into the world as monastic landlords and formed political pressure groups to guard those institutions that made possible their status position and style of life.

What effect does all this have on the Buddhist sub-system? Historical records, scanty in other ways, are instructive in this respect. Eighteen attempts by kings to purify the monastic order are recorded in the chronicles and commentaries. The first is said to have occurred in the third century A.D., the last in the eighteenth century. It is quite possible that there were more attempts than this, and it is equally possible that many were not successful. In theory, whenever scandal rent the monkhood, the king would induce monks to extirpate it by an ecclesiastical or "regulative" act, *dhamma ḳammena,* founded on the rules of the Vinaya or Book of Discipline; thus the king is said to have purified the doctrine (*sodhesi sāsanam*) (see Geiger, 1960:205; Rahula, 1956:67, 306–307; Codrington, 1947).

Higher ordination in the monkhood, an apostolic succession allegedly derived from

Buddha himself, is said to have been lost on four occasions and consequently reintroduced or restored from abroad by various kings, thrice from Burma in the eleventh, sixteenth, and seventeenth centuries, once from India in the thirteenth, once from Siam in the eighteenth century (Geiger, 1960:198).

As Rahula observes, "the life of monks . . . began to change in conformity with time and place as social and economic conditions changed" (1956:153). The principle is simple, and common to all monastic systems. The more holy a monk, the more meritorious it is to give to him; and the more he receives in gifts and favors, the more difficult it becomes for him to retain his holiness. The Sinhalese, especially the monk, is constantly being seduced by the world before he can flee it. This is certainly true today, whatever happened in the past. Sinhalese are universal in their complaint about monastic corruption and lay iniquity. Exploitation of temple properties is widespread (see Guneratne, 1959, and the temporalities reports cited above). Monks are deeply involved in politics (Wriggens, 1960:169–210) and business enterprises.

It is in the estate and state systems especially that Sinhalese religion articulates closely with secular institutions—with caste and land tenure, government and politics. It is here that strains seem to develop most easily. Once corruption sets in, it ramifies throughout the entire religious system and contaminates sacred institutions as well. That sacred pursuits for most people are limited strictly to attaining pleasant rebirths and worldly benefits through *pinkama* and magic only serves to encourage the worldliness and materialism that are already endemic.

The government has retained to this day the right to intervene in Sinhalese religious affairs; but since about 1850 it has refrained as much as possible from exercising that right. Ecclesiastical laws pertaining to affairs within the monkhood are no longer enforced by the government. The church in effect has been "disestablished"; it suffers the same consequences as it would under a corrupt or ineffectual king.

Modern Buddhist intelligentsia are quite aware of the many problems now confronting their religion and are today desperately trying to work out a new program for church-state-estate relations (see Buddhist Committee, 1956; Pannasekere, 1959; Perera, 1952; Siriwardene, 1960). It would not be farfetched to describe these efforts as an attempted Reformation (Ames, 1963; Mendis, 1957:116). In fact, an editorial writer in a scholarly Ceylon journal (Anonymous, 1951) even goes so far as to hope that a reformed Buddhism would "usher into Ceylon the Peace on Earth that Calvin hoped for England"!

Summary and Conclusions

The purpose of this paper is to describe the dominant ideals of Sinhalese religion, to show how these ideals are put into practice, and to suggest some of the problems this implementation involves. It is a preliminary attempt to subject a total religious system to sociological analysis. A next important step would be to explore more fully the relations between this system and secular institutions such as kinship, caste, and politics.

Now let me list the threads of the argument that runs throughout the paper.

1. Other-worldly salvation from a life of suffering is the ideal all Sinhalese Buddhists venerate and the one that conditions or dominates all religious action. It is the ultimate goal of the system.

2. But it is an ideal that is both difficult to understand and even more difficult to attain. For most people it takes thousands and thousands of rebirths.

3. Sinhalese must therefore find temporary ways of combatting suffering until salvation is possible. These temporary means—happy rebirth, consolation through magic—become important secondary goals of the religious system. They may even become ends in themselves rather than means to something higher.

4. The division of labor within the religious system and within the Buddhist sub-system reflects this multiplicity of goals and the emphasis placed on those that are secondary.

5. Within the Buddhist sub-system, for example, people specialize at being hermit monks, or village monks, or lay devotees, or ordinary householders. But in practice, most people follow the vocations of householder and village monk. They are people concerned with merit-making rituals and rebirth, with combatting *duka* rather than eradicating it, with preaching the doctrine rather than practicing it. There are only a few who are hermits and lay devotees actively seeking salvation through meditation. Buddhism is a low pyramid with a very wide base.

6. The spirit cults are entirely devoted to combatting misfortune and providing consolation in the present existence. By alleviating mental disturbances, they enable Buddhists to concentrate on meritorious and meditating activities, both of which involve mental development. Magical-animism therefore caters to both types of Buddhists: the few virtuosos and the masses.

7. The estate and state sub-systems are also primarily concerned with facilitating those pursuits (rebirth and consolation) that are secondary in theory but primary in practice. Hermit monks need a minimum of facilities. But there are vast estates dedicated to providing economic support for village monks and spirit priests, their temples, and their ceremonies. There is in addition the state that gives protection and patronage to these popular institutions.

8. In contrast to Buddhism, the economic, political, and therapeutic sub-systems are considered quasi-sacred or wholly profane because of the worldly functions they perform.

9. There are certain strains both within each sub-system and in the relations between them. But strain and instability are especially evident in those institutions (estate, state, magic) most deeply involved in the world and whose members are consequently in greatest danger of becoming seduced by the very things from which they must flee. Perhaps this is why these worldly religious institutions always seem to be the first to adapt to changes that occur at the secular, societal level.

10. The structured strains in conjunction with a world-affirming, materialistic emphasis resulting from a radical, unobtainable salvation ideal lead naturally, inevitably, to corruption and disorder within the religious system. Sinhalese religion may be defined as the "business of earning salvation," but repeatedly people pay more attention to the business than to its purpose. Wealthy temple estates are always a source of temptation both to monks and laity; they make possible the same kind of material rewards that people seek through a happy rebirth.

The fundamental paradox facing the Sinhalese is that they have such a high and noble ideal they can never fully realize it in this life. Not only are they unhappily bound to endless rebirth, they *need* rebirth. Then they must somehow learn to escape from it.

Change the concept of *nirvānaya*—bring it "closer" to realization—and the value placed on auxiliary religious institutions would also change. It is precisely the modern Buddhist enthusiast who believes that salvation is attainable within this or the next few lives who also claims that magic is superfluous, happy rebirth a waste of time, and materialism sinful. Who needs these things if he believes he can attain salvation now? Who can do without them while redemption is not available? It is in this way, among others, that abstract religious ideals condition concrete actions.

This is my interpretation of the facts. I believe it helps to account for the peculiar ways in which Sinhalese religious life is organized and for the fact that the auxiliary institutions such as magical-animism, although distinguished from Buddhism by the Sinhalese, are nevertheless closely related to Buddhism in a special way.

The moral of my story is quite simple. Sinhalese religion faces the dilemma all redemption religions are confronted with: although it offers salvation from the world, it must nevertheless itself remain very much a part of the world. There is no escape from this seduction. The only question is how to handle it. And it is the religious ideal that determines how this question will be answered. There is a more general proposition involved in this moral, concerning the relations between abstract values and concrete actions. Even though values themselves are not realized, not put into practice, perhaps not even fully understood by people, they nevertheless do continue to influence and guide what is practiced. The absence of salvation striving does not mean absence of concern.

Do not mistake my analysis for a negative criticism of Sinhalese religion. I have no intention of being derogatory. In fact, much can be said in favor of this religion. No complex religious system is immune to strain and corruption and the Sinhalese have fared no worse than others in this respect. Second, judging by the historical records, Sinhalese religion with its four-pillar structure (Buddhism, magic cults, temple estates, political patronage) appears to have persisted for perhaps two thousand years. Even if corruption was frequent and endemic, the system appears always to have reasserted itself again. From the point of view of survival, therefore, Sinhalese religion seems to be highly successful. It has persisted in one small island perhaps for a longer period than Christianity has persisted anywhere, and with far fewer changes.

At one time or another Mahayana Buddhism, Hinduism, Islam, and Christianity were all introduced to Ceylon. But there is no evidence to suggest that more than a few Sinhalese ever converted to these other faiths. Today, at least, perhaps only five percent of the Sinhalese are Christian, another three percent are Muslim, and there are almost no Hindus.

What is more, inspection of the early written records, myths, and legends, scanty as they are, nevertheless strongly suggests that the ancient religion was little different from its contemporary version in basic ideals. In one of the commentaries to the Pali Canon that the famous monk Buddhagosha (fifth century A.D.) was said to have translated into Pali, he himself expresses the wish to be reborn during the time of Maitri Buddha thousands of years hence so that he can attain salvation under the guidance of a Buddha (Adikaram, 1955:153). Apparently even then salvation was not considered imminently attainable. But constantly in the early records, the importance of *pinkamas* and rebirth is stressed. These records also indicate that temple estates, state patronage, and spirit cults were always closely associated with *pinkama* Buddhism. (For surveys of the evidence, partly myth, partly fact, see Adikaram, 1953; Devendra, 1960; Geiger, 1960, Rahula, 1956.)

From the point of view of structural stability and survival of ideas, therefore, Sinhalese religion appears to have been remarkably successful. But perhaps the really crucial evaluation lies in the attitudes of the people themselves towards their religion. Again today, at least, there is little doubt that Sinhalese are devout and loyal Buddhists. They are entirely satisfied that it is the best of all religions, the only true one. They are even sending missionaries now to convert the heathens of India and Europe. Even though they complain about the present state of Buddhism, they never question Buddhism's validity, its value. The Buddha's name is never taken in vain; his teachings are universally venerated. Can a religion really ask more than this of man?

References Cited

Adikaram, E. W.
1953 *Early History of Buddhism in Ceylon*. Colombo: Gunasena.

Ames, Michael M.
1962a Religious Syncretism in Buddhist Ceylon. Unpubl. Ph.D. dissertation, Harvard University.
1962b Popular Ideology and Village Rites of the Sinhalese Buddhists. *In: Laity and Buddhism*, ed. by R. J. Miller and A. Wayman (in press).
1962c Ritual Prestations and the Structure of the Sinhalese Pantheon. *In:* Proceedings of the Chicago Conference on Theravada Buddhism, ed. by M. Nash (in press).
1962d The Buddha and the Dancing Goblins: a Theory of Magic and Religion. Ms.
1963 Ideological and Social Change in Ceylon. Human Organization. 22:45–53.

Anonymous
1951 Notes and Comments on Some Aspects of the Buddhist Revival (editorial). Ceylon Historical Journal. 1:7–12.

Ariyapala, M. B.
1956 *Society in Mediaeval Ceylon*. Colombo: K. V. G. de Silva.

Bareau, André
1957 La vie et l'organisation des communautés bouddhiques modernes de Ceylan, Publ. de L'Institut Français D'Indologies No. 10, Pondichéry (India).

Bell, H. C. P.
1916–17 Mahā Saman Dēvālē and its Sannasa. Ceylon Antiquary and Literary Register. 2:36–46.
1889 Paddy Cultivation Ceremonies in the Four Kōralēs, Kēgalla District. Journal (Ceylon Branch) Royal Asiatic Society. 11:167–171.

Buddhist Committee of Inquiry
1956 *The Betrayal of Buddhism*. Balangoda (Ceylon): Dharmavijaya Press.

Callaway, John (trans.)
1829 *Yakkun nattannavā and kolan nattannavā*, Cingalese poems (descriptive of Ceylon system of demonology and masks). London: Oriental Translation Fund.

Ceylon Government
1938 Buddhist Temporalities, an Ordinance to Amend and Consolidate the Law Relating to Buddhist Temporalities. Ordinance No. 19 of 1931, 1938 revision. Colombo: Ceylon Government Press.

Codrington, H. W.
1938 *Ancient Land Tenure and Revenue in Ceylon*. Colombo: Ceylon Government Press.
1947 *A Short History of Ceylon*. London: Macmillan.

Copleston, R. S.
1908 *Buddhism Primitive and Present in Magadha and in Ceylon.* London: Longmans, Green.

Crawford, H. L.
1910 Papers on the Buddhist Temporalities Ordinance of 1905. Sessional Papers 23 of 1910. Colombo: Ceylon Government Press.

Davy, John
1821 *An Account of the Interior of Ceylon and of Its Inhabitants.* London: Longman, Hurst, Rees, Orme and Brown.

Devendra, D. T.
1960 A Mirror of Ancient Ceylon. The Buddhist, Vesak number. 31:31–36.

Dickson, J. F.
1870 Report of the Service Tenures Commissioner for 1870. Administration Reports, pp. 277–287. Colombo: Ceylon Government Press.
1886 Notes Illustrative of Buddhism as the Daily Religion of the Buddhists of Ceylon, and Some Account of Their Ceremonies Before and After Death. Journal (Ceylon Branch) Royal Asiatic Society. 8:297–330.

Durkheim, Emile
1915 *The Elementary Forms of the Religious Life.* London: Allen and Unwin.

Geiger, Wm.
1938 *A Grammar of the Sinhalese Language.* Colombo: (Ceylon Branch) Royal Asiatic Society.
1950 *The Mahāvamsa or the Great Chronicle of Ceylon.* Trans. by Wm. Geiger. Colombo: Ceylon Government Information Department.
1953 *Cūlavamsa, Being the More Recent Part of the Mahāvamsa,* Parts I & II. Trans. by Wm. Geiger. Colombo: Ceylon Government Information Department.
1960 *Culture of Ceylon in Mediaeval Times.* Wiesbaden: Harrassowitz.

Gogerly, D. J.
1908 *Ceylon Buddhism.* Colombo.

Gooneratne, D. de S.
1865–66 On Demonology and Witchcraft in Ceylon. Journal (Ceylon Branch) Royal Asiatic Society. 4:1–117. (Reprinted, 1954.)

Green, A. L.
1961 Sangha and King: The Structure of Authority in Medieval Ceylon. Paper presented at the symposium on Theravada Buddhism, Tenth Pacific Science Congress, Honolulu, August 1961.

Guneratne, V. F.
1959 Malpractices of Trustees: Report of the Public Trustee. *In:* Buddhist Sasana Commission Report (draft of English language translation), ed. by K. Pannasekere, *et. al.* Colombo.

Hardy, R. S.
1860 *Eastern Monachism.* London: Williams and Norgate.

Hocart, A. M.
1931 Temple of the Tooth in Kandy. Memoir of Archaeological Survey of Ceylon IV. London: Luzac.

Ivers, R. W.
1880 Customs and Ceremonies Connected with Rice Cultivation. Journal (Ceylon Branch) Royal Asiatic Society. 6:46–52.

Layard, C. P., *et. al.*
1876 Report of the Commissioners Appointed to Inquire into the Administration of the Buddhist Temporalities. Sessional Paper 17 of 1876. Colombo: Ceylon Government Press.
Leach, E. R.
1962 Pulleyar and the Lord Buddha: An Aspect of Religious Syncretism in Ceylon. Psychoanalysis and Psychoanalytic Review. 49:80–102.
Le Mesurier, C. J. R.
1884 An-keliya. Journal (Ceylon Branch) Royal Asiatic Society. 8:368–394.
Liyanage, K. C.
1958 Popular Elements in Buddhism Today. University of Ceylon Buddhist Annual, pp. 34–39.
Madsen, W.
1957 Christo-paganism: A Study of Mexican Religious Syncretism. Middle American Research Institute, Tulane University. (Reprinted, 1960.)
Meerwarth-Levina, Ludmila
1915–16 The Hindu Goddess Pattini in the Buddhist Popular Beliefs of Ceylon. Ceylon Antiquary and Literary Register. 1:29–37.
Mendis, G. C.
1957 *Ceylon Today and Yesterday.* Colombo: Associated Newspapers.
Obeyesekere, G.
1958 The Structure of Sinhalese Ritual. Ceylon Journal of Historical and Social Studies. 1:192–202.
1962 The Sinhalese Pantheon and Its Extension. *In:* Proceedings of the Chicago Conference on Theravada Buddhism, ed. by M. Nash (in press).
Pannasekere, K., *et. al.* (eds.)
1959 *Buddhist Sasana Commission Report.* (Draft of English language translation.) Colombo.
Parsons, T. and N. J. Smelser
1958 *Economy and Society.* Glencoe: Free Press.
Perera, G. K. W.
1952 A Constitution for Buddhists. Negombo (Ceylon), pamphlet.
Pertold, O.
1930 The Ceremonial Dances of the Sinhalese. Archiv Orientalni 2, Parts I, II, III, IV.
Pieris, Ralph
1956 *Sinhalese Social Organization: The Kandyan Period.* Colombo: Ceylon University Press.
Rahula, Walpola
1956 *History of Buddhism in Ceylon.* Colombo: Gunasena.
Ripley, Rev. F. J.
1960 *This is the Faith.* New York: Guild Press.
Ryan, Bryce
1953 *Caste in Modern Ceylon.* New Brunswick, N. Y.: Rutgers University Press.
Seligman, B.
1908 A Devil Ceremony of the Peasant Sinhalese. Journal Royal Anthropological Institute. 38:368–379.
Sessional Papers
1904 Relating to the Proposed Amendment of the Buddhist Temporalities Ordinance, No. 3 of 1899. Sessional Paper 23 of 1904. Colombo: Ceylon Government Press.

de Silva, W. A.
1911 Note on the *Bali* Ceremonies of the Sinhalese. Journal (Ceylon Branch) Royal Asiatic Society. 22:140–160.
Siriwarden, C. D. S.
1960 The Proposed Incorporation of the Sangha. The Buddhist, Vesak number. Vol. 31, No. 1, 3:83–84.
Thompson, D. E.
1954 Maya Paganism and Christianity: A History of the Fusion of Two Religions. Middle American Research Institute, Tulane University. (Reprinted, 1960.)
Tillich, P.
1962 *The Courage to Be.* New Haven: Yale University Press.
Upham, E.
1829 *History and Doctrine of Buddhism, with Notices of the Kappooism or Demon Worship and Bali, or Planetary Incantations of Ceylon.* London: Ackermann.
Weber, Max
1958 *The Religion of India.* Glencoe: Free Press.
Wijeyewardene, E. A. L., *et. al.*
1956 Report of the Commission on Tenure of Lands of Viharagam, Dewalagam and Nindagam. Sessional Paper 1–1956. Colombo: Ceylon Government Press.
Wirz, Paul
1954 *Exorcism and the Art of Healing in Ceylon.* Leyden: Brill.
Wriggens, W. Howard
1960 *Ceylon, Dilemmas of a New Nation.* Princeton, N. J.: Princeton University Press.
Yalman, Nur
1962a On Some Binary Categories in Sinhalese Religious Thought. Transactions of the New York Academy of Sciences (Ser. 2, 24).
1962b The Ascetic Buddhist Monks of Ceylon. Bulletin London School of Oriental and African Studies (in press).
1962c The Structure of Sinhalese Healing Rituals. Proceedings of the Berkeley Conference on Indian Religions.
1962d An Keliya. *In:* Proceedings of the Chicago Conference on Theravada Buddhism, ed. by M. Nash (in press).
de Zoysa, A. P.
1948–49 *Sinhala sabda kosaya.* Colombo: Dharma Samaya Yantralaya. Vols. I, III.

Brahmins and Shamans in Pahari Religion

GERALD D. BERREMAN

Introduction

THE roles of various castes (*jatis*) in Hindu religious activities have been of interest to many students of rural Indian society. As a result, we are quite familiar with the patterns of ceremonial activity of Brahmin priests and of other participants in Brahmanical ritual such as temple keepers of various castes, barbers, carpenters, musicians, etc. (Dube, 1955; Opler and Singh, 1948; Planalp, 1956; Srinivas, 1952). Many of these patterns of religious participation are described and prescribed in the Sanskritic literature of Hinduism, and so fall within the "great tradition" of Hinduism (Redfield, 1956).

Also of interest have been those religious activities of village Hindus which, while not necessarily incompatible with great traditional, Sanskritic, or Brahmanical Hinduism, are in many ways distinguishable from it. These include the myriad religious observances followed by village Hindus which are not described in Sanskritic literature. Many of these appear to be variations on Sanskritic themes, i.e., local deviations from Sanskritic norms (cf. Marriott, 1955), but many are of a different order. They supplement Sanskritic ritual but are not derived from it. Among these are the activities of a variety of religious practitioners such as shamans, diviners, exorcists, curers, and propitiators of particular gods.

The purpose of this paper is to contrast the religious roles of Brahmin priests in Brahmanical or Sanskritic ritual, on the one hand, and of shamans, an important category of non-Brahmanical, non-Sanskritic practitioners, on the other, with special reference to their roles in religious change—i.e., as religious innovators and policy makers. This will be done not for India at large, but for one culture area.

The area to be described is that of the lower Himalayas of North India and Nepal —a region occupied by Indo-Aryan-speaking Hindus who are known as Paharis ("of the mountains"), a term which also denotes their language. The sub-region known best to me is the central section of this extensive area, in and about the district and former princely state of Tehri Garhwal. My field research was carried out during 1957–58 in Sirkanda, a Garhwali village in Dehra Dun district on the western border of Tehri Garhwal.[1]

The culture of this area has been described in general terms elsewhere (Berreman, 1960b; 1961; 1962a; 1962b; 1963). For the purposes of this paper, only a few preliminary points need be made.

The author is Associate Professor of Anthropology at the University of California, Berkeley.

[1] The research upon which this paper is based was carried out under a Ford Foundation Foreign Area Training Fellowship in 1957–58. The writing was supported by a summer research appointment with the Himalayan Border Countries Project of the Center for South Asia Studies, Institute of International Studies, University of California, Berkeley.

Pahari caste distribution and ranking differ from those of the nearby but culturally distinct Indo-Gangetic plain in that there are relatively few Pahari castes, none of whom are classed as Sudras or Vaisyas. Everyone is either one of the twice-born *Khasiya* castes (sometimes spelled *Khasa*—a term which includes Pahari Brahmins and Rajputs), or one of the untouchable *Dom* castes. Artisans are nearly all in the latter category, while full-time agriculturists, who make up nearly ninety per cent of the population, are in the former category. Priests are Brahmins but few Brahmins are priests. Even in those cases where a Brahmin family performs priestly functions and has a traditional clientele (and by no means all do), only one or two members pursue this specialty, while the rest till the family fields.

It is important to note that religious belief and practice, like other aspects of Pahari culture, vary little from caste to caste. This is in notable contrast to the situation in villages of the North Indian plains (cf. Berreman, 1960b).

Finally, Pahari Hinduism deviates from Hinduism in the plains, and by plains standards is not only unorthodox but actually degraded. This differential status may be suggested by the following quotations from an anthropologist who did research in a western Pahari area. They reflect the difficulty of assessing the quality of Pahari Hinduism by plains standards:

> The Khasas are Hindus; their customary rites in temples, the manner and mode of offering sacrifices . . . periodical festivals . . . all indicate their Hindu origin. . . . (Majumdar, 1944:139f.)
>
> While the Khasas claim to be Hindus . . . their social life as well as their beliefs and practices connected with their religion do not identify them with the Hindus of the plains. They re-marry their widows, practice levirate, sororate and polyandry, recognize divorce as legal, while inter-marriage between the various Khasa groups is not tabooed and children born of such marriages do not suffer any social stigma. While they worship Hindu gods and goddesses, they have a partiality for ancestor spirits, and queer and fantastic demons and gods and for the worship of stones, weapons, dyed rags and symbols. The sun, the moon and the constellations are their gods. (Majumdar, 1944:150)

There can be no doubt that these people are Hindus. Their religious beliefs and behaviors are not outside the range found in Hindu villages throughout India (Berreman, 1961; Cf. Cohn, 1954:174ff.; Dube, 1955:88ff.; Lewis, 1958:197ff., 249ff.; P. Mahar, 1957; 1960; Marriott, 1955; Opler, 1958; Planalp, 1956; Srinivas, 1952). Much of their unorthodoxy stems from the fact that even high-caste Khasiya Paharis tend to exhibit religious and social behavior which on the plains is associated primarily with low-caste groups.

Brahmins

Traditional religious functions of Pahari Brahmin priests are similar to those well known for other parts of India. The priests perform or direct life cycle rites for individuals, and they participate in a variety of periodic and special religious observances on family, lineage, and village levels.

For example, the priest is called shortly after a birth in order to read the child's horoscope, name him, purify him and his family, and secure the blessing of the gods to insure him a long and successful life. A year later the priest performs a brief ceremony when the child takes his first solid food. When a boy has his first haircut, three to seven years after birth, the priest again performs a ceremony while the local Dom barber cuts the child's hair. Likewise, the Brahmin officiates in the elaborate ceremonies of weddings and funerals much as he does in plains villages, though the details of the ceremonies often vary significantly from those carried out elsewhere in North India.

In addition, some annual or calendrical ceremonies require the participation of Brahmin priests. At *Rakri,* a ceremony readily identifiable with *Raksha Bandhan, Silono, Saluno,* and *Upa-karma,* as it is called in other areas (Lewis, 1958:208f.; Marriott, 1955:198; Atkinson, 1884:850), the priests go from house to house tying string bracelets on the wrists of household members, and receiving gifts of grain in return. Although this ceremony is believed to benefit the participants, it lacks the overt implications of brother-sister devotion which characterize it on the plains, and its meaning is obscure to those who engage in it. Another calendrical ceremony led by Brahmins is the annual worship of lineage ancestors.

Priests perform the worship to various Sanskritic gods which accompanies many other religious observances in this area. If the local version of Shiva is to be honored in the spectacular (and non-Sanskritic) rope-sliding ceremony in order to alleviate village-wide difficulties, a Brahmin is employed to worship Ganesh, a god who is honored at the initiation of almost any undertaking, and to worship Shiva, the god to whom the ceremony is directed (Berreman, 1961). In the village protection rite held every ten years or so (Berreman, 1963:102; 383–385), a Brahmin directs much of the worship to the several gods in whose honor the rite is held. He leads the group of villagers who perambulate the village boundaries, and his blessings of the boundaries make the village safe from intrusion of evil spirits. He officiates similarly in the propitiation of most village gods, though he does so infrequently in the case of specifically household deities (Berreman, 1963:96–103). He may be called upon to perform special types of worship such as that intended to bring about the birth of children to barren couples.

In all of these activities, the Brahmin performs prescribed religious actions and recites standard sacred verses or *mantras.* This is done within the context of the *jajmani* system of exchange of ritual services for goods (cf. Berreman, 1962b). By this system a Brahmin performs for those families for whom he is traditional, and usually hereditary, family priest (*purohit*). In return he receives from each family a standard amount of grain annually, plus periodic gifts and prescribed additional remuneration on special occasions and for special services. If the purohit is not competent or available to perform service, another Brahmin priest may be hired to play his role in the family ritual. Whether the purohit's unavailability is temporary or permanent, he continues to get his traditional annual and periodic gifts from his hereditary clientele and the substitute priest is paid only for services rendered on each occasion that he is called. Priests who perform in this capacity will be discussed later.

A Brahmin priest performs or directs virtually all of that part of village religious activity which is of the learned, literate, or great tradition. In this he is a purveyor of carefully prescribed, stereotyped, highly ritualized religious activity. Even when he participates in non-great traditional ceremonies, his function is usually to inject an element of the great tradition into the performance; to propitiate the great traditional deities who will not ignore the ceremony even though it may be directed elsewhere.

He may also, on occasion, lend a Sanskritic air to the worship of non-Sanskritic, local gods, by worshiping them as he would Sanskritic gods.

Priests therefore deal with maintenance of the system in ways prescribed in the great tradition of Hinduism. It is they who help people achieve a favorable afterlife and rebirth. Their primary responsibility is the long-range welfare of their clients. They perform the annual ceremonies and life-cycle rites as well as many special ceremonies. In addition they perform worship to village gods and they practice astrology and some forms of divination based on written prescriptions of Hinduism. Although Brahmin priests are considered local experts on the great traditions, their beliefs and daily practices do not seem to differ materially from those of other castes.

Brahmin priests serve primarily the high-caste Khasiyas, i.e., other Brahmins and Rajputs, although even the lowest castes occasionally secure their services. Many Pahari Brahmins will not deny their services to anyone who will pay, regardless of the client's caste.

Shamans

A variety of non-Brahmanical religious practitioners function in Pahari religion as they do in village Hinduism throughout India. In the area of my research these can be categorized according to the functions they perform as temple keepers, shamans, pujaris (propitiators of particular household gods), diviners, exorcists, and curers (Berreman, 1963:114–117). These categories are not necessarily mutually exclusive nor do they necessarily exclude Brahmins. Brahmin priests are often temple keepers, and frequently they perform some of the functions of diviners and curers, though they usually do so according to certain textual prescriptions.

With the exception of temple keepers—who oversee worship of gods ranging from the Sanskritic to the purely local, in temples dedicated to them—these non-Brahmanical religious functionaries deal with the exigencies of daily life relative to the supernatural. Their primary responsibility is the immediate and worldly welfare of their clients. The shaman diagnoses difficulties through the use of his personal deity. The pujari performs worship to propitiate household deities and plays drums to let the spirits dance. These two functionaries enable people to find the cause and cure of supernaturally caused troubles. Pujaris also help to satisfy the supernatural's demands. Diviners are people who can see the past, present, and future by use of various magical techniques. Exorcists are adept at driving harmful ghosts or other spirits away from their victims. These two types of practitioners overlap in their functions with shamans. Curers include a variety of practitioners of curing arts depending in most cases upon a combination of magical formulae, herbal remedies, and other folk treatments. In function, they overlap diviners and exorcists. Practitioners of all these specialties range from the lowliest shoemakers to Brahmins, but the majority are drawn from among the lower castes.

In this paper I shall concentrate on those practitioners known in the hills as *bāḳī*. Such a person is properly called a shaman because he has direct contact with the supernatural world through a personal, familiar spirit which can possess his body (literally "come to his head") and speak through his mouth to communicate with people who call upon him for information. The activities of shamans in various parts of India have been commented upon by other authors (Harper, 1957; Opler, 1958; Planalp, 1956:636ff.).

Shamans are turned to by people experiencing acute or chronic difficulty bothersome enough to require remedial attention. When an individual, a family, or some other social group has experienced persistent difficulties, such as illness, accidents, poor crops, dry cows, barrenness, lack of male heirs, unfaithful wives, bickering sons or unaccountable losses of property, those who suffer the misfortune usually assume that it is punishment or torment deriving from a supernatural source, and they seek to find the source of the difficulty and to determine the measures necessary to alleviate the trouble (cf. Opler, 1958:554).

In order to get the necessary information, a shaman (bākī) is usually consulted. The shaman is devoted to a particular personal deity or spirit for whom he acts as medium in the diagnosis of difficulties of supernatural origin. Generally the shaman holds regular sessions open to anyone who wants, and can pay for, his advice. First he conducts a short ceremony in honor of the supernatural to which he is personally devoted, and then beats a small drum and sings prayers in its honor. Gradually the spirit takes possession of him, causing him to twitch or even dance in evident unawareness of his environment. When the spirit is in complete control, it acts in the body of the shaman and it calls out the names of those who have come to seek its knowledge, telling first the nature of the troubles experienced by each client and then identifying their source. The spirit's accuracy in identifying the nature of the troubles determines to a large extent the client's confidence in that particular shaman. The personal spirit possessing the shaman identifies the supernatural being responsible for the difficulty and the circumstances which have offended that being. It may also identify human spell-casters, thieves, or other culprits, as well as objects or actions which have had deleterious magical effects. If the client is not satisfied with the diagnosis, he can seek another shaman, with access to a more knowledgeable spirit.

In addition to identifying the source of a client's difficulties, the spirit possessing a shaman will tell the client the steps necessary to alleviate his difficulties. The advice is almost invariably to hold a ceremony worshiping the offended deity. Part of such a ceremony involves the beating of drums, which gives the deity a chance to dance in the body of a worshiper (an activity said to be enjoyed by supernaturals) and also to make known any further demands by speaking through a worshiper. If the source of difficulty is a ghost rather than a deity, the shaman will tell the client what ghost it is so that he may seek out the appropriate exorcist. Although the shaman may make specific recommendations for remedial action, he often merely indicates the intensity of the spirit's anger and vaguely suggests the kind and extent of worship required to appease it.

From that point on, it is up to the family of the victim to carry out the shaman's recommendations. In this respect the Pahari shaman functions in a way similar to that described for South India by Harper (1957), and differently from the North Indian plains shamans reported by Opler (1958) and Planalp (1956). The Pahari and South Indian shamans are primarily sources of advice and knowledge; the North Indian plains shaman takes part in contacting the supernatural entity responsible for the difficulty and inducing it to make known its demands.

After receiving the shaman's diagnosis, special non-shaman practitioners are required in order to contact the being inflicting the difficulty. These are specialists in the propitiation of particular supernaturals but they themselves have no direct access to these supernaturals. Rather, they know how to honor them and how to induce them to possess their victims and make known their demands It is a member of the victim's family, never the practitioner, who is possessed. The specialists, known simply as pujaris (those who perfom worship), like shamans, may be of any caste, but are usually Doms. They usually work in two-man teams, arranging and performing the ceremony in honor of the supernatural, and playing the percussion accompaniment for the dancing that is a part of every such performance and which brings the spirit to possess a worshiper. The possessed person goes into a trance and, after dancing for some time, becomes quiescent, indicating that the supernatural is prepared to talk. The worshipers then ask the supernatural what it wants, and not infrequently plead for less stringent demands When the demands have become final, the worshipers vow to fulfill them. At this point the spirit leaves and the difficulties imposed by him should terminate. The family members must then set about to fulfill their vow or face even more dire torment at the hands of the same spirit. In most cases, the demand is for a minor ceremony culminating in the sacrifice of a goat, or for some other relatively easily accomplished form of worship. However, it may be for some more elaborate and expensive ceremony ranging up to the spectacular rope-sliding ceremony (Berreman, 1961).

Shamans are consulted and pujaris are employed by Brahmins and Rajputs as well as by Doms. It is upon the shaman's advice, and upon the advice of the deity which he has identified and which pujaris have brought to the presence of those he is troubling, that most religious activity, other than annual and life-cycle ceremonies, takes place in the Pahari village.

There are a number of shamans within consultation distance of any village, and people are willing to travel some distance to obtain the services of a successful shaman. In fact, there is a consistent tendency not to consult a shaman of one's own village, for village-fellows are known too well to have acquired an aura of infallibility. Payment is on a per consultation basis with no trace of lasting mutual obligations between practitioner and client, in contrast to the purohit's jajmani relationship with his client.

Shamans may attribute their clients' difficulties to any one of the great traditional gods well known in Hinduism or to a variety of regional and local deities worshiped either on a village-wide basis or by particular households. They may also attribute difficulties to family ancestors, witches, malevolent ghosts of various kinds, irresponsible sprites, practitioners of spell-casting, evil eye, or the presence of some inauspicious person or object. In each case the shaman is, of course, bound by his own experience and by the expectations of his clients who can go elsewhere if his advice seems faulty. On the other hand, he has considerable leeway for choice and originality, a fact demonstrated by the diversity and the constant and surprisingly rapid turnover in gods worshiped in the Pahari village. In the past twenty years many families in Sirkanda have begun worshiping new gods and/or ceased worshiping old ones. Following consultation with a shaman, a family may learn that a previously quiescent ancestor has finally come to demand attention, or that an entirely alien god has made his appearance. An influential shaman might introduce a new deity to a large area, giving it attributes of his own choosing, and specifying the form of its worship.

Those who have been troubled by a supernatural may be advised to honor a god with a ceremony or to make a pilgrimage, or to consult an exorciser in order to repel the spirit. The inconvenience consequent upon following a shaman's advice may vary from the minor expense of sacrificing a goat to the financial calamity that occasionally accompanies the fulfillment of a vow to meet a god's demand for an elaborate series of sacrifices and ceremonies. An insolvable problem may elicit advice requiring the client or his representative to be in two places offering worship at the same time, or to sacrifice a cow (which is sacred and cannot be sacrificed), thus helping to maintain the practitioner's reputation for infallibility.

Shamans as Religious Policy Makers

Shamans (and to a lesser extent certain other non-Brahmanical practitioners whose functions overlap those of shamans, such as diviners and exorcists) play an important creative role in Pahari religion. As a result of their pronouncements, particular deities appear, gain prominence, lose prominence, and disappear in the village pantheon. They are often in a position to decide responsibility or guilt in interpersonal difficulties, and then to influence, if not actually decide, the atonement to be made They are asked the source of supernatural punishment and they usually rationalize this punishment by specifying the misdeeds and oversights of their clients. Since particular kinds and degrees of antonement are characteristically required by particular supernaturals, the shaman can, by designating as responsible one agent rather than another, partially determine the sacrifice a family will have to make. If he attributes misfortune to a new and hence unknown supernatural, he will characterize it to his clients, thereby achieving the same end. Consequently, it is largely as a result of the shaman's decision that one family will have to spend hundreds of rupees and weeks of effort in an elaborate ceremony while another spends only a few hours and gives only a goat in a simple sacrifice. The shaman exercises this influence over Brahmins and Rajputs as freely as over Doms.

Thus the shaman functions as a decision-maker or "gate-keeper" in Pahari religion, and is a "cultural policy maker" (Singer, 1955:30) who influences the lives of others in important ways.

The power of the shaman is curbed by three circumstances: (1) There are many shamans competing freely for clients, and hence no one is obligated to consult a particular shaman. (2) Even when a shaman has been consulted, his advice may be accepted or rejected by the client as he sees fit. The only criterion applied is whether or not the shaman is believed to be correct in his advice. The shaman has no means to enforce adherence to his advice except by assuring the client of its accuracy and of the supernatural sanctions which the punishing deity will impose if its demands are not met. (3) In most cases the punishing supernatural speaks directly to his worshipers by possessing one of them. As a result, final judgment is usually made through the mouth of one of the shaman's clients. Thus the severity of the required atonement may be mitigated when worshipers of the god plead with the supernatural who speaks to them in the person of one of their relatives. For example, a shaman may say that illness and crop failure in a Rajput family are due to inconsiderate treatment of a young bride in that family, and that one of the deities from her natal household has come to torment her tormentors. The family members know, or are told by the shaman, that this god often demands a particular ceremony and that he is intensely angry with them at present. Later, when the family holds a ceremony and dances to honor this deity and to ascertain his specific demands, he will possess the mistreated bride, or possibly another household member, and probably demand an expensive ceremony. Family members may then plead poverty and perhaps innocence or non-culpability in their alleged misbehavior, vowing to mend their ways. At this point it is up to the possessed to stand firm or modify the demands,

These checks on the shaman's power do not alter the fact that he is influential. He remains a key individual in determining the nature of religious behavior in the Pahari village.

Traditional Brahmins as Religious Policy Makers

Within the context of traditional Pahari religion, Brahmin priests, when contrasted with shamans, appear primarily as religious technicians. They are called in to perform stereotyped ritual actions at prescribed life-cycle or periodic ceremonial occasions, or they perform prescribed ritual at other times as a result of a shaman's advice. On other than life-cycle and periodic ritual occasions, the shaman often determines or heavily influences whether or not a ceremony will be performed and to which deity it will be directed. The Brahmin priest's actions, once the ceremony has been specified, are determined by well-known precedents. He is rewarded with public esteem and, in the case of a purohit, with a secure livelihood.

The Brahmin priest is not, however, without areas of influence and creativity; in his role of horoscope reader, he is in a position to pass on the suitability of proposed marriages, and on occasion to advise the auspicious or inauspicious portent of particular undertakings, acquisitions, etc. However, except in the case of marriage arrangements, non-Brahmanical diviners are more likely to be consulted than Brahmin priests.

Brahmins and Shamins in Pahari Society

In assessing the relative roles of Brahmins and shamans in traditional Pahari religion, their places in society in terms of recruitment, training, source of income, and prestige are relevant.

Brahmins are eligible to become priests by birth, and whether or not they perform priestly functions, they are assured of high ritual status and the advantages which accrue thereto. Those few who become priests do so because of their own interests and capabilities or because of their place in the social structure of the Brahmin community. A Brahmin will not become a purohit unless he can inherit a clientele from his father or another relative. Inheritance of a clientele tends to be on the basis of primogeniture, but other factors such as ability and inclination to learn the necessary rituals play some part. Brahmins who become priests but who are not purohits are usually sons or other close relatives of practicing priests.

The priest learns his profession by dint of long effort, memorizing verses, rituals, gestures, and associated features of religious activity. Since he can become a priest only if he is a Brahmin, he is not competing with people of lower status. In the case of a purohit, his clientele is largely inherited, so he is not competing overtly with other Brahmins. Much of his income from priestly activities is obtained in exchange for the routine functions performed for particular families who are his regular clients. He has little fear of losing their patronage and little hope of acquiring the patronage of others. Finally, most traditional Pahari Brahmin priests are relatively well-off farmers who do not have to rely for their livelihood on income from their religious duties.

The Brahmin's prestige comes from his inherited status, his style of life, and the competence with which he performs his ritual activities. These contribute to his advantageous economic position. A good Brahmin is a conservative, learned man who performs his prescribed duties with accuracy. The Brahmin is, almost by definition, a cultural and social conservative. Brahmin priests to whom these generalizations do not apply are often advocates of religious change in the form of emulation of plains Hinduism, a point to be discussed below.

Shamans are differently recruited, and their social position and rewards are different from those of Brahmin priests in ways which are crucial to a consideration of their roles as cultural innovators and policy makers. They are generally Doms, a fact which is attributable partly to a widespread feeling that low castes have rapport with supernatural beings, and perhaps partly to a feeling of danger or risk inherent in such dealings which makes this specialty most attractive to people without other adequate and reliable means of subsistence.[2] However, Rajputs and even Brahmins occasionally become shamans.

The shaman depends for his training upon his observation and knowledge of other shamans—often he learns from a close relative—but he is not recruited by birth. Rather, he is to a large degree self-selected, and he acquires his clientele as a result of his reputation for accuracy. The requisite lore is learned with relatively little effort. The shaman depends for his competence more upon the ability to achieve the appropriate psychological state and to portray convincingly the supernatural than, as in the case of a priest, on the ability to memorize age-old formulae. He learns to respond properly in unrehearsed but highly stylized situations when his familiar spirit "comes to his head" and speaks through him. He is not expected to perform exactly as does any other shaman. The general style of a shamanistic performance is well known, but the details of a particular shaman's style are unique.

He acquires his clientele in competition with other shamans, some of whom earn a good living at this work and others of whom rarely get a client. Showmanship, persuasive oratory, an imaginative flair, and knowledge of Pahari "human nature" are undoubtedly assets to become a successful shaman, but one must not only be able to describe a colorful and dangerous tormentor convincingly and confidently recommend a means to appease him, one must also be able to recount authoritatively, without asking, the kinds of difficulties which have prompted the client to seek aid. This requires an ability to judge character, to analyze social structure, to respond to minimal cues, to keep abreast of gossip in a fairly wide region, and to speak wisely in convincing generalities.

Thus, a shaman's prestige is acquired as a result of a reputation for successful diagnosis and treatment. Clients are not reluctant to shop around and compare the advice of different shamans on important problems. Payment is made at each consultation. Since many shamans have no other major source of income, they are highly motivated to perform their specialty in a way that will attract customers, and they do this with originality and imagination. Every successful shaman has a distinctive style as his trademark.

---

[2] It is for precisely the latter reason that illegal distillation of liquor, selling of women, and other risky jobs are most often undertaken by low-caste people.

The vast majority of Pahari shamans come from the depressed castes. Shamanism affords people who would otherwise spend their lives deferring to others a role in which they can hope to acquire not only prestige and economic well being, but a large measure of influence in the lives of others, and especially in the lives of their caste superiors who otherwise exert authority over them. Just as there are situational exemptions from the strict regulations of low-caste deference and subservience, as on the festive occasion of Holi, so it may be that religious roles, such as that of shaman or pujari, which exempt those who play them from the full implications of their caste status, often attract those who most resent their status. There can be no doubt that low-caste people derive considerable satisfaction, personally if they are practitioners and vicariously if they are not, from the power non-Brahmanical practitioners exercise in overtly manipulating their caste superiors.

Brahmins and Shamans as Religious Innovators

Brahmin purohits, by the nature of their position and practice, are discouraged from innovating in the traditional religious context. They have a vested interest, as a group, in the religious *status quo,* in the continuation of religious practice and belief precisely as it is, for it provides them with their inherited priestly occupation, clientele, income, and the superior ritual and social status of their caste. In achieving proficiency in their specialty, they have memorized great amounts of material which they are then supposed to be able to reproduce without deviation from the original. They belong to a well-organized caste which can act to regulate their behavior as priests. They are subject to pressures for conformity from their clients. They embody the highest religious ideals of their society, and innovation is not one of these. They are not socially mobile in the traditional context.

Shamans, on the other hand, by the nature of their position and practice, are encouraged to innovate, within prescribed limits, in traditional religious matters. Their position is achieved in competition with others with the same aspirations. To attempt to become a shaman is in itself unconventional behavior, and it requires unusual capabilities. Not only is there selection of people who are able easily to go into psychological states of "possession," but also of people who are socially and economically ambitious—who want to improve their prestige, influence, and income. The shamans' practice does not rely on precise adherence to established precedents as does that of Brahmin purohits. Originality within conventional limits is rewarded by the society, whose members regularly seek the advice of shamans. Moreover, since there is no caste of shamans nor any association among shamans as such, there is no regulatory agency to control their behavior; there is only that exercised by the society at large by its individual members' approval or disapproval

That shamans have not become a powerful élite is perhaps partly attributable to the open competitiveness of this profession. There is no traditional practitioner-client arrangement comparable to the jajmani relationship enjoyed by the Brahmin purohit. Thus, their clientele shifts easily, public opinion is a limiting factor, and no shaman has a monopoly on the market.

If there are characteristic circumstances and attitudes which correlate with innovation as a recurrent activity in some individuals, as Barnett (1953:378ff.) has hypothesized, it seems that Pahari shamans have these and traditional Brahmin priests do not. It is in line with Barnett's hypotheses that innovative shamans come predominantly from the low castes, for it is low-caste people who are most often dissatisfied with their lives as they are (cf. Berreman, 1960a). Dissatisfaction with things as they are, according to Barnett, often leads to innovation or acceptance of change, for innovation serves to change the *status quo* and hence may eliminate the cause for dissatisfaction. Innovation seems to be a means to alleviate the frustrations of the shamans' inherited social and economic position.

Shamans are, therefore, innovators in the sphere of traditional Pahari religion. Most of their innovations, however, take place within relatively narrow limits. They seek to enhance their own position in the system, but they seek to perpetuate the religious system which validates their role. Most traditional Brahmins also seek to perpetuate that religious system, but they perpetuate their own advantageous position within it by conformity rather than by innovation.

Atraditional Brahmins

Increasing contacts with plains people in the past twenty to thirty years have led many Paharis, especially those with education (mostly from the high castes) to adopt high-caste people of the plains as a reference group. They find that adherence to the customary usages of Pahari Hinduism earns them disrespect and even derision by people from the plains. While they have long been aware of this fact, only relatively recently have contacts been sufficiently intense—through teachers, community development workers, vote-seekers, etc.—to induce them to try to change their ways. They increasingly aspire to emulate religious and social customs of plains people. In so doing, they demand ritual services which traditional Pahari Brahmin priests do not know how to provide. Other Brahmin priests have come forward to meet this demand.

For the most part, these atraditional priests are Pahari Brahmins who have no traditional, inherited clientele. They are Brahmins who traditionally were either exclusively farmers or were farmers who performed priestly functions as a minor adjunct to their farming, supplementing the services of local purohits. These individuals have responded to the demand for priestly practitioners of sophisticated plains Hinduism by undertaking to master its lore and techniques, and have found that by devoting themselves to learning the great tradition in the plains idiom they can increase their income and enhance their status. Therefore they cease merely to respond to the demand for religious change, but become instead active advocates of it. With increasing demand for plains religious forms, their clients increase in number as does the frequency of service required per client.

Innovative, atraditional priests, like shamans, have no inherited, fixed clientele. They seek to acquire clients by recruiting converts to plains emulation and by advertising themselves as being more sophisticated and knowledgeable than their competitors. The competition among such entrepreneurial priests is readily apparent. I have never heard purohits disparage one another, but among atraditional priests this is a regular practice.

Innovative priests often refer to their clients, after the fashion of purohits, as their jajmans, but nevertheless the relationship of client to priest is quite different. Clients may exhibit considerable loyalty to such a priest but payment remains on a per-service basis and the priest's family or successors have no firm assurances that they will continue to receive the clients' patronage. Atraditional priests, always on the lookout for new customers, have a relatively aggressive, innovative approach to religion. Competition among such priests is often tempered by jajmani-like loyalties on the part of their clients and by the fact that in any given area most Brahmins belong to a single caste which has some degree of control over its members' behavior, even those who are atraditional in outlook.

Atraditional priests attempt to undermine purohits by criticizing their unorthodox Hinduism and by advocating that their clients give nothing but traditional charity to their purohits and that they hire more sophisticated priests—namely, themselves—for ritual purposes.

To some extent atraditional priests, unlike purohits, also compete with shamans. They see shamans as obstacles to plains emulation or Sanskritization because shamans are alien to the Sanskritic religious image to which they encourage Paharis to aspire. Shamans are a symbol of traditional Pahari Hinduism which it is to the atraditional Brahmin priest's advantage to discredit and replace. Whereas the functions of traditional Brahmin priests and shamans are compatible and even complementary, those of atraditional priests and shamans are at odds. Atraditional priests attempt to discourage people from consulting shamans, pointing out that heavy reliance upon shamans is one of the reasons that Paharis are considered backward by plains people. They advocate instead the worship of great traditional gods, adherence to Brahmanical rites, and consultation with practitioners of great traditional curing techniques. One of the grounds upon which they criticize traditional priests is that they tolerate and even themselves consult shamans. While the purohit flourishes in the traditional religious context of which shamanism is an integral part (and vice versa), the innovative, atraditional priest profits from its displacement.

Shamans, like purohits, are conservative in those contexts wherein atraditional priests are innovators. They see in plains emulation a threat to their position and livelihood. Since they lack lasting ties to their clients, they are extremely vulnerable to these changes; they see and respond to the threat more immediately and concretely than do purohits. They know that advocates of, and adherents to, the new Hinduism tend to look askance at much shamanistic practice. Their resistance to such charges has not been without effect. In the vicinity of Sirkanda, despite the best efforts of an atraditional Brahmin priest, plains emulation has been limited largely to such conspicuous and relatively superficial spheres as the ceremonies at marriage and investiture with the sacred thread. Most villagers do not feel an acute conflict between this behavior and local traditions They have adopted and adapted Sanskritic ritual but they continue to rely on shamans for advice on their troubles and to worship traditional deities and such new ones as shamans describe rather than Sanskritic deities of the plains. They perform most of the traditional annual and other periodic ceremonies rather than alien Sanskritic ones. Plains emulation in the religious sphere (i.e., Sanskritization) of a very thoroughgoing kind has apparently been inhibited partly because it does not get the sanction of the most important cultural policy makers in the field of traditional religion—the shamans. A conspicuous instance of overt resistance from shamans to the concerted innovative efforts of atraditional priests is the fact that they and other local non-Brahmin practitioners have encouraged the Pahari belief that the Sanskritic marriage ceremony of the plains, wherein no brideprice is given, results in short-lived, barren wives. They have done so by diagnosing this as a cause of such troubles.

Brahmin purohits, like shamans, have tended to remain conservative in the face of plains emulation. They have an assured clientele, income, and status. Although atraditional priests encroach to a degree on their profession, they continue to reap most of its traditional rewards. As conservatives with a stake in the religious *status quo,* they have been reluctant to change and have evidently been slow to see the implications of the changes which their innovative caste-fellows are exploiting. Plains emulation usually means that villagers will depend upon priests more learned in plains Hinduism in contexts where purohits were formerly employed. Plains emulation, therefore, threatens the purohit, as it does the shaman, with loss of religious importance and hence of income and esteem. That they have perceived the threat less clearly than shamans can be attributed in large part to their relative security of status and income. Also, they have open to them an avenue of escape which, by the structure of the society, is denied to shamans, namely to emulate the atraditional Brahmin priests by becoming knowledgeable in plains Hinduism themselves. Evidently in some other Pahari areas, this has already happened and it may well occur in the vicinity of Sirkanda. So far, however, among religious practitioners in and around Sirkanda, it is only the atraditional priests who see plains emulation as a means to economic and status enhancement.

Plains emulation or Sanskritization can be expected to accelerate as increasing plains influence through direct contacts, education, and mass media makes of plains people a more pervasive and important reference group. The role of sophisticated priests—whether in competition with purohits or as modernized members of purohit families—will increase and that of traditional priests and of shamans can be expected to decline. Eventually, secularization may occur, first among the younger men of high caste if, as has been the case elsewhere, these individuals are the first to acquire secular values through further education. This might shift emphasis on plains emulaation or Sanskritization to the low castes, at least until they become secularized themselves. Such a trend would undermine the religious functions of Brahmins as well as shamans. Speculation about this sequence of religious change is based upon projection, in the Pahari context, of trends observed by Cohn (1954:263f.; 1955:73ff.) and others in villages of the plains.

Atraditional Brahmins as Innovators

While conservatism is characteristic of Brahmin priests in the traditional context (and they contrast significantly with shamans in this regard), there are critical differences between such purohits and atraditional priests. These differences can account for the differences in their innovative behavior. Although both are Brahmins and of high ritual status, and often have property, only the atraditional priests are self-selected. If they wish to become practicing priests, they have to set out to acquire a clientele and work to keep it. In addition, they are often people who have had more contact with plains Hinduism than most of their fellows and hence have felt more acutely the disparagement which comes from high-caste plains people, based on the ethnocentrism of the latter. To them these plainsmen—especially Brahmins—are likely to be an extremely important reference group. Such atraditional priests have been advocates of a kind of change which appears to be a direct response to their dissatisfaction with the relatively low status accorded them by plains Brahmins. Although I lack information on whether atraditional priests come from economically marginal families, it is certain that most of them come from families who lack the prestige and relatively large income of traditional purohit families. Their new role offers them an opportunity to compensate for this lack. In short, they seem to be dissatisfied in precisely those crucial respects in which traditional Brahmin priests are presumably satisfied. Thus, their innovative nature does not necessarily contradict Barnett's hypotheses regarding the relationship between relative dissatisfaction and innovative potential.

Neither are the hypotheses contradicted by the fact that, relative to the atraditional Brahmin priests, shamans are in some spheres conservatives. Their conservatism is exhibited in response to a perceived threat to their livelihood, prestige, and influence. That is, plains-style Sanskritization threatens to degrade or destroy the role of the shaman, a role which has provided those who perform it with a means to alleviate the dissatisfaction with their economic and social position which they presumably felt and which in part led them to become shamans.

The changes advocated by enterprising atraditional Brahmins are spectacular and of considerable significance in Pahari religion and society. They involve new religious and social conceptions. The influence of shamans has been primarily in introducing variations on traditional Pahari religious themes and in invoking sanctions on individuals and groups. It is worth noting, however, that the sanctions can be invoked even against Brahmin priests who, in the traditional setting, have consulted shamans as avidly as anyone else. It can be argued that through use of such sanctions, shamans may have influenced their society as greatly as atraditional Brahmin priests now seem likely to do. It can also be argued that priests who advocate plains emulation, rather than being innovators, are often merely responding to a widespread demand among sophisticated Paharis. As Brahmins without a stake in the traditional religious system, they have been in an exceptionally good position to participate in and benefit from this trend. Therefore, the Pahari shaman has innovated in different ways, under different conditions and with different, but not necessarily less important, effects than has been the case with the atraditional priest.

Summary and Conclusions

In traditional Pahari religion, Brahmin priests appear to be religious "technicians"—learned men who utilize and transmit their knowledge efficiently but who have relatively little influence in the changes which constantly occur in religious belief and practice. Shamans, on the other hand, appear to be strategically important in policy making and in effecting changes within the context of traditional Pahari religion. There is an air of excitement about the pronouncements of a shaman which never surrounds those of a Brahmin priest. People wonder what the shaman will tell them and they regard him with awe or wonderment; in most cases they know what a Brahmin will tell them, and they regard him with respect rather than awe.

Shamans are the key men in many kinds of religious worship. They determine which supernatural being is to be worshiped, placated, or exorcised, which ceremony will be performed, which sacrifice will be offered, which pilgrimage undertaken, which new supernatural will be worshiped and which old one will fall by the wayside. Styles and fads of worship, means to correction of troubles, and treatment of disease emanate largely from them. They are often in positions to decide or influence the decision regarding human guilt or innocence and the nature of restitution to be made. To be sure, the range within which shamans innovate and exert influence is quite restricted. Public opinion holds them in check because they practice only in response to demand for their services, and the demand can quickly turn away. Within these limits, however, they exert considerable innovative and policy-making influence. Attitudes towards shamans condition their clients' attitudes toward, and responses to, other practitioners. Thus, a major complaint about Western doctors and urban practitioners of non-Western medicine is that these ask the patient to tell his symptoms. In the eyes of a Pahari, this is a ridiculous procedure for an allegedly competent diagnostician. Any good shaman can tell the patient's troubles as well as their cause and cure without a word from the patient. In fact, this is evidence by which the patient judges the shaman's competence.

The shaman's role as a religious innovator seems to be conditioned by a number of factors deriving from his place in society, his recruitment, training, source of income (clientele), and prestige. The contrasting nature of these same factors in the case of traditional Brahmin priests helps account for their predominantly conservative role. Of special interest in this regard is the analysis of shamanism as one of several religious means by which a dissatisfied low-caste person can alleviate some of the disadvantages of his caste status.

Traditional Pahari religion is focused on anxiety about the difficulties which afflict people and which are assumed to be the result of the machinations of supernaturals (cf. Opler, 1958). The shaman is invested with the responsibility to diagnose the sources of such difficulties and to recommend means to their solution. Therefore the shaman is in a position which calls for important decisions and which gives opportunity for innovation. The Brahmin priest, by contrast, is expected to perform prescribed ritual acts in prescribed situations and consequently is infrequently in a decision-making or innovative role. He, too, is a key person, but in a different way.

With increasing knowledge of the Sanskritic Hinduism of the plains, some Pahari Brahmins have become advocates of religious change and hence innovators, while shamans, like traditional priests, have held to the old traditions. Each group has self-interest at stake. The motives impelling Brahmins to become atraditional priests are to be found in a combination of their priestly caste status, their lack of a traditional clientele, and the presence of an increasing demand for Brahmin priests more learned in plains Hinduism than most traditional priests. The changes which atraditional priests encourage promise to have far-reaching ramifications in Pahari culture. This group of priests is responding and contributing to changes which seem likely to alter drastically traditional Pahari religion, culture, and social organization, i.e., the very context within which their caste fellows have been conservatives and shamans have been innovators. Now shamans join purohits as conservatives—as advocates of the traditional religion which supported their roles—relative to the "new" Brahmin priests who advocate innovations which will give to themselves an enhanced status. In the region I studied, tradition seems still to hold the upper hand, but the balance has begun to shift and is sure to continue to do so.

Village Hinduism cannot be understood without reference to its dynamics and these cannot be understood without reference to all of those who participate in it. Shamans and other non-Brahmanical practitioners are not within the great tradition of Hinduism, but they are all-India in spread and hence are part of the pan-Indian Hindu vernacular, or little, tradition. They play a crucial role in that tradition, and in the changes it is undergoing. Regional variations in the functions of such specialists are doubtless many and important, but these are largely unexplored. Their influence as religious "policy makers" is only one, and perhaps not the most fruitful, point of view from which they can be studied and compared. From whatever viewpoint they are studied, they must be studied in the total setting of village religion, including all of the behavior and attitudes pertaining to the supernatural, rather than in a category entirely separate from that in which Brahmin priests are studied. In the region of my research, such a dichotomous distinction was not often volunteered by the people themselves, while the realm of religion, defined as behavior and beliefs pertaining to the supernatural, was one which came readily and naturally to them and which was a rich and varied topic for conversation. Such conversation ranged from the machinations of local evil spirits to the epics of the great traditions of Hinduism. Brahmin priests, shamans, and a variety of lesser practitioners were important human figures in these conversations. An analysis of both categories is necessary in order to understand Pahari concepts of the supernatural and the human agents associated with them.

References Cited

Atkinson, Edwin T.

1884 *The Himalayan Districts of the North-Western Provinces of India.* Vol. II (comprising Vol. XI of The Gazetteer of the North-Western Provinces and Oudh). Allahabad: North-Western Provinces and Oudh Press.

Barnett, Homer G.

1953 *Innovation, the Basis of Cultural Change.* New York: McGraw-Hill.

Berreman, Gerald D.

1960a Caste in India and the United States. American Journal of Sociology. 66: 120–127.

1960b Cultural variability and drift in the Himalayan hills. American Anthropologist. 62:774–794.

1961 Himalayan rope sliding and village Hinduism: An analysis. Southwestern Journal of Anthropology. 17:326–342.

1962a Pahari Polyandry: A comparison. American Anthropologist. 64:60–75.

1962b Caste and economy in the Himalayas. Economic Development and Cultural Change. 10:386–394.

1963 *Hindus of the Himalayas.* Berkeley: University of California Press.

Cohn, Bernard S.

1954 The Camars of Senapur: A Study of the Changing Status of a Depressed Caste. Ph.D. dissertation, Cornell University. Ann Arbor: University Microfilms.

1955 The changing status of a depressed caste. In: *Village India,* ed. by M. Marriott, Memoir No. 83. The American Anthropological Association. 57: 53–77.

Dube, S. C.

1955 *Indian Village.* Ithaca: Cornell University Press.

Harper, Edward B.

1957 Shamanism in South India. Southwestern Journal of Anthropology. 13: 267–287.

Lewis, Oscar
1958 *Village Life in Northern India.* Urbana: University of Illinois Press.

Mahar, Pauline Moller
1957 The Functional Relations of a Hindu Cult. Paper read before the meeting of the Society for Scientific Study of Religion. Cambridge, Massachusetts, November 2, 1957.
1960 Changing religious practices of an untouchable caste. Economic Development and Cultural Change. 8:279–287.

Majumdar, D. N.
1944 *The Fortunes of Primitive Tribes.* Lucknow: The Universal Publishers.

Marriott, McKim
1955 Little communities in an indigenous civilization. In: *Village India,* ed. by M. Marriott, Memoir No. 83, The American Anthropological Association. 57:171–222.

Opler, Morris E.
1958 Spirit possession in a rural area of Northern India. In: *Reader in Comparative Religion,* ed. by W. Lessa and E. Vogt Evanston: Row, Peterson and Company. 553–566.

Opler, Morris E. and R. D. Singh
1948 The division of labor in an Indian village. In: *A Reader in General Anthropology,* ed. by C. S. Coon New York: Henry Holt. 464–496.

Planalp, Jack M.
1956 Religious Life and Values in a North Indian Village. Ph.D. dissertation, Cornell University. Ann Arbor: University Microfilms.

Redfield, Robert
1955 The social organization of tradition. The Far Eastern Quarterly. 15:13–22.

Singer, Milton
1955 The cultural pattern of Indian civilization. The Far Eastern Quarterly. 15:23–36.

Srinivas, M. N.
1952 *Religion and Society Among the Coorgs of South India.* Oxford: Clarendon Press.

Religious Anxiety and Hindu Fate

PAULINE MAHAR KOLENDA

HOW do ordinary people of India adapt themselves to the Hindu theory of *karma* and rebirth? It is said that these concepts justify and reconcile Hindus to the inequalities of the caste system and that they result in fatalism and "other-worldiness." These, in turn, are said to obstruct interest in modernization and progress. Although hypotheses such as these have been formulated by students of Hindu *texts* (Singer, 1961; Weber, 1958; Schweitzer, 1936), there have been few investigations of the living *contexts* within which Hindu philosophical ideas operate.

In this paper I shall first review village studies to glean information on the place of philosophical concepts in Hindu peasant thought and religious life. I shall then discuss some ideas about karma held by a group of north Indian Untouchables. These latter data may be considered an instance of "parochialization," the process whereby elements of the great tradition in an indigenous civilization are localized, simplified, limited, and refracted in the forms in which they are adopted and maintained in the little tradition of peasant life.[1]

Philosophical Concepts in Hindu Peasant Culture

Introductions to Hinduism invariably present the concepts of transmigration, karma, *dharma,* and *moksha* as the heart of Hinduism (e.g., see de Bary, 1958:203–366); yet we have little information about the place of these ideas in the thought and life of Indian villagers. A perusal of the literature at hand suggests five conclusions. First, most of the recent village studies make no mention of Hindu philosophical concepts (this is true of most of the studies in Marriott, 1955, and in Srinivas, 1955). Even some writers concerned specifically with village religion concentrate on other problems and say little or nothing about these basic concepts (e.g., Naik, 1958; Opler, 1959).

Second, with a few notable exceptions, most of the information available appears to be impressionistic; observations and interviews are seldom specified.

Third, there is a tendency either to minimize the importance of the philosophical concepts (Whitehead, 1916:138–139; Crooke, 1897:243) or to assert their importance with little supporting evidence (Srinivas, 1952:222; Young, 1931:67). Three of the recent studies discussed below are more detailed, however, and suggest the complexity of issues that may arise when individuals attempt to apply these concepts to life.

Fourth, two kinds of religious parochialization can be noticed. First, the achievement of moksha (release from rebirth) is not a serious goal for most villagers. Instead, they are said to be preoccupied either with attaining a better next life (Young, 1931:

The author is Associate Professor of Sociology and Anthropology at the University of Houston.

[1] Marriott (1955:200) defines parochialization as "a process of localization, of limitation upon the scope of intelligibility, of deprivation of literary form, of reduction to less systematic and less reflective dimensions. The process of parochialization constitutes the characteristic creative work of little communities within India's indigenous civilization."

175–176; Dube, 1955:91) or with attaining heaven and avoiding hell (Burn, 1902: 76–77; Dube, 1955:91). Second, *punya* (merit) is generally thought to be derived from outward religious observances such as bathing in sacred rivers, giving charity to Brahmins, and going on pilgrimages rather than from good moral character or ethical action (Crooke, 1897:245; O'Malley, 1935:70–71; Dube, 1955:92; Young, 1931: 179).

Fifth, most observers indicate that the salient feature of village Hinduism is the propitiation of godlings, ghosts, and demons, usually local and non-Sanskritic (for exceptions, see Beals, 1962; Lewis, 1958). The older writers (e.g., Whitehead, 1916:12; O'Malley, 1935:37; Crooke, 1897:240–241) as well as at least one modern writer (Carstairs, 1957:89; see also Dube, 1955:88) have labeled this tradition as animism, and have often considered it to be Dravidian or tribal in origin rather than Hindu or Sanskritic (Crooke, 1897:249–252; O'Malley, 1935:129; Whitehead, 1916:12–14).

Some writers mention the presence of *bhakti* movements in the villages (Young, 1931:177–178; Cohn, 1958:418–419; Carstairs, 1957:94). Few speak of fatalism as an attitude of the villagers (for an exception, see Young, 1931:175). Dube, for example, states that fate (karma) is blamed only after all efforts to avert misfortune have failed (1955:90).

One investigator explicitly states that Untouchable Chamar informants in a Uttar Pradesh village do not have ideas about rebirth, nor do they rationalize their low status in terms of karma and dharma (Cohn, 1958:413). Another states that the Nayars of Kottayam, a high warrior caste, seem to use the karma theory chiefly as a legitimation for their own high-caste status (Gough, 1958:462).

The studies by Beals (1962:45–57), Steed (1955), Carstairs (1957:95–102; 145–147), and Lewis (1958:249–259) present different views of philosophic ideas in village life. Although these four studies were done in different parts of India, most of the informants were high-caste males. All of these authors suggest that their informants were concerned with moksha, reincarnation, and heaven and hell as they related to merit derived from a system of ethical action.

Beals describes members of a Hyderabad village as confused about what constitutes virtuous behavior. They see a conflict between caste dharma (rightful duty) and virtuous behavior. For example, caste dharma may include *hinsa* (violence) by requiring blood sacrifices to village godlings, while virtuous behavior generally requires *ahimsa* (non-violence). Gopalpur villagers evidently believe that the only way to avoid rebirth is to become a holy man; yet they scorn this as a cowardly way out and believe that a sinful father who provides for his children is a better man than a sinless ascetic. Also, there is confusion in their minds about righteous behavior when two equally accepted authorities direct opposing action. These villagers tend to avoid dilemmas about virtue by shifting the responsibility for decision to the headman of the village.

The studies of Steed and Carstairs are based upon intensive interviewing of informants with whom they had established good rapport. Steed (1955:142–143) presents an analysis of a high-caste Rajput who in his mid-twenties decided to devote himself to three goddesses, presumably as a path to salvation. She shows that such a decision resulted from his life experience and his feelings of inadequacy. Her analysis suggests something of the interplay between philosophical concepts and specific personality needs.

Carstairs (1957:95) found that sixteen of his thirty-seven high-caste male subjects were trying to advance themselves spiritually toward a better next life or to moksha. All his subjects believed in the "inevitability of fate and the need to acquiesce in all that comes, calling upon God's name" (Carstairs, 1957:144). They knew about karma, moksha, transmigration, and also more refined philosophical ideas like *maya, karma yoga,* and the *ashramas.* Carstairs presents his informants' views of self-discipline, which involve ritual purity, sexual celibacy, abstinence with respect to food and alcohol, emotional self-control, yogic concentration, and devotion to God.

Lewis (1958:249–259) interviewed twenty high-caste Brahmins and Jats, and five low-caste Potters and Chamars, all but one of whom were males. Besides being asked to identify a list of Sanskritic gods and mythological characters, and to give the incarnations of Vishnu, they were asked to give their ideas of heaven, hell, reincarnation, salvation, God, soul, illusion, the cosmos, and life. In defining these nine terms, there were two types of respondents: those (mostly Brahmins) who gave a traditional theory of transmigration, moksha, and karma; and those (mostly Jat farmers) who denied belief in reincarnation, moksha, or an afterlife and emphasized life on earth, claiming that heaven and hell are to be found on earth. Lewis suggests (Lewis, 1958:254) that the latter view may be considered an alternative ideology to the traditional philosophical theory.

In the rest of this paper, I shall present the theory of fate held by a group of low-caste villagers whom I knew well for twenty months.[2] Their ideas represent another kind of refraction or parochialization of philosophical concepts. Interpretations of such data must be approached cautiously, for lower castes and members of all castes in villages distant from urban centers may have only recently had access to the philosophical concepts of the Great Tradition (see Marriott, 1959; Srinivas, 1952:218).

Theory of Fate Among a Group of North Indian Sweepers

Members of Khalapur village in Uttar Pradesh believe that only very important events in life are part of an individual's karma. These include time of death, length of life, identity of spouse, serious illnesses, number and sex of children, illnesses and deaths of children, lameness and maimedness, level of poverty or prosperity, caste affiliation, and life occupation.

In checking through my field notes on the Sweepers for spontaneous mention of the word karma, I found instances such as the following:

1. The mother of a twelve-year old son who had lost several other children compared herself to her sister. She said, "My sister has eight children, five sons with wives. She has a full household. She is younger than I am. She is very happy. My fate wasn't so good. I don't grumble. May God give my one son a good life. That is all I wish . . . I feel that if it were in my fate to have children, my other children would have lived. God would have made them live. Now when we quarrel, my husband blames me for not having children."

2. In discussing various jobs held in cities of the area, a young man said that in one place he had obtained the job of a man who had just resigned and that finding such a job was a matter of karma.

---

[2] I carried on the field research upon which this paper is based between October 1954 and May 1956 as a Post-doctoral Fellow of the Cornell University India Program. The Cornell India Project, directed by Morris E. Opler, was located in village Khalapur, Uttar Pradesh, between 1953 and 1956.

3. A neighbor's pigs had gotten into the grain supply of a Sweeper woman. While she was berating the owner of the pigs, the headman was heard to mutter, "Certain mishaps are fated."

4. In talking to a very old illiterate woman about education for women, we asked if education wouldn't spoil a woman's mind, a local belief we had heard. She said that only those whose minds were so fated would be spoiled. She mentioned a Brahmin whose mind had been deranged from excessive study.

Phrases besides karma were used to suggest the concept of fate: "it is written," "it is his," or "it is given by the one above." Villagers believe that God (*Xhudah, Parmatma,* or most often, *Bhagwan*) writes an individual's fate before his birth. It is important to emphasize that even though fate is believed to be directed by God, it is nevertheless believed to be unchangeable.[3] Here, I am limiting my concern with karma to events in this life which are due to sin or to merit in past lives, not with the karma one is currently storing up for the future by means of his present actions.

I shall consider three kinds of misfortune believed to be associated with karma: low-caste status, illness, and fate of children. In each context, we may ask: (1) How did the villagers understand karma? (2) What other ideas did they introduce to explain the misfortune? (3) Were these ideas consistent with the karma theory? (4) What conclusions can we draw?

Untouchable Caste Status

Sinfulness in a past life is reflected in low-caste status in this life, according to the transmigration-karma theory. The *Laws of Manu,* for example, say that the Sudras or low serving castes were dominated in past lives by *tamas*—that is, by "covetousness, sleepiness, pusillanimity, cruelty, atheism, leading an evil life, a habit of soliciting favours, and inattentiveness" (Buhler, 1886:491).

Sweeper thinking on this theory was indicated by my discussions with three men of the lowest caste in Khalapur, one with no education, one with about four years, and one with nine years. Two things stand out in their explanations. First, while they understand and can explain the ideas of transmigration and karma, indicating the connection between sins in past lives and present life condition, they refuse to admit that low-caste persons were less virtuous in past lives than members of castes which rank immediately above them. Instead, they introduce other explanations of caste status of a mythical-historical sort.

The uneducated young man explained:

> One's position in life reflects the deeds done in the past. If one did bad deeds, one is in a poor place. If one did better, one is in a good place. If one did some good deeds, he would be in man's form, but if he had also done some bad deeds, he would come to *serve* others. If we had done better, others would have served us. God does not create people as Rajputs, Chamars, or Sweepers. He determines only whether they shall serve or be served. Some are made beggars; some are on a throne.

The Sweepers emphasize the benefit of being in man's estate at all, rather than in animal's, and they group themselves with all those who are servants, rather than differentiating ranks among the servants. One man, the elderly headman with four years of schooling, refused to admit any ranking among men. He claimed that the

[3] For a similar conception of God directing fate, see Harper, 1959.

four *varnas* or classes of castes, the Brahmins, Warriors, Merchants, and Servants, were merely a convenience in the division of labor. "Man is all the same. For convenience a division was made," he said.

Here we can use the concept of religious anxiety for anxiety aroused by accepting certain religious beliefs (Weber, 1930:112). We may then say that the Sweepers' conception of why they have a low-caste status protects them from anxiety which would result if they accepted the full karma theory with its requirement that members of the lowest caste must have been those who were most sinful in past incarnations.

The Sweepers explain the rank of the caste itself not as a synthesis of multiple individual rebirths reflecting punishment for deeds in past lives, but rather in terms of a caste history. They console themselves that their low-caste rank may all be just a terrible historical accident, and they told at least three different status-legends to justify this position.

One, a story widespread among Untouchable castes, is about four original Brahmin brothers, one of whom was their founding ancestor. In a spirit of cooperation and brotherly love, their ancestor removed a dead cow from the brothers' common kitchen. The other three gave priority over kinship to their concept of pollution and thus banished the "'scavenger" brother, who was for all time defiled. The injustice of their position is tied in, then, with the injustice of pollution.

Like many other middle and low castes, these Sweepers claim ancient Twice-Born status. In a second myth, they say that their ancestors were Bhil Rajputs, tribal rulers of olden times who were defeated by Asoka and banished to the forest for many centuries. When they were later again accepted back into village life, their true identity was not acknowledged.

A different refraction of this myth is the Sweepers' claimed descent from Valmiki, a thief converted to the good path, who later wrote the *Ramayana,* and whom Sweepers sometimes equate with the One God who writes Fate. Sweepers support the Rajput claim of descent from Ram, the hero of this Hindu epic, but add that they should be of higher status than Rajputs since their ancestor, Valmiki, actually composed it one hundred and eighty thousand years before Ram's birth.

Note that these historical explanations of caste rank are not in any way reconciled with karma; instead, they are concerned with group destiny rather than with individual fate. Since the historical status-legends are so commonly found among middle and low castes (Cohn, 1955:59; Baines, 1912:19–20; Rowe, 1960; Srinivas, 1952:33) we may ask whether, in fact, the transmigration doctrine does justify the differences in caste rank for these castes, or whether it is usually outweighed by myths explaining the injustice of the low status of the group. Perhaps the theory is a justification for rank for only the highest castes, as Max Weber has suggested (Weber, 1946:271).

To summarize—if the Sweepers accepted the full karma theory, they could be expected to explain their low-caste status as the result of the sinful past lives of the members of their castes, but they do not draw this conclusion. Rather, they ignore all but gross differences in caste rankings. They do feel compelled to explain their low rank, but they do so by a different set of theories, which seem to say, "We originally had very high rank, but were tricked out of it," or "We should have high status, but others do not recognize our claims." In the case of the karma theory, low status is not admitted, and in the case of the alternative theories, high status is claimed. The anxiety that might be caused by a karma explanation for low status is avoided by the supplementary explanations.

Illness and Death

Serious illnesses and death, Khalapur villagers believe, are predetermined as a part of an individual's karma. However, many of the religious and magical activities of the village are based upon the premise that an individual may die before his fated time.

Such premature death may occur in two ways. A person may die a sudden death from drowning, snake-bite, war, being burned to death, being gored by a bull, falling from a tree, or being struck by lightning. Second, he may die because some malevolent supernatural has "stuck" to him. These creatures include a complicated pantheon of disease goddesses either centering around the Small Pox Mother Goddess Sitala, or those angry voracious mothers and various ghosts and godlings associated with Kali, or again, ghosts of dead family members or ghosts who have led unfulfilled lives.

In the Khalapur system of classifying supernaturals, there are a number of categories of creatures who have led unfulfilled lives; *bhuut* is a general term for a ghost. *Preets* are ghosts of dead boys; *uuts* are ghosts of men who died childless, and *churails* are ghosts of women who died childless or in childbirth. Sweepers state explicitly that these premature deaths are ones which occur before an individual's fated time.[4]

This extra-fate type of death creates a self-perpetuating society of malevolent beings. The ghost of an individual who dies an accidental death or who is taken by a voracious supernatural may cause other people illness or death. Such a process was described by a young Sweeper man:

> *Bhuut-preets* wander around. Their own salvation has not been settled by God. I don't know why they cause trouble; maybe because they are crazy. They have the same thoughts as a thief or a wicked man. A thief might see something good and take it away. A wicked man might have any intentions. When the bhuut resides in someone, it causes fever, deliriousness, senselessness, and pain. One may go months without eating. If a bhuut kills someone, that person becomes a bhuut and joins a gang of bhuuts, although the stronger ones stay alone.

Such ghosts must haunt the earth until the time of their fated death. Another Sweeper explained it this way:

> Suppose that in God's place, it is written that a man shall live until he is thirty. Then he dies at twenty-five. Unless he spends those five years in either bhuut or preet form, he can't go to God. After he has spent those five years, he goes to God. Then if he has been good, he goes to heaven. Otherwise, he is reborn.

These bhuuts are but one category of agents working outside of fate. Another category are all those supernaturals who have gained a measure of autonomus power

[4] Belief in bhuuts, disease goddesses, forms of Kali and premature death is common in northern India (see Crooke, 1926; O'Malley, 1935; Carstairs, 1957) and in other parts of India as well (Dube, 1955:93–96, 127–130; Srinivas, 1952; Beals, 1962:47–48). Dube calls the same type of premature death "abnormal death," and he suggests that persons dying abnormal deaths "reside permanently in the village and create difficulties in the normal life of the community" (Dube 1955:125–126). Crooke speaks of "natural death" and death "through evil magic or by the attacks of a Bhūt" (Crooke, 1907:239). Carstairs speaks of ghosts of the recently dead as "inhabiting a vague limbo until their next rebirth" (Carstairs, 1957:92).

from God through mortifications, or devotion either to him, or to another of these same autonomous creatures. Supposedly, during the *Satyug* (ancient age of pure morality), the important mother goddesses and male godlings were devout mystics who died in religious trance. Through their austerities and closeness to God, they gained power from him, but power independent of his will. Thus, it is explained, there is monism in supernatural power. All power is God's, but nevertheless these creatures who take their power from him are independent of him.

The frequently cited principle used to explain this paradox is *Bhagat kee bans men Bhagwan,* that is, God is in the hands of his devoted, or God is bound in obligation to those devoted to him. Devotion may be shown through prayer, praise, sacrifice, or austerities and mortifications. Much religious activity proceeds on this premise. Through devotion to God or to a godling, one may at least gain a measure of protection, not from the working out of God's fate, but from the caprices of the myriad extra-fate supernaturals. It is frequently pointed out by the more educated that those "who take God's name (a single supreme God, usually called Bhagwan) are not troubled by bhuuts, preets, *devidevtas* (goddesses-and-gods), *devpittars* (ghostly ancestors) and *piirs* (Muslim saint ghosts)."[5]

Devotion to one or more of the extra-fate creatures themselves also protects a devotee from the others. An elderly Sweeper woman recounted an incident illustrating the reassurance derived from devotion to a mother goddess.

> Once my brother's wife, Champia, and I were out in the fields in the evening, and suddenly I felt something, perhaps a bhuut, behind me. I ran to Champia, but Champia was not afraid, because Kanthi Mai (a goddess) "plays" on her.

The term "playing" refers to the capacity to become possessed by an extra-fate creature. Although every Sweeper family is devoted to one or more of the *opRii* (godlings and ghosts), whom they worship by offering pujas of pig meat, country liquor, fried sweets, or puddings, only a few ardent ones become *bhagats* (devotees), and thus a shaman can "play" with the (a) supernatural(s) to determine the causes of illness or perhaps perform sorcery. The powers of such shamans, drawn largely from the lower castes, are relevant only to curing illnesses caused by the opRii, the extra-fate supernaturals. Shamans cannot cure illnesses that are "natural," "bodily," or "God-given," in other words, those that are fated.

Sweepers sometimes pontificate that a death is the result of God's fate, but in almost the same breath accuse a bhuut or godling. When a young Sweeper mother died shortly after giving birth to a child, an older lady said: "She's gone to God's. . . . If it had been her fate she would have lived. It was not fated." She then added, "Everyone wanted her to live, but what could we do? No one disliked her." However, other members of the community attributed the death to the husband's neglect of the family's main ghost (a servant of Kali), saying that the death was in retaliation for his failure to give to this supernatural the four sacrificial pigs which he had previously promised.

The Fate of Children

When a female child is born, the number of children she will bear and the span of their lives supposedly are already determined by God's fate. The time of her

[5] Carstairs also cites this principle (1957:93).

husband's death and whether she will suffer the lot of widowhood are also predestined. However, despite a belief in the inevitability of fate, women participate in many religious and magical activities directed toward the preservation of their husbands and children, especially sons. A series of calendrical rites are dedicated to Sanskritic and local deities for the protection of animals, sons, and husbands. Women of all castes vow to make offerings at local and distant shrines if a child lives to be, say, a year and a half, or six, or old enough to be married. For the women of Khalapur, the hundred-and-one mother goddesses at Kankhal and Raiwala, suburbs of Hardwar, are popular for this purpose. When it is time to fulfill such a vow, the woman makes a pilgrimage to the site of the protective deity. In return, the mother goddess is believed to protect the child from extra-fate dangers.

Miscarriages are attributed to various malevolent female ghosts and godlings. Women sometimes protect their children from such ghosts and from the evil eye, an evil human power, by putting lampblack around their children's eyes, by calling them by lowly names, or by dressing boys like girls.

These villagers do not acquiesce before the hand of fate. Mothers perform acts of a magical and religious nature which they believe to be helpful in preserving the health of their children. This is a society characterized by high infant mortality rates and one in which a woman's worth is measured largely by the number of her living children. The Hindu philosophical directives of non-attachment and of stoic acceptance of one's fate seem to be incompatible with her feelings as a member of a social community, and by themselves would lead to feelings of helplessness and anxiety. The beliefs concerning ways whereby fate can be subverted seem to function to allay such anxieties—to give the individual mother some feeling of control over her social environment.[6]

Educated men of the Sweeper and of several other castes who have been influenced by the Hindu *Arya Samaj* reform movement criticize the vows, pilgrimages, offerings, and sacrifices made to the mother goddesses, godlings, and bhuut-preets. These reformists insist that one should believe in only one God and should acquiesce to God's fate. Yet these men do not state baldly that these supernaturals do not exist, and they acquiesce to the entreaty of their anxious wives who rebel against inactivity in such important matters of life and death.

Conclusion

There are themes in the religion of these Sweepers which might be described as "austerity-compulsion" and "devotion-boon" relationships to God and lesser deities. Through austerities, an ascetic can compel a supernatural to give him power; through devotion, boons may be granted by a supernatural. Both of these are ancient themes in Hinduism. The first theme goes back to the earliest days of the Aryans, when through sacrifices, and later through asceticism, it was possible for an individual to gain such powers. There are many classic instances. In the story of Ram, for example, the tyrant-demon Ravana derived his power from austerities which lasted ten thousand years. The devotional-boon theme is also old. Devotional rela-

[6] Dube, taking a leaf from Malinowski and Radcliffe-Brown, describes the religion of a Hyderabad village as psychologically and socially reinforcing. He says, "It strengthens and fortifies the individual and the group in situations where technical competence and practical intelligence are of no avail, and at the same time acts as a bond of cohesion for maintaining the structural unity of the society" (1955:93).

tionships with God were emphasized in the medieval bhakti movements when the poets, philosophers, and preachers proclaimed that salvation could be attained by passionate devotion. Both themes are to be found in the *Bhagavad Gita* (Edgerton, 1952).

The uneasy reconciliation the Sweepers have made between their concept of devotional religion and their belief in the theory of karma and transmigration reflects on a small scale the difficulty members of the bhakti sects have in accepting both doctrines. Ramanuja, one of the medieval bhakti preachers, attempted to resolve the matter by suggesting that through devotion the karmic rewards and punishments destined for one could be changed by a grace-giving God (Basham, 1954:332). The Sweepers reconcile the two by saying that God and fate are not absolute—that there are events and supernaturals independent of fate and God.

It should be clear, however, that the goal of this Sweeper religion is not salvation or a better next life; instead, it is concerned with preventing or relieving misfortunes in this world. Philosophical Hinduism is a heroic religion in that it sets forth the highest of goals. Hindu holy books rail against those who are caught in maya, those attached to the "real" world. Yet these are the kind of Hindus generally found living in villages, not people fulfilling the heroic ideals held up by the scriptures. Certainly a few of the latter are there, and perhaps more are concerned at times in their lives with moksha. The gap between the heroic and people's real capacities is always great.

References Cited

Baines, Sir Athelstane
1912 *Ethnography.* Strassburg: Karl J. Trübner.

Basham, A. L.
1954 *The Wonder That Was India.* New York: Grove Press Inc.

Beals, Alan R.
1962 *Gopalpur: A South Indian Village.* New York: Holt, Rinehart & Winston.

Buhler, G. (translator)
1886 *The Laws of Manu.* Sacred Books of the East. Oxford: At the Clarendon Press.

Burn, R.
1902 *Census Report: North Western Provinces of Oudh.* Allahabad: Government Press.

Carstairs, G. Morris
1957 *The Twice-Born.* London: Hogarth Press.

Cohn, Bernard S.
1955 The changing status of a depressed caste. In Marriott (ed.), 1955:53–77.
1958 Changing traditions of a low caste. In Singer (ed.), 1958:413–421.

Crooke, William
1897 *The North-Western Provinces of India.* London: Methuen & Co.
1907 *Natives of Northern India.* London: Archibald Constable & Co.
1926 *Religion and Folklore of Northern India.* London: Oxford University Press.

de Bary, William Theodore (ed.)
1958 *Sources of Indian Traditions.* New York: Columbia University Press.

Dube, S. C.
1955 *Indian Village* London: Routledge and Kegan Paul Ltd.

Edgerton, Franklin (translator)
1952 *The Bhagavad Gītā.* Cambridge: Harvard University Press.

Gough, E. Kathleen
1958 Cults of the dead among the Nāyars. In Singer (ed.), 1958:446–478.

Harper, Edward B.
1959 A Hindu village pantheon. Southwestern Journal of Anthropology. 15:227–234.

Lewis, Oscar
1958 *Village Life in Northern India.* Urbana: University of Illinois Press.

Mahar, Pauline
1960 Changing religious practices of an untouchable caste. Economic Development and Cultural Change. 8:279–287.

Marriott, McKim
1955 Little communities in an indigenous civilization. In Marriott (ed.), 1955:171–222.
1959 Changing channels of cultural transmission in Indian civilization. In: *Intermediate Societies, Social Mobility and Communication,* ed. by Verne F. Fay. Proceedings of 1959 Annual Spring Meeting of the American Ethnological Society, pp. 66–74.

Marriott, McKim (ed.)
1955 *Village India.* American Anthropological Association Memoir No. 83.

Naik, T. B.
1958 Religion of the Anāvils of Surat. In Singer (ed.), 1958:389–396.

O'Malley, L. S. S.
1935 *Popular Hinduism.* London: Cambridge University Press.

Opler, M. E.
1959 The place of religion in a north Indian village. Southwestern Journal of Anthropology. 15:219–226.

Rowe, William L.
1960 Social and Economic Mobility in a Low-Caste North Indian Community. Ph.D. dissertation, Cornell University.

Schweitzer, Albert
1936 *Indian Thought and its Development.* Boston: Beacon Press.

Singer, Milton
1961 Text and context in the study of religion and social change in India. The Adyar Library Bulletin XXV, Parts 1–4:274–303.

Singer, Milton (ed.)
1958 Traditional India: structure and change. Journal of American Folklore. 71:191–518.

Srinivas, M. N.
1952 *Religion and Society Among the Coorgs of South India.* London: Oxford University Press.

Srinivas, M. N. (ed.)
1955 *India's Villages.* India: West Bengal Government Press.

Steed, Gitel P.
1955 Notes on an approach to the study of personality formation in a Hindu village in Gujarat. In Marriott (ed.), 1955:102–144.

Weber, Max
1930 *The Protestant Ethic and the Spirit of Capitalism.* New York: Charles Scribner's Sons.

1946 The social psychology of the world religions. In: *From Max Weber: Essays in Sociology*, by Hans Gerth and C. Wright Mills (translators and editors). New York: Oxford University Press, 267–301.

1958 *The Religion of India*. Glencoe, Illinois: The Free Press.

Whitehead, Henry

1916 *Village Gods of South India*. Calcutta: The Association Press.

Young, M.

1931 *Seen and Heard in a Punjab Village*. London: Student Christian Movement Press.

Particularization and Generalization as Processes in Ritual and Culture

MORRIS E. OPLER

IN November, 1949, I witnessed the ritual events of the tenth day of the month of Muharram in a village of north India inhabited by Muslims of the Shiah sect. According to Shiah tradition, on this day of the year in 680 A.D., Husain, the grandson of Mohammed, sacrificed his life in the battle of Kerbela rather than swear allegiance to one whom he did not consider fit to be caliph and a successor to the Prophet. To mark the occasion, the villagers had gathered to recount the heroic resistance offered by Husain and his tiny band of seventy-two persons against fearful odds to preserve their religion and honor. *Tazias* (colored paper representations of the tombs of Husain and his brother Husan) were placed under a canopy, and a tall, grey-bearded elder read a long narrative poem describing the tragic struggle. His voice broke and tears streamed down his face as he detailed the acts of sacrifice and devotion performed by Husain and his followers and as he pictured the suffering of the women and children when enemy forces cut them off from water and supplies. His account was punctuated by cries of grief and distress from the audience.

At the conclusion of this deeply dramatic and moving reading, another man rose and spoke. He reminded his listeners that prophets and saints have arisen ever since the time of Adam to light the way for mankind but that they have always been opposed by others who have tried to put out the light. Jesus Christ was one of those who sought to help mortals, and he was put to death; Mohammed was a great prophet, but he had to flee for his life. Many, he added, claim that they are willing to die for their faith or sacrifice all for righteousness, but in spite of their talk most of them manage to live comfortable lives. Husain and his followers, however, belonged to that small but noble group of men who really did what they promised. Because it is a lesson from which all can profit, their story should be told not only for the benefit of Muslims and Islam but for the good of the entire world. This speaker, too, graphically described the suffering, the resolution, and the piety of the members of the beseiged and outnumbered group, and at times he sobbed, wiped his eyes, and paused to regain composure. But while his point of departure was the unequal contest which occurred so long ago, his emphasis throughout was upon the need to accept Husain's spirit and message in these times and, if necessary, to suffer for faith and religion in the modern world.

At the end of this talk the drums began to beat, the tazias were lifted on poles to be carried on the shoulders of men, and a procession of drummers, singers, and bearers of the tazias made its way to a raised platform in another quarter of the village. During the journey the young men of the chorus of singers beat their breasts

The author is Professor of Anthropology at Cornell University.

rhythmically as they lamented the fate of the martyrs. When the destination was reached, garlands which had been carried in the tazias were buried in a hole prepared for the purpose, and food was distributed. Then the tazias were borne back to the point in the village from which the procession had started. Later they were carried to the Jumna River, towed into the stream, weighted with rocks, and sunk.

This is a much abbreviated account of a moving, colorful, and dramatic ceremony. Yet perhaps it is sufficient, since here I am less interested in furnishing complete details than in calling attention to a process distinguishable in the rite that I shall term "particularization." The battle of Kerbela occurred nearly thirteen hundred years ago. It involved such important personages as the immediate descendants of Mohammed and claimants to the succession and resulted in the martyrdom of saints. Yet its main function is to act as a model for contemporary behavior and individual decision. It is a call to courage and faith for a minority group within Islam. It is a claim on the conscience of every Shiah.

I use the Muharram as an example of a principle found in religious systems which may be identified as "particularization," that is, a process or direction of ideological flow in which values and concepts associated with the remote, the vast, and the important become translated into effective guides and stimuli for the immediate, the humble, and the individual. The movement is from overriding forces and meanings to particular applications. In particularization it is the act, rather than the person, which presses for identification with divinity.

The Hindu religious festival, Holi, offers another instance of what I call particularization. The principle mythic account which forms the background for Holi describes how Prahlad, a virtuous youth, persisted in worshipping Lord Vishnu in the face of strong family opposition. Finally, to accomplish Prahlad's destruction, the evil supernatural, Holika, who was believed to be immune to the ravages of fire, carried him into the flames. Through the intervention of Vishnu the devout Prahlad emerged unharmed, while Holika, the embodiment of evil, was burned to ashes. In commemoration of the triumph of virtue over evil, of religion over sacrilege, large bonfires are kindled all over India on the night of Holi.

Yet Holi is much more than an annual salute to piety and God's protection. Its central conception has been translated into very concrete acts and becomes the justification for dealing with continuing situations in the lives of finite men. The new year begins immediately after Holi, and people seek during the Holi season to rid themselves of the evils, impurities, and conflicts that may have accumulated during the preceding months. It is a period when debts are paid or forgiven, inhibitions and conventions in speech and behavior are relaxed in the interests of frankness, and quarreling persons or factions are reconciled. Symbols of the sicknesses, filth, and impurities of the past year are thrown into the Holi fire. It is considered inauspicious to fail to see the Holi conflagration.

This is admittedly an oversimplified portrayal of Holi, but even in this brief treatment the feature that I call particularization is evident. For the emphasis is on present dangers, present impurities, present relationships. The interest is in beginning a year as free from sickness, conflict, and evil as possible. The difficulties of the past are symbolically consigned to the flames. The lofty tradition concerning Prahlad, Holika, and Vishnu provides a convenient frame and justification for specific behavior. It asserts that evil and malice can be overcome with God's help. But this does not remain merely a philosophical conviction about a test of strength among powerful supernaturals during a remote mythological era. It becomes objectified in the recurring attempts to ease individual conscience and to deal with existing perplexities. Though the starting point may be the abstract confrontation of good and evil, it is not long before we meet the Indian villager, seeking, as the Holi fire flares, to improve his prospects for the coming year.

The type of process in religious thought and ritual we have been examining can be profitably compared with another for which "generalization" seems an appropriate designation. In generalization, as the term implies, the progression is from the specific to the more comprehensive. We start with the immediate, the personal, the present and move toward the timeless, the inclusive, the abstract. Again, to provide context, an example chosen from religious practice in a north Indian village may prove helpful.

The status and happiness of a north Indian woman are more than a little dependent upon whether or not she is the mother of sons. Understandably, therefore, her desire for sons and her hope for the continued health and longevity of her sons are frequently expressed in word and act. The concern of the mother for her son culminates ritually in Jiutia, a calendrical ceremony which falls on the eighth day of the dark half of Kuar (September-October). The term Jiutia, probably related to the word for life (*jiu*), is the name given not only to the ceremony but also to a necklace worn by a woman at the time of the ceremony. Small pendants of silver or gold hang from such a necklace, one for each of the woman's sons.

Normally a woman does not begin to observe Jiutia until she has borne a son, although a married woman who is without a son occasionally does so in the hope that such participation may aid her in bearing a male child. When a woman celebrates Jiutia for the first time, she does not make this known publicly and does not go with the other women to the bathing place or take part in the group worship. Instead, she quietly fasts and bathes alone in the cattle shed. It is not until the Jiutia of the following year that she joins the others in procession. Thus her initial participation in the rite begins in a highly individualized manner.

Not long before sundown on the day of Jiutia, the other married women with sons, led by a band of musicians, walk together to a bathing place. Each carries a brass tray containing a number of objects and substances to be used in the rite. As soon as the group reaches the place of ceremony, a Kaharin (a woman of the water-carrier caste) plasters a large circular area with cow dung. Within this she then molds a cow-dung representation of Jiut Baba, the personification of life and of this ceremony, identified by many villagers with Lord Shiva. A Brahman marks the image of Jiut Baba with vermilion and arranges sticks of wood around it. At this point another highly individual note is sounded. In turn, a woman of each family enters the circle and makes offerings. After that, the women participate in other ritual acts and finally bathe. A woman guards her jiutia ceremonial necklace carefully, lest some person without a son attempt to make off with it. It is now time for the ritual fire, and the Brahman ignites the wood covering Jiut Baba. The women throw wood upon the fire and, sitting in concentric circles, also toss rice and cotton seeds into it. To feed the fire, the Brahman collects some clarified butter from each of the women and pours it on the image as he recites sacred texts.

For the return journey, which begins at sunset, each woman lights a small earthen lamp and tries to preserve the flame until she reaches her home. As she walks, she strews rice and other materials along the path. She takes both parts in an imaginary conversation between two persons, one of whom is directing the other to tell God that this particular mother has kept a very strict fast on Jiutia for her son and that therefore the boy should be protected and blessed. Once home, the women spend the rest of the night preparing dishes considered to be the favorites of the female sex. At dawn they break their fast by eating a preparation made of five grains. Then, after offerings are made to the female ancestors of the house, all family members dine.

Jiutia obviously has its impetus in the individual mother's concern for the well-being of her son, and this personal interest is never entirely erased in the course of the rite. A woman guards the pendant and the flame that represent her son. She calls the attention of God to the fast she has maintained in the name of her son. Nevertheless, in attempting to attain her goal, she moves far toward the merging of her need and her protective devices with those of others. She joins with the other women to go to worship at a sacred spot where one Brahman serves all who are there. The women bathe together and honor the same improvised image of the God. The ceremony has as its prime objective the placing of all the sons of all the women involved under the protection of Jiut Baba. The single sacred fire is fed through the efforts of the entire body of women, and the clarified butter poured on it is their joint contribution. Jiutia may have its psychological roots in the personal anxiety felt by the individual mother for her son, but through a process of generalization it has become a standard ritual means by which the whole community acts to safeguard its sons and to place them under the divine protection of a God who is the abstract essence of life itself.

It will readily occur to anyone who has given much thought to the theoretical aspects of comparative religion that life cycle ceremonies are certain to contribute many striking examples of the process of generalization. After all, a life cycle rite, the taking on of a new role, is ordinarily precipitated by a change of age, physiology, or condition which temporarily disturbs bonds and solidarities that the individual has enjoyed and consequently isolates him. Often, to facilitate a transition, the person is brought under the protection of powerful forces or supernaturals. The ceremony is the ritual recognition of his absorption into some other, usually some larger, more important, or more inclusive, grouping and of his identification with the symbols and attributes that attend such a progression. In fact, the logical affinities of the life cycle ceremony and of the process of generalization are so close that other rites in which generalization plays a prominent part may be overlooked. Because of that very danger of overemphasis, I deliberately chose Jiutia, instead of a life cycle rite, as my key example. I would suggest, also, that rituals aimed at restoring those who have fallen into an unclean state are very likely to harbor a strong element of generalization.

There is no doubt that Arnold Van Gennep in *The Rites of Passage* and in his terms "separation" (*séparation*) and "incorporation" (*agrégation*) has discussed processes which in some ways are not far removed from those I have termed particularization and generalization. But there are some very fundamental differences, too. Because Van Gennep dealt so exclusively with life cycle ceremonies, he saw a one-way progression from "separation," through "transition" (*marge*), to "incorporation." I tend, rather, to view particularization and generalization as polar tendencies, though I am conscious of a certain amount of overlap and coexistence. In fact, I would argue that Van Gennep depicts his stages as much more uniform and absolute than actual data and experience justify. Despite the strong pull of generalization, something of particularization is usually preserved. It will be remembered that in Jiutia, during the return from the ceremony in which she has merged her prayers with those of the other mothers, the Hindu woman reminds God that she has personally maintained a strict fast on behalf of her own son.

There are many fruitful ways in which to compare and analyze rites, and what I have submitted is but an introduction to one of them. Nevertheless, it is one which I believe will repay some attention and effort, for it has roots in one of man's most poignant dilemmas, the need to find meaning for individual existence and the parallel urge to seek the assurance and the ties which can come only with the transcendence of the self.

I strongly suspect, too, that these philosophical components of religious systems are rather sensitive barometers of cultural orientation. I have seen some evidence which would suggest that in cultures where comparatively little expression of individuality is normally encouraged the process of particularization in ritual is rather marked, and that in cultures where group cohesion is relatively weak a compensatory process of generalization can be discerned. I would not offer this as a settled principle at the present stage of our inquiries, but it does appeal to me as a hypothesis well worth investigating.

Religion and Social Communication in Village North India

JOHN J. GUMPERZ

ALTHOUGH India presents a scene of great local cultural diversity, in the study of religion the subcontinent may be viewed as a single large field of social action. Within this field new movements are constantly arising, whose practices and ideas interact with others and penetrate from one section of the subcontinent to the other, filtering across deep political and social barriers. Thus in ancient times Brahminical Hinduism spread south from the Northwest, and Hinduism and Jainism, originating in the Northeast, followed closely upon its path. In medieval times the various bhakti movements which arose in South India spread northward, but have continued to play an important part in the life of all regions. Similarly reform Hinduism, born under the impact of contact with the West, affects areas far from its points of origin.

Action and interaction on this large scale are hardly possible without a highly developed system of mass communication. In fact, communication is a major function of many Indian religious institutions. Side by side with the local priest and the scholastic, who confine their activities to officiating at religious rites and to commentaries on traditional texts, we find the religious communicators: the *sanyasi,* the *guru,* the theatrical performer, and the musician. These often wander from region to region, penetrating into remote areas far from public transportation. In assuming their religious role, they are freed from many restrictions of the caste system, they interact freely with many individuals with whom they otherwise would not come into contact, and their message is assured a more sympathetic hearing than that of ordinary strangers.

Anthropologists studying the media employed in the communication of religious values have recently pointed out the importance of religious performances (Singer, 1957:141; McCormack 1959:119; Damle 1959). The present paper deals with such performances in a single village and attempts to analyze their social function in respect to other aspects of the local communication network. Observations made here are based on an eighteen-month study of rural Hindi dialects carried out in cooperation with a team of American and Indian anthropologists in and around the village of Khalapur.

Khalapur is located in the Gangetic valley, about eighty miles north of Delhi, not far from the main communication arteries leading to the Punjab in the West. With its population of about five thousand, it is somewhat larger than the surrounding villages, but its economy and social organization are typically rural. Inhabitants fall into thirty-one endogamous caste or *jati* groups, ninety per cent Hindu and ten per cent Muslim. Rajputs constitute the dominant caste and make up forty-eight per

The author is Associate Professor of Linguistics at the University of California, Berkeley.

cent of the total population. Untouchable Chamars are next with twelve per cent, and after them come Brahmans with five per cent. The remaining thirty-five per cent of the population is divided into twenty-eight caste groups (Hitchcock 1956, 1959).

From the point of view of communication, we may visualize Khalapur as part of a complex grid, of the type proposed by Cohn and Marriott (1958), consisting of a series of major and minor religious, commercial, and administrative centers, each with its own hinterland. Innovations arising in one center spread both to other centers and into the hinterland. On the village level, we find a further process of diffusion, which seems to be determined largely by networks of social relationships such as the marriage networks recently described by Rowe (1960:299).

The town of Deoband, six miles away, is the most important of the many centers affecting the life of Khalapur. Formerly the seat of a local Muslim feudal ruler, it now serves as the *tahsil* (sub-district) headquarters. Among its attractions are a well-known mosque and several Hindu shrines, a sugar mill, and the bazaar which is the closest and most convenient of several surrounding marketing facilities. Muzzarfarnagar, sixteen miles south of Deoband and twelve miles from Khalapur, the headquarters of the neighboring district with its large bazaar and extensive wholesale grain market, offers a somewhat greater selection of goods and services. Saharanpur, the district headquarters for Khalapur, thirty miles to the north of Deoband, is primarily of administrative and religious importance. Both Muzzarfarnagar and Saharanpur are easily accessible from Deoband via the main Delhi-Saharanpur railroad or by bus via the paved highway following the same route. Hardwar, in the Himalayan foothills at a distance of five hours by bus or train, is the chief religious center of the area. Here the ashes of the dead are consigned to the Ganges. Hardwar has a great variety of well-known shrines, and many of the most important Hindu sects maintain their headquarters there.

In addition, a number of religious fairs are regularly held in the countryside, and some shrines located as far away as Rajasthan are well known to Khalapur villagers. Marriage relationships for the upper castes extend as far as Ambala and Patiala, about one hundred miles to the west, to Moradabad, one hundred miles to the east, and to Delhi, to the south; the lower castes tend to marry within a circle of about thirty miles.

Most information filtering into the village from these various sources reaches the average villager via oral channels either through travellers returning from abroad or through visitors. Although Khalapur has never been very isolated as Indian villages go, contacts with the outside have increased manyfold within the last fifteen years. The railroad and the interurban road system have been in operation ever since the turn of the century, but the village itself was cut off from this urban grid. It is surrounded on three sides by a stream and a swampy tract fordable only in the dry season. Roads leading to the main Deoband-Muzzarfarnagar arteries were unimproved and almost impassable to vehicular traffic. Construction of an all-weather bridge and a paved road during the last ten years has eliminated most obstacles to regular travel. Villagers may now travel to Saharanpur and back within a single day. Horse tongas have begun to ply between the village and the Deoband railroad station. Most upper castes and many artisan castes have family members who visit Deoband several times a week on foot or by bicycle. For the lower castes such trips are only slightly rarer. Longer trips outside the Deoband, Saharanpur, Muzzarfarnagar area, made either for religious pilgrimage purposes, to visit relatives, or in connection wth marriage parties, also seem to have increased in number.

While villagers have begun to travel more, their opportunities for informal contact with strangers are less extensive than one might suppose. Trade negotiations are accompanied by a great deal of suspicion on both sides, a fact which limits the nature of the social relationship. Individuals who visit a city frequently have a regular circle of contacts there. In each bazaar in fact, there are shops frequented by members of one caste group, where individuals may congregate and smoke a *hukka* (waterpipe) without fear of pollution. Longer trips in connection with marriage parties often lead through large cities such as Merut or Delhi and often there is as much as eight hours delay between trains. On the occasion of such delays, villagers rarely venture outside the railroad station into the strange city. They show little desire to sightsee in places where they have no personal relations. If for any reason it is necessary to stay overnight in a strange location, the preferred spot is a *dharmshala,* a place for religious pilgrims, or if that is not available, the railroad platform. All these restrictions on outside contact limit the ways in which innovations may reach the village.

The recent improvements in communication have also materially increased the number of non-resident visitors to the village. A great variety of peddlers arrive daily and sell their wares from house to house among the well-to-do. This is a recent phenomenon since most villagers still recall the day when any stranger would find himself harassed by groups of children, and strange peddlers from abroad had reason to feel unsafe in the village lanes. The number of outside visitors to the village is further increased by the new inter-college (junior college) established in the early 1950's, which attracts students from many surrounding villages, where they mingle with the local boys. In addition since the establishment of the village development project in 1953, a village level worker has been permanently stationed in the village and block development officers frequently arrive for special visits. Other officials come in connection with collection of taxes, cooperative society business, or tubewell or canal irrigation.

Within the village itself, the spread of innovations is greatly hampered by caste- and kinship-determined restrictions on free social interaction. Although in Khalapur, as in most small village communities, the division of labor is such that most members of all castes come into regular contact, interaction among different groups is limited to certain neutral spheres. A low-caste person will not ordinarily engage in free and equal discussion with those of greatly superior status. One frequently finds a lower-caste individual sitting or standing at a slight distance from a higher group engaged in discussion, listening to what is said, but not participating. Although news of current events may spread with relative ease, intergroup contact is not sufficiently intense to eliminate differences in attitude on such matters as home life, social and religious values, village politics, etc., which thus tends to restrict conversational subject matter. We find some evidence in support of this in a study of social dialects, which shows that the speech of untouchable Sweepers diverges significantly from that of the majority. These Sweepers spend a great deal of their day in the homes of their upper-caste masters, talk to them regularly, but do not adopt their speech patterns (Gumperz, 1958).

Observations on social interaction in the village show that free discussion and interchange of opinion are most likely to occur in small groups which we might call social nuclei. These are made up of men of one or more joint agricultural families, i.e., those who jointly own and operate their farm or business or share in the income from wage labor. They congregate either in the family *chopal* (men's house) or in cattle compounds or workshops, which are often hidden from public view. Group members are usually but not always of the some caste. It is possible for one person to be part of more than one nucleus. As a matter of fact, intercaste friendships are fairly frequent among touchable classes with roughly similar position in the hierarchy, so that a Rajput may have Brahman, merchant, or goldsmith friends; a carpenter may be in close contact with a group including merchants and goldsmiths; other carpenters may in turn be friendly with potters; and so on down the hierarchy. Among the Rajputs, many of the wealthier joint farm families divide their work in such a way as to allow some members enough time for cultivating other social groups.

Most informal social life in the village takes place within individual social nuclei. We find no functioning public assembly hall or square, accessible to all, where members of different groups may mingle. Village lanes are empty during leisure hours, and it is rare to find anyone just strolling or visiting from house to house. The community center, built with government funds, serves as a school during the day and is usually empty in the evening. Occasionally the local youth group uses the hall for some evening of devotional songs. Membership in this group is limited to a few upper-caste social nuclei and is by no means representative of the community as a whole.

Direct contacts of outsiders with villagers also tend to be channeled through indivdiual nuclei. Casual visitors usually see only their own friends and relatives. Government officials, including development officers whose task it is to promote social change, invariably stop at a selected family chopal. If they require information about the village, this is obtained by enquiries from members of their host's social nucleus. If direct contact with other villagers is necessary, these villagers are called to see the officer at the host's chopal. Whatever information the officer has to convey reaches the public through the host group. The village level worker similarly must work through the dominant caste. The fact that he has no public offices but is forced to seek quarters in a village home further limits his freedom of movement.

In the absence of any central mechanism which would provide simultaneous access to a variety of groups, the flow of innovations within the village is dependent primarily on intergroup contact. The study of dialect distribution, for example, shows a direct correlation between speech differences and the number of intercaste friendships. Those untouchable groups which are the most divergent linguistically also show the lowest number of intergroup friendships. Similar conditions might be expected to hold in the field of social values.

A number of the newer media of mass communication have recently been added to the already mentioned outside contacts, but these have done little so far to disturb the described pattern of dependence on person-to-person oral channels. Newspapers are not sold in the shops; they reach the villager primarily through individual subscriptions. Periodical literature and pamphlets intended for general distribution through the *panchayat* ordinarily circulate no further than the village headman's social nucleus. Moreover, the number of individuals capable of reading these papers is much smaller than would appear from the literary statistics, since the style employed in the news stories is quite different from either the village dialect or the conversational style of standard Hindi. Those few individuals who do read may often be found reading aloud to their own friends and commenting on the content of the news in the local dialect, thus reverting to oral communication.

The local youth group receives a number of posters dealing with village development. Some of these can be found adorning the chopal of the youth group leader; others are placed in his private room within the women's quarters, and are accessible to none except close family members. There is no public place in which to display posters. A lending library made available to the youth group is also stored in a private home and suffers from the same limitations of accessibility.

There are at least five radios in the village. Two of them are publicly owned. The one belonging to the village council fell into disrepair two months after it was purchased and no effort was made to have it repaired, in spite of the fact that repairmen are easily available in the neighboring bazaar town. Another one, which is owned by the local junior college, is occasionally used by small groups of students. The three private radios serve only a few of the social nuclei. They are used with such discretion that anthropologists working in the village were not aware of their existence for several months. This contrasts sharply with Muslim or Christian villages in the Near East where radios are set up in most public places and the voice of Radio Cairo is heard by all.

To summarize, therefore, if we leave aside the nature of a particular item, the spread of innovations in the village is determined by: (1) the nature of the message source and, if the source is human, its position in the social hierarchy; (2) the nucleus or nuclei through which it is channeled into the village and their relative status in the hierarchy; (3) the number of intergroup friendship ties of the mediating nuclei. It is obvious that high-caste families whose representatives travel frequently and who receive the greatest number of outside visitors have the best access to information from the outside. In the absence of a functioning system of mass communication, low-caste groups who, for economic reasons, tend to be confined to the village are the most isolated.

Religious performances avoid many of the limitations which the village social structure imposes on other media of communication. They may take place during the spring or fall seasons of religious festivals or in connection with weddings or sometimes whenever a troupe happens to pass through the village. In view of the almost total absence of any form of public entertainment, they form a welcome break in the daily routine and tend to draw large audiences.

Performances observed in the village are of two types. The first are religious lectures, based on traditional texts either read or spoken by a single performer. The narrative alternates with song. Often they are presented in dialogue form and acted out with vivid gestures. The lecturer is sometimes accompanied by a group of musicians, or he may provide his own accompaniment with his own instrument. Performers usually are members of a particular religious sect or order.

The second type, dramatic troupes, consist of several people acting out mythological themes usually on a platform stage. Dialogue is again interspersed with song, and music is provided by a group of musicians. Performances follow the general pattern outlined by Hein for the Ram Lila spectacle (1959).

Drama troupes or religious lecturers frequently visit the village on invitation of a particular family. But the actual performances are held in a public place, an open square or a field, and members of all castes including untouchables may attend. One performance was observed in the untouchable Chamar section of the village and much of the audience consisted of upper-caste individuals. This section of the village is not ordinarily frequented by touchables except when on business.

The troupe receives food, lodging, and occasionally presents of clothing and money from the inviting family. Most of the cash income derives from voluntary audience contributions. Individuals pass their money over to the actors in public during the performance. Their names and the amount contributed are then announced.

Of special interest is the caste composition of the various performing groups. In the case of religious lecturers, caste varies with the nature of the sect. Some sects draw their members exclusively from a Brahmin caste; in others, members of a single non-Brahmin caste predominate; while others, like the Arya Samaj troupe mentioned below, are of mixed composition. Dramatic troupes, as a rule, are composed of persons whose families are engaged in agriculture and who travel about for part of the year. Some come from neighboring villages, others are drawn from villages which may be several hundred miles distant from one another. One of the troupes observed was entirely Brahmin; another included only Dooms (a traditional Muslim caste of musicians and beggars). Several other troupes had intercaste composition. One combined Rajputs and Brahmins, another Rajputs, Brahmins, as well as Dooms, who occupy a place close to that of untouchable in the caste hierarchy. Regardless of caste, performers tend to be well treated on their travels and are accorded a measure of respect which recalls that given to the sanyasi, who is casteless by definition. When the performers take up their roles, the audience tends to forget their secular states and accepts their message as if it were spoken by the characters they represent.

The communicative advantages of religious performances are thus twofold. They differ from other types of social interaction in that they take place in a public location and are capable of simultaneously reaching a large number of diverse social nuclei. By virtue of their religious character, they are able to overcome many of the usual limitations of caste and social status. These features make them effective mass communication media.

An examination of the structure of traditional performances shows that they lend themselves to the transmission of a variety of messages, not always related to the overt religious theme. Let us take an example from music to illustrate the mechanics of this process. The basis of Indian music is the *rag* or melody type, consisting of a fixed sequence of notes within a certain interval. A piece of music or composition consists of variations on one or another of the rags in the traditional repertory. The result is closer to what in Western music we might call variations on a theme than to free composition. In classical Indian music, the number of available rags and the permitted range of variations are so large that a great degree of melodic variety is possible. The village system, however, is much more limited. Melodies as a rule are few and well known and rarely present a new esthetic experience. Rags are usually associated with certain themes: the holi rag or the *biaahii* rag sung at weddings is associated with festivals; the *malhar* is sung in the rainy season; the *shair* is suitable for love themes, the *ragni* for ballads, and the *bhajan* for devotional songs. Villagers are primarily interested in the words rather than the tune of a song. Lyrics are in fact composed for special occasions. Villagers fail to understand, for example, the fact that the anthropologist could enjoy a song without understanding its words. The function of the rag is to set the mood for the story or to provide a clue about the nature of the information to be conveyed by the words of the song.

The structure of dramatic performances and lectures is in many ways similar to that of music. The main components are the religious plot or story, prose dialogue, and the musical accompaniment. Chanting may or may not be used. The plot, the cast of characters, and the music are fixed, but the prose dialogue permits a great deal of improvisation. Subject matter of plots tends to be limited to a finite number of themes drawn from the epics, the Puranas, the Upanishads, or perhaps Rajput heroic tales. Since most of these themes are a matter of common knowledge, they convey little if any new information. Furthermore, the language of the chants is, as a rule, unintelligible to uneducated members of the audience. In information theory terms, we might say that the message is conveyed through the prose dialogue. Plot, music, and chant are part of what Hymes (1961:21) has called the form of the message. Like the rag, they set the mood and provide advance information about the message. Mythological themes can be elaborated in certain limited directions. Stories from the Ramayana provide scope for emphasizing the traditional martial values of the Rajput; the stories of Nal and Damayanti from the Mahabharata are suitable for domestic topics. Just as the musician is allowed to perform variations on a rag, the individual actor is given a great deal of freedom in prose dialogue, and this provides him with an opportunity to put his message across.

There are several instances of performances in which the message differs considerably from the overt religious theme. In one performance a Doom actor inserted a long plea for Hindi-Muslim amity into the mythological story of Nal and Damayanti. Even as a government official, he would never have been accorded the attention he received nor the audience, had he attempted to make a prose speech.

Another instance is the *Bhajan* group, sponsored by the Arya Samaj sect of reform Hinduism, in which a single lecturer performs while accompanied by a group of musicians. The message of one of these lectures concerned fixed prices and honesty in business, a subject introduced in the guise of a story from the Upanishads. The lecturer started by telling of a sage who arrived at the home of a famous raja. The raja paid him respect and offered him food, but the sage refused, saying, "How do I know that your kingdom is not full of tightwads and profiteers?" The raja replied, "Sir, there are no sinners in my kingdom. All goods in my kingdom are sold at fixed prices." This last statement was repeated in song with musical accompaniment, using the Bhajan rag, a rag associated with devotional songs. The lecturer went on to tell how he met a sanyasi who had been in America who told him that goods are sold at fixed prices there and that Americans are so honest they leave money for their milk on their doorstep. This statement, accentuated by musical underscoring, was followed by a discussion on the need for more honesty in business dealing.

The intercaste audience listened to the lecture with seeming interest and several people later commented favorably on the honesty of Americans. This interest contrasts sharply with the reception accorded to a group of students from Merut who wrote a modern play dealing with village development. In spite of the fact that intermissions were filled with movie songs and other light entertainment, the attitude of the village audience remained negative and even hostile. Many of them walked away before the end of the performance, criticising the fact that the theme was from daily life and had no connection with mythology.

In at least one instance, the Bhajan party technique was adapted to village development propaganda. A traditional Arya Samaj singer was employed by the Community Development Block. He collected a group of followers and lectured and sang about village uplift, using the Bhajan rag for songs about public health, the Japanese method for rice cultivation, etc. His activities have been singularly effective —he has been known to hold an audience of several hundred in bitter cold winter weather. Although a carpenter by caste, his followers included young people from a number of castes, including Tyagis and Brahmans. Caste status does not seem to impede his effectiveness. His followers stay with him for a while in a traditional teacher-disciple relationship and then return to their villages where they continue singing his songs to their own groups. If he were to attempt to disseminate propaganda as a village level worker, his effectiveness would be severely limited by his low caste.

The use of traditional performances as instruments of social reform in Khalapur is by no means unknown or new in Indian society. Medieval bhakti preachers like Kabir and the Virashaiva saints were essentially social reformers who spent much of their time preaching against the evils of caste. The evidence suggests that the roles of the religious preacher and of the secular social and economic reformer, which to some Westerners seem quite separate, are closely associated within the Indian social system. This would provide an explanation for the extraordinary popularity of individuals like Tilak, Gandhi, and Vinoba Bhave (compared with secular leaders like Gokhale, Rajendra Prasad, or even Pandit Nehru) who associate their message of egalitarian social reform with traditional symbolism, and thus at least assure it a hearing.

Marriott (1959) has recently suggested that traditional channels of cultural transmission in India are changing. He notes that the newer channels of radio, newspapers, and cinema are beginning to carry more and more of the burden of mass communication. Even so, the most popular of these media, the cinema, shows a high incidence of mythological themes performed in a manner reminiscent of village drama. The change is thus neither so fast nor so abrupt as one might imagine.

References Cited

Cohn, Bernard S. and McKim Marriott

1958 Networks and centers in the integration of Indian civilization. Journal of Social Research, Ranchi Bihar.

Damle, Y. B.

1959 Harikatha—a study in communication. Bulletin, Deccan College Research Institute. S. K. de Felicitation Volume, Poona.

Gumperz, John J.

1958 Dialect differences and social stratification in a North Indian village. American Anthropologist. 60:668–682.

Hein, Norvin

1959 The Ram Lila. In: Singer, 1958:279–304.

Hitchcock, John T.
1956 The Rajputs of Khaalaapur. A Study of Kinship, Social Stratification, and Politics. Ph.D. dissertation, Cornell University.
1959 Leadership in a North Indian village: Two case studies. In: *Leadership and Political Institutions in India,* ed. by Richard L. Park and Irene Tinker. Princeton: Princeton University Press.

Hymes, Dell H.
1962 The ethnography of speaking. In: *Anthropology and Human Behavior,* ed. by Thomas Gladwin and W. C. Sturtevant. The Anthropological Society of Washington.

Marriott, McKim
1959 Changing channels of cultural transmission in Indian Civilization. In: Intermediate Societies, Social Mobility and Social Communication, Proceedings of the 1959 Annual Spring Meeting of the American Ethnological Society, pp. 63–73.

McCormack, William
1959 Forms of communication in Virashaiva religion. In: Singer, ed., 1958: 119–129.

Rowe, William L.
1960 The marriage network and structural change in a North Indian community. Southwestern Journal of Anthropology. 16:299–311.

Singer, Milton (editor)
1958 Traditional India: Structure and Change. Journal of American Folklore 71.
1959 The Great Tradition in a metropolitan center: Madras. In: Singer, 1958: 347–388.

Conflict and Interlocal Festivals in a South Indian Region

ALAN R. BEALS

IN Yadgiri Tahsil, an administrative subdivision of Mysore State, many villages stage annual fairs or festivals in honor of local deities.[1] These festivals, known locally as "*jātras*," usually involve the enactment of ritual, competition between villages, public entertainment, commercial activities, and feasting and celebrating. Description of the jātra as an "interlocal festival" emphasizes its distinguishing feature, the entertainment of reified guest villages by an equally reified host village. Participants in a jātra consist of guests representing neighboring villages and of hosts representing the village where the jātra is held. Comparison of the jātra with such cultural features as the American county fair, the Creek Indian ball game, the Olympic games, the Mexican fiesta, Pueblo Indian ceremonials, and medieval European tournaments may well, at a later date, make possible the establishment of the concept of interlocal festivals as a basis for cross-cultural generalizations. For the present, four jātras held in Yadgiri Tahsil will be described and some of their possible functions suggested.[2]

These jātras, referred to here as A, B, C, and D, were held in the four neighboring villages of Maylapūr, Yelhēri, Gannapūr, and Gopālpūr, respectively. Because jātras require complicated planning and involve complex performances, it is not possible to describe any one in detail, but we will attempt to present the major features of each. The A (Maylapūr) jātra, although held in a small community, is a regional or model jātra in the sense that it attracts many visitors from a large area and is considered to be a "great jātra" well worth imitating. The B (Yelhēri) and C (Gannapūr) jātras are held in medium-sized communities, while the D (Gopālpūr) jātra is associated with a small community.

Participants

Participants in each jātra consist of contributors (of money, grain, or labor), directors, actors, and audience. The government is said to be the most important contributor to the A jātra, through a tax collected on coconuts offered to the deity during the ritual performance. In the B and C jātras, grain, money, and labor are collected from every household in the village. For the C jātra, fifty per cent of the contribution comes from a wealthy landlord, who probably obtains assistance from the government. In the D jātra there is no collection of money, but each household

The author is Associate Professor of Anthropology at Stanford University.

[1] The collaboration of Dr. K. Gnanambal of the Government of India, Department of Anthropology, in the collection of some of the observations upon which this paper is based and in the revision of a preliminary draft is gratefully acknowledged.

[2] The fieldwork upon which this paper is based was supported by a grant from the National Science Foundation and was carried out between December 1958 and January 1960 in Yadgiri Tahsil.

contributes an animal to be sacrificed. In all four villages, traditional leaders and priests, persons who are especially devout, and those whose poverty prevents them from making other kinds of contributions make additional contributions of labor by assisting in ritual performances, sweeping and decorating the temple, or playing drums. As will become evident, the nature of an individual's contribution to the jātra tends to vary according to caste (*jāti,* or endogamous group), economic status, and social position. Wealthy landlords give money, members of a priestly caste give their services, and poor people or members of low-ranking castes give menial services. Outside of these variations, contributions tend to come more or less equally from every household in the village.

The four jātras are organized and directed by village leaders and hereditary village officials. In the A jātra these are assisted and perhaps to some extent supplanted by the many policemen and government officials present. Village officials in the other three jātras are assisted by local men of importance who play informal roles in directing ritual, quelling disturbances, and keeping the audience in good humor. At the B and C jātras "great" landlords, to whom many persons owe money, personally direct portions of the ritual.

In all except the A jātra, the performers, that is, the enactors of ritual, the musicians, the actors in dramas, and the sellers of merchandise, are mainly or exclusively members of the host village, drawn from a wide range of social groups. The contributors, directors, and performers in all four jātras likewise represent the entire village rather than just one of its segments. Hand wrestling, the main form of competition, draws performers only from the guest villages although members of the host village participate as referees.

The Audience

Most jātras' audiences are drawn from nearby friendly villages. In the regional A jātra, visitors are said to number over 50,000 and to represent more than thirty-four villages, towns, and small cities. The organizers of B, C, and D jātras invite and entertain a specific group of villages with whom they maintain ties of marriage and economic exchange and with whom they frequently share a common village boundary. The jātra is an occasion for members of a host village to entertain members of a guest village. In the A and B jātras, neighboring villages considered to be the birthplace respectively of the deity's wife and of the deity herself are treated with special honor. Members of the host village frequently extend personal invitations to kinsmen in more distant villages which are not invited as a whole.

In all cases, representatives of the guest villages appear in procession and form the bulk of the audience. During the festival, social divisions in the host and guest villages are temporarily eclipsed by the reified village group.

The Myth

A jātra is generally accompanied by an explanatory tale suggesting some unique and miraculous property of the festival, the village, or the village deity in whose honor it is performed. At one village, the jātra focuses upon a stone which is said to be moving; when it reaches a particular spot, the present age will come to an end. The tale accompanying the A jātra, which is held twice a year, states that at these times the local form of the more widely known Hindu deity Maḷḷayya emerges from the Maylapūr hill and attempts to find and slaughter the demon Mārgasura. Maḷḷayya's hunting at the time of the jātra, according to the tale, has been carried on for 902 years. When Maḷḷayya catches Mārgasura, the jātra "will come to an end." At the B jātra the face of the goddess is so terrifying that it must be covered lest those who see it be struck dead. The D jātra stems from an agreement between Cā Hussayn and the villagers among whom he resides: he protects them and they in return worship him. The explanatory tales apparently add an element of awesomeness, stressing a particular jātra's unique ritual. The honored deity, considered to be a resident of the host village, also has special powers which are generally used for the benefit of the village.

The Performance of Ritual

Only portions of the week-long A jātra were observed, and accounts of the ritual obtained afterwards were contradictory because informants and interviewers repeatedly confused details of the fall and winter performances. According to one description, Maḷḷayya leaves his temple three days before the beginning of the jātra and is taken in procession to his mother-in-law's house in a neighboring village. There he and his human attendants are entertained until the morning of the third day, when a procession comes from the A jātra village to return Maḷḷayya and his betrothed to their home. On the night of the third day, Maḷḷayya emerges from his temple three times: first, to call together his worshippers; second, to accept the offerings of food which have been brought to him; and third, to hunt for the demon Mārgasura. At this latter time, members of the Kancavīraru "caste,"[3] who claim descent from Mārgasura, hide in their houses and make offerings to the goddess Kāḷika. Some of them put stakes through their tongues so that they cannot be compelled to reveal the hiding place of Mārgasura.

When Maḷḷayya has finished his hunting, he is taken to the *cāvadi,* a structure designed to shelter travelers. An official (Sēthasīndi) from a middle-ranking caste, whose function it is to call people together and to direct certain portions of ritual performances, then goes to the houses of the Kancavīraru people and informs them that the hunting is over. The Kancavīraru go to the Temple of Vīrabhadra and make offerings.

Several days later, on Sankranti, the major day of the jātra and the day of a great Pan-Indian festival, Maḷḷayya is taken in procession to the irrigation tank (reservoir) which he is said to have constructed 902 years ago. The route is lined with such crowds of visitors that policemen have difficulty opening up a pathway for the procession. When the procession reaches the tank, Maḷḷayya is immersed five times, and then worshipped by priests of the Jīraru (Flower Vendor) caste. The procession then returns to the foot of the hill on which the temple is located. There, priests of the Kuruba (Shepherd) caste attach a chain eight feet long and about two inches in diameter to a stone pillar, upon which is placed a lighted lamp. Nearby members of the audience, with hands folded prayerfully and whispering the name of Maḷḷayya, watch the chain, while more distant onlookers, seated on rooftops, discharge clouds of red and yellow powder in the direction of the deity. One of the Kuruba priests,

[3] Probably not a "caste" at all; but a lineage of the Kuruba or Shepherd caste which maintains a special relationship with the deity Maḷḷayya.

who has been possessed by Maḷḷayya, suddenly with a great cry grabs and pulls the chain. The number of pulls required to break the chain is believed to indicate whether or not the following year will be prosperous. Following the chain-breaking ceremony, Maḷḷayya is returned to the temple to receive offerings. In the evening a Brahmin priest celebrates the marriage of Maḷḷayya to his bride while groups from various villages sing appropriate songs. Although minor rituals occur throughout the six to eight days of the jātra, the other days are devoted mostly to secular entertainment and commercial activities.

B Jātra Ritual

The B jātra is in honor of Mariamma, a goddess said to have been born in the Vōḍḍaru (Stoneworker) colony in Gopālpūr, the village in which the D jātra is held. In the 1959 jātra, the two village headmen (one of the high-ranking Reddi caste, the other a Muslim) and the village account keeper (a Brahmin) gave one sheep and sixteen measures of *jōḷa* (sorghum vulgare) as well as other edibles such as chilies and grams to each of the Boyīns, (officials of the middle-ranking Kabliga or Farmer caste who take an important part in ceremonial activities and are supposed to bring water for dignitaries who visit the village). The Boyīns took these to their houses and prepared a thick jōḷa mush. By dawn on the following morning, they had placed the foodstuffs in decorated pottery vessels. On top of each pot, they placed leaves of the sacred *nīm* tree, and upon these another pot full of water, and then garlands of flowers. Outside of the Boyīns' houses, a procession was waiting. Two women of the lowest-ranking caste (Māḍaru) came holding winnowing fans into which the Boyīns placed offerings. These two women then washed the heads of the sheep and decorated them with turmeric (*ārsina*) powder before garlanding them. Nīm leaves were then waved around the heads of the sheep while the onlookers said, *"eḳālige,"* an utterance believed to induce Mariamma to come and stand beside them. The pots were then worshipped with offerings of fire and sandalwood sticks. Outside, men of the Māḍaru caste began drumming, and four other men of middle-ranking castes put each pot on the head of a member of the household of the village official who contributed it. The pot-carriers, each accompanied by four men—a necessary precaution as the pot-carriers must be supported and restrained if they are possessed by the goddess—proceeded to the village gate and waited until the representatives of each household in the village had assembled with their offerings. The procession which formed included women of B village who carried sacred lamps (*jyōti*) to the temple, and persons from Gopālpūr, Mariamma's birthplace and site of the D jātra, who also carried sacred lamps and pots full of offerings.

The procession moved to Mariamma's temple and circled it five times in a counterclockwise direction. Offerings were placed near a large flat stone in front of the temple. The stone was washed with water and divided into quadrants with diagonal lines of jōḷa flour. Three half-circles of turmeric powder were drawn in each quadrant. Women from Gopālpūr then removed large double handfuls of jōḷa mush from each pot to build a three- or four-foot high heap (*ḳumba*) on the stone. Others placed a lamp made from wheat flour on top of the heap and decorated it with lines of saffron and turmeric. A kind of pancake (*holigi*) stuffed with gram and brown sugar were placed in a circle around the heap, and a canopy of mango leaves and flowers was placed over the heap.

The Māḍaru women who had washed the sheep received the unused Jōla mush from the women of Gopālpūr and made a separate undecorated heap in front of which they placed toddy, pancakes, fire, and coconuts as offerings to Mariamma. Inside the temple, similar offerings to Mariamma were being made by priests of higher-ranking castes. The Boyīns then sacrificed the sheep contributed by each household, arranging the heads in a line in front of the heaps and placing the left leg of each in its mouth. The sheep's stomachs were removed, stuffed with turmeric, pancakes, mush, and other foodstuffs, and thrown in different directions around the temple area. Water was then sprinkled in the same area. The sheep were butchered by the Boyīns and distributed among the caste groups, who cooked in separate places in the temple area. The visitors from Gopālpūr included nearly all of the castes resident there—Muslims, Shepherds, Stoneworkers, Farmers, and Saltmakers. At this point in the ceremony, the host group was restricted to Farmers (Kabliga) and Leatherworkers (Māḍaru). Shepherds from the host village ate in their own houses; no vegetarians were present.

D Jātra Ritual

At Gopālpūr, the home of the D jātra, the ritual starts the night before the jātra's official opening. In 1959, a party of about twenty young men belonging to various castes went in procession with drums to the tomb (*darga*) of Cā Hussayn (Shah Hussein). When they reached it, a young man of the Muslim butcher caste (*Kaṭegāru*) was possessed by the deity who said through the young man's lip, "Bring the water when you feel happy; if you do not feel happy, don't bring it." Following this the procession left with drums and lanterns for the Bhima River ten miles away. There, a Muslim from a weaver caste (Pinjāra) took the pot of water from the Brahmin priest who carried it from the river, and was then possessed by Cā Hussayn. Dancing and trembling, he walked three times around the tomb counter-clockwise and poured the water over the image of the deity which had been placed on top of the tomb.

Towards evening of the following day host families of all non-vegetarian castes appeared with goats, sheep, or chickens and cooking equipment. The animals to be eaten were ritually killed by the Muslim priest (Mavla). Muslims and Shepherds then chopped up the carcasses and distributed the meat to the owners of each animal. After nightfall, while women were preparing the food, the priest offered sandalwood sticks (*lōbhana*) to the deity and read some passages from the *Koran*. A procession of men went through the village to the house of one of the village Boyīns (Farmer caste). The priest and his assistants went inside. The householder had filled a pot with offerings of *gallip,* composed of flowers, sugar, and sandalwood sticks. The pot was decorated in the same way as those offered in the B jātra. The Muslim priest repeated *mantrams* (sacred recitations) and burned sandalwood sticks before the pot. Ashes taken from a small fire kindled in front of the pots were mixed with water and pasted on the foreheads of those present, some of whom had gone all day without food and drink. A similar enactment took place at the house of the Village Crier, a member of the Saltmaker caste. The Brahmin village headman did not participate in the jātra; the Muslim village headman was the priest. The Brahmin priest who carried water from the river was the temporarily resident village school teacher. The pots were carried by two Muslims of the Butcher caste.

As the procession moved toward the tomb, one of the pot carriers began to tremble and dance. His attendants rushed up to prevent him from falling and the Muslim priest handed him a bundle of peacock feathers. The deity then said in Urdu, "Clear out of my path, otherwise you will suffer; however much you wish to worship, you worship that much. Get moving, get moving, otherwise you will suffer." A little later, the priest was possessed, trembled violently, and fell to the ground. Almost instantly he recovered. The other pot carrier then began to tremble and dance. The carrier of the pressure lantern then said in Kannada, "Ask him what he wants. Why is that god again and again coming on everyone? Let us know his purposes." The possessed man then beat the lantern carrier with a bundle of peacock feathers and said in Urdu, "Why are you so proud? It is you have brought him out." The carrier of the pressure lantern replied in Kannada, "Why are you scolding those who ask why the god is coming on top of everyone? Why are you performing the jātra if you don't really want to see this?" A crowd began to gather, but the Crier parted the disputants and the procession entered the enclosure surrounding the tomb.

Following the arrival of the decorated pots, a new procession formed, led by the Carpenter caste, the only vegetarian group present and hence the highest-ranking. The new procession, composed of all persons present, circled the *darga* counter-clockwise five times. One representative of each family, usually a small boy, carried a brass plate containing a sacred lamp and an offering of coins. When these offerings had been given, the Muslim priest read from the *Koran* and then placed burning sandalwood sticks before the deity. This finished, the priest, facing outwards from the temple enclosure, repeated some mantrams, presumably passages from the *Koran,* over a four- or five-year-old Māḍaru boy who had been brought to the jātra by his parents, and cut off a lock of his hair. The non-vegetarian participants then went to their respective cooking places to consume rice with meat and chili, and members of the vegetarian Carpenter caste returned to their houses for food.

C Jātra Ritual

The ritual part of the C jātra is carried out in honor of Bhimarayya and Hanumantha, who figure prominently in the *Mahabharata* and the *Ramayana.* The main outlines of the C. Jātra ritual are parallel to those of the B and D, although the primary ritualist is a Brahmin priest who tends to follow more closely the Sanskritic aspect of the Hindu great tradition than do the ritualists of the other jātras. Many of the participants are vegetarian Lingayats.

Common Ritual Elements

Common features of the ritual include: the presence of priests; possession of some individuals by the deity; washing an image of the deity; giving *namaskārams* (salutations made by placing the two hands together) to the deity; carrying the offerings in pottery vessels; carrying lamps; dancing, playing music, and singing; and making offerings of such items as saffron, turmeric, sandalwood sticks, and coconuts. Although animal sacrifice occurs at all four jātras, it is not part of the public ritual at the A and C jātras.

Within this common ceremonial language, there is wide variation. Priests are drawn from many different castes including Brahmin, Muslim, Shepherd, and Flower Vendor, and their assistants from as many different castes. Each jātra honors a different deity: Mariamma is the goddess of cholera and presumably of Dravidian or at least non-Brahminical origin; Cā Hussayn is a Muslim deity; Maḷḷaya and Bhimarayya both seem to be of Sanskritic or Brahminical origin although Maḷḷayya's antecedents are not so easily traced. Maḷḷayya and Bhimarayya both receive vegetarian offerings, while Mariamma and Cā Hussayn receive offerings of meat.

The myth and ritual of these jātras involve a weaving together of local, regional, and pan-Indian traditions. Despite their differences, the evident intention and effect of the myth and ritual are to make each jātra a unique and dramatic performance. The worshipped deity is regarded as local in origin even though identified with less parochial Hindu or Muslim deities. Although Cā Hussayn presents the outward features of the Muslim saint,[4] he is regarded as a unique and powerful defender and supporter of Gopālpūr where the D jārta is performed. In Gopālpūr, Hanumantha, a vegetarian god, is the official village deity, yet the jātra honors Cā Hussayn, possibly because over ninety per cent of the population of the village eat meat. The choice of Cā Hussayn in preference to a Hindu goddess may have been influenced by the fact that ritual honoring of goddesses requires the participation of Māḍaru priests, none of whom live in Gopālpūr. The C jātra village has a large proportion of vegetarian Lingayats who cannot in good conscience participate in animal sacrifice, a fact relevant to their worship of the vegetarian Bhimarayya, even though he is not a Lingayat deity.

Religious rituals of each jātra are so structured as to permit almost every resident caste and sect to attend and participate. The amalgamation of Sanskritic, non-Sanskritic, and Muslim rituals is particularly evident in the many similarities between the B and D jātras. The myth and ritual appear to be an expression of the entire village, a further indication of the temporary submergence of internal social segmentation.

Feasting and Celebration

Feasting and celebration are virtually identical in all of the jātras, although variation occurs in the type of food served and in the degree to which dining and feasting are communal. At the B and D jātras, meat is served and the castes dine in separate rows about ten feet apart, in the vicinity of the temple. At the A jātra, where many strangers assemble, there is no organized communal meal, but persons of all castes eat together in the coffee shops and restaurants set up for the occasion. Communal dining is completely absent at the C jātra, probably because of the marked social distance between the vegetarian Lingayats and the non-vegetarian Farmers and Shepherds.

For most people, the pattern of communal dining is less important than the entertainment of relatives. Political power in the region is based largely upon the extension of kinship bonds between families residing in different villages. Because most marriages involve the coming of the bride to the village of her husband, the key relatives are those who are classified as "mother's brother," who are potential

[4] Although on some occasions, Gopālpūr's Muslims identify Cā Hissayn as a saint, he is, in this context, a village deity. All of the deities honored at jātras are human and local in origin despite the fact that all have temples and all bear the names of pan-Indian saints and deities. In the local dialect of Kannada, all deities are referred to in the plural and all benevolent supernaturals are referred to as deities. Cā Hussayn may be a saint in Urdu, but he can only be a "God" (dēvaru) in Kannada.

fathers-in-law, and women classified as "father's sister," and "sister," who are potential mothers-in-law, to males born in the village. For example, fathers and older brothers in the non-vegetarian castes consider it particularly important to insure a plentiful supply of toddy or brandy to their daughters or sisters who return home for the jātra. Far into the night, groups of women meet in friendly conclave, sing, and pass the bottle. The number of invited relatives depends upon the wealth and political ambition of the host, and they must be lavishly entertained.

Formal Competition

As part of the jātra, men engage in "hand play" or "hand wrestling," while the women "exist inside happiness." For young men, this competition is the most important part of the jātra. Adolescents and young married men practice hand wrestling for weeks before the jātra season in order to defend the reputation of their village or to demonstrate its superiority. When the jātra season starts, teams of young men from almost every village in the region visit as many jātras as possible, avoiding only those jātras performed by the one or two villages known to be hostile toward their own.

A space for hand wrestling is cleared in a field near the village, players and audience sitting in a circle surrounding the arena. Members of each village sit together. Referees, who do not participate in the wrestling, are selected from the host village. At the opening of the competition, one of the referees addresses the audience and the players, saying that the rules must be observed and that any player who defeats five opponents in a row will be awarded a coconut and, sometimes, a money prize. The referees then ask that a player step forward. For ten or fifteen minutes the referees beg and browbeat the players, saying, "Come on, somebody please step forward. Are you all women?" Finally, one of the guest villages sends out a young boy, the smallest member of its team. The boy comes forward with determination, hitches up his *dhōti* with great emphasis and savoir faire, carefully adjusts his turban to protect his head, and squats in the ring to wait for an opponent. After another period of exhortation by the referees, a second player is found. Ideally, the opponent should represent an "enemy" village. Most villages in the region have one or two "enemy" villages, enmity being largely expressed in terms of a desire to best the "enemy" village in what can only be called an unfriendly wrestling match. If the team from the "enemy" village is absent, the opponent is drawn from a distant or neutral village and a "friendly" match is held, in which, initially at least, both teams attempt to behave in a sportsmanlike manner. Matches between villages which have strong economic or marital ties are apparently never arranged.

When the wrestling begins, the representative of the first team, holding up his right arm, approaches the second player, who seizes the proffered arm with a ferocious two-handed grip. Suddenly the second player releases his grip and slowly and solemnly rubs dirt over his hands. With ominous deliberation, he then resumes his grip. The two referees begin to circle about the players, warning them not to trip each other or otherwise violate the rules. The first player begins to twist about, attempting to win by breaking the grip of his opponent. The players spin around and around each other. In the half-light of the kerosene pressure lantern, some members of the audience see an illegal leg or knee brought into play. The two players fall to the ground with a bone-cracking thump and begin wrestling in earnest. The referees leap on the players and try to separate them before they injure each other. Sometimes a player graciously accepts defeat saying, "Finished" (*aytu*). At other times the apparently defeated player wails, "He kicked me" or "He tripped me." There are hot words; the audience stands. Men from opposing villages raise their five- to six-feet-long staves, and wave them threateningly. If a policeman is present, the noise awakens him and he comes sleepily into the ring and administers a stern warning. Sometimes older men from the two opposing villages make peace, telling their representatives to calm down and be sportsmanlike. If there is a fight, they threaten, there will be no more hand wrestling. Sometimes peacemaking efforts fail and, perhaps once a year, one out of thirty or forty villages will be the scene of a bloody riot. In 1958 at one of the jātras, members of two villages began to quarrel and some of the young men began hitting each other with staves. Persons in the audience, fearful that the quarreling might disrupt the match and angry at the exhibition of unsportsmanlike conduct, began pitching stones at the offenders. At this point members of at least one small village melted away into the night, later explaining, "We are a small village and cannot afford to offend people." Of those who remained, eight are said to have been killed before the rioting ended.

In the normal course of events, the defeated player leaves the ring and his village sends in another, larger player. Any man who wins by defeating five successive opponents becomes a village hero. At the B jātra, when a man from Gopālpūr, where the D jātra is held, won a coconut, the prized possession was brought home in procession, offered to the village deity, and then consumed in a spirit of triumph. The victor was widely praised, but later debunked, as is the fate of heroes.

The fact that the weakest players of each village wrestle first allows the inclusion of all who wish to be members of the village team. The only caste that appears to be excluded from the hand wrestling is the lowest-ranking Māḍaru. Although members of the high-ranking Brahmin caste have not been observed participating, the audience appears to find nothing incongruous in a wrestling match between a wealthy college graduate from a high-ranking land-owning caste and a landless illiterate from a caste which is of sufficiently low rank to be required to live apart from other castes. A team from one village contained two men who had sworn to murder each other. In the hand wrestling as in other aspects of the jātra, intra-village differences of status are minimized in order to create a representation of village unity.

Dramatic Performances and Commercial Activities

Dramatic performances are frequently given on nights when there is no hand wrestling. This is most marked at the larger A jātra, where dramas, motion pictures, and other performances may last for six or seven nights. The C jātra sponsored one all-night performance, while in the B and D jātras there were none. This was felt to be regrettable because a performance is considered essential to a really perfect jātra. By January of 1960 the D jātra village had plans to perform no less than three dramas during their next jātra. General participation is less marked in the dramatic performances than in other aspects of the jātra, but it is worth noting that although the dramatic performance is organized by a relatively small group of individuals, the performers are rarely, if ever, drawn from a single caste.

Commercial activity is a major feature of the A jātra, though not so important in the others; the D jātra village had only one or two shops selling edibles, tobacco, and other small items. There were several shops at the B and C jātras selling candy, tea, utensils, and cloth. Persons attending jātras expect to be able to make purchases, but only in the A jātra, where everything from electric motion picture projectors for children to brass bells for village temples was available, is commercial activity an essential feature.

Analysis

Although each of the jātras described above is designed to be a unique event, the evidence suggests that all jātras meet certain requirements: There must be inter-village participation. The host village must be sufficiently united so that its members may contribute financially and work together to make the jātra a success. Relatives must be invited and entertained. There must be an elaborate ritual supported by a suitable mythology. The ritual, to say nothing of other activities, must be adapted from the general jātra model in such a way as to allow virtually all local castes and religious sects to participate. Feasting and joyous celebration must take place. There must be hand wrestling, dramatic performances and commercial activities if they can be arranged.

The jātra has many manifest functions and purposes. People say, "We hold a jātra so that the god will be happy," or "We hold the jātra to entertain our relatives," or "We hold the jātra so our village will be famous." From an analytic standpoint, it is easy to list a number of its economic, recreational, and social functions. But to demonstrate that the jātra actually fills these functions, or does so more effectively than some other available device, is by no means easy.

For example, the ritual performance is intended to please the local deity and encourage him to be benevolent. One participant in the D jātra explained, "We worship Cā Hussayn so he will stay in the village and bring us good fortune." But when Cā Hussayn appeared at the jātra he behaved discourteously and threateningly. The audience clearly felt that Cā Hussayn might well have been insulted by the small size of the jātra and by possible errors in the conduct of ritual. At the A jātra, where six tries were required before the chain could be broken, many felt that the deity was less than pleased. If performed properly, the propitiation and ritual might have a compelling effect on the deity, but mistakes inevitably occur. Those who believe that a particular jātra is insufficiently grand or that the ritual has not been carried out properly are plainly not reassured by the performance of ritual. One of the leaders of the A jātra said, "Maḷḷayya does to us as he wishes," meaning that performance of ritual had no compelling effect.

The issuing of invitations to relatives or to related villages and the entertainment of these visitors suggest a number of integrative functions. Possibly the jātra facilitates the communication of new and old ideas and behavior patterns. This communication function is most highly developed at the A jātra, where government demonstrations, motion pictures, and special shops may widen perspectives and encourage the diffusion of new ideas. Most interlocal festivals draw their audiences from neighboring villages and the individual jātra represents a rearrangement of traditional materials rather than the introduction of new forms. It is difficult to envision the communication in such a situation of much beyond the usual sort of gossip exchanged among people who see each other quite frequently in any case.

The jātra is designed to bring together one's relatives, friends, and members of neighboring villages and instill in them a warm friendly feeling for the host family and village. But, like the gods, neighbors and relatives are not easily pleased, and the assumption that close interaction leads to integration hardly describes the behavior of kinsmen. Fancied failures of hospitality ("Why don't you give me some brandy?"), remembrances of past disappointments ("When are you going to give us that leg chain you promised as part of the bride price?"), and fatigue resulting from travel and excessive celebration lead almost inevitably to quarrels and conflict.

The carrying out of a jātra is supposed to present the image of the host village as a good, friendly, and cooperative place in which to live. This is important for marriage negotiations as well as for trade and employment. On the other hand, the very act of presenting such an image is a part of the competitive aspect of the jātra. Visitors from one village do not go to another in order to be convinced that it is better than their own. There is a great deal of criticism and faultfinding; the disgraceful failure of a particular jātra may be discussed for months or even years afterwards.

This discussion suggests that the success of the jātra in satisfying the overt purposes of the organizers is by no means unequivocal. Jātras are expensive and time-consuming. Possibly they create (or at least make manifest) tensions which are sufficiently strong to lead to pitched battles between villages. Further, it is difficult to identify any single overt purpose of the jātra sufficiently unique to make it an essential part of the local social organization. Propitiating deities, entertaining relatives, participating in games and dramas, and carrying out commercial activities may all be accomplished by other means.

The uniqueness of the jātra as a social institution appears to lie in the fact that it creates the only situation in which one village entertains other villages and in which competition between villages takes place. The competition occurs covertly in the comparison of the host village with all others and overtly in the wrestling matches between guest villages.

On the surface, hand wrestling serves the prestige needs of adolescents and young married men. The young men from each of the visiting villages hope to become famous for their heroic performances in the ring. The usual fate of the would-be hero is to be tripped up, slammed onto the ground, and badly bruised. The young man, if he loses, is likely to be accused of cowardice by his team mates; if he wins, of unsportsmanlike conduct by members of the opposing team. It is far easier for a competitor to acquire shame and defeat than to win the coconut denoting victory. As each village has a fifty-fifty chance of winning, it is not as likely to encounter defeat and dishonor as are its individual members. The chance of defeat can be decreased by picking a quarrel before the match and thus having reason to refuse to participate, or by attributing defeat to foul play. Although consistent defeat sometimes leads to demoralization and the temporary abandonment of hand wrestling by a particular village, defeat is more likely to stimulate a greater interest in hand wrestling which leads in turn to more intensive practice for next year's matches. Other alternatives, such as catching a group of people from the "enemy" village and beating them with sticks, become the cowardly actions of persons who cannot succeed at hand wrestling.

The broader competition between villages based upon the size and quality of each village's jātra is one which few villages can lose. One village may have a grander festival, but the food served by another may be superior. Visitors leaving a jātra talk about "our village," about how well "our village" behaved, and about the superiority of "our village's jātra." Even the notably small D jātra is considered by its performers to possess special attributes which make it in various ways superior to all other jātras.

Except upon the occasions when rioting occurs, the jātra restricts conflict between villages to a particular time, place, and form. Such conflict is channeled so as to prevent any permanent disruption of normal patterns of relationship. Even when the competition turns into unlawful conflict, it may still be channeled and arbitrated. It is suggested, then, that one of the unique and necessary functions of the jātra, and perhaps of other kinds of interlocal festivals as well, lies in the fact that it provides a legitimate means of expressing hostility between villages and of restricting the occurrence of violent conflict to a particular time and place.

This use of the jātra as a kind of safety valve mechanism for regulating relationships between villages does not explain why a particular village undertakes to perform a jātra.[5] Because only about half of the villages in the region actually hold jātras, it may be supposed that the decision to sponsor one arises from some characteristic or set of characteristics of the host villages. In any event, it appears extremely unlikely that the leaders of any single village would decide to hold a jātra solely on the grounds that it would be beneficial in the regulation of inter-village conflict.

A comparison of thirty villages in the region where the four jātras were observed appears to shed some light upon the question of why some villages have jātras and others do not. The thirty villages fall into four size categories: seven, which might be called "hamlets," contain between 15 and 78 households; six, "small villages," contain between 92 and 137 households; ten, "medium villages," contain between 168 and 307 households; and seven, "large villages," contain between 379 and 512 households. Households average about five persons. Only one of the seven hamlets has a jātra while about half of the twenty-three villages have them. Thus, although population size can be identified as an important determinant of the presence or absence of jātras, a second variable is needed to explain their distribution among communities larger than hamlets.

A Second Variable?

Identification of a second variable which might affect the distribution of jātras in the region requires a consideration of some further aspects of regional social organization. The most powerful source of regional social and cultural unity lies in the belief that men should choose brides from villages other than their own on the basis of previous ties of real or fictitious consanguinity. The pattern established by this belief compels each village and each family within a village to maintain a circle of friendly villages and friendly relatives. Maintenance of such circles of relationship depends ultimately upon the exchange of brides between families in the different villages. This exchange, in turn, depends upon the reputation of the village as a good place to send one's daughter to live. One of the outstanding characteristics of a "good place to live" is an absence of quarrels, fights, and thefts. Demonstration

[5] The role of jātras in regulating conflict between villages in another region of India is discussed by Roy, 1915:312–318.

of such an absence is effectively accomplished by the jātra because it is the only occasion upon which all of the members of a particular village publicly cooperate before an audience composed largely of visitors from other villages. Villages which are, in fact, free of overt conflict, would hardly feel an imperative need to demonstrate that point at great cost. This leads to the perverse conclusion that the village which advertises its state of harmony by performing a jātra may in fact be a village which is in an actual state of disharmony.

The most prominent diagnostic feature of disunity within a village is its division into two conflicting parties. In the group of thirty villages, fifteen were reported to be so divided by persons living in the villages. The presence of parties within particular villages is public knowledge and a source of discreditable gossip in neighboring villages, so that it is unlikely that the presence of parties could be successfully concealed. A comparison of the distribution of jātras and parties in the four types of communities follows:

	Parties, Jātras	No Parties, No Jātras	Parties, No Jātras	No Parties, Jātras
Hamlets	0	6	0	1
Small Villages	3	1	2	0
Medium Villages	3	4	1	2
Large Villages	4	1	2	0
Totals	10	12	5	3

The hypothesis of an association between the distribution of parties and of jātras is supported within each of the size categories in the above table. A chi square test applied to the column totals of the table indicates that the distribution of column totals could occur by chance once in one hundred trials.[6] The small size of the sample precludes any attack upon the relative importance of community size and the presence of parties in predicting the presence of jātras.

An indirect approach to the problem of the relationship between the presence of jātras and the presence of conflict within the villages in which they are held can be made by attempting to scale the incidence of public cooperation and public conflict in each of the thirty villages. The incidence of public cooperation in each village can be calculated by counting the incidence of such activities as construction of public buildings, the organization of hymn singing groups and drama companies, or the holding of jātras, as these activities require the cooperation of all or most members of the community. Public conflict can be measured in terms of the reported incidence of thefts, quarrels, fights, and parties within each of the villages.

When these rather crude calculations are correlated with population size and wealth, as indicated by village land revenue, using a four-variable multiple correlation technique, the adjusted coefficient of partial determination between public conflict and public cooperation indicates that public conflict accounts for forty-two per cent of the variation in public cooperation. The partial correlation coefficient is +.65. The data for this correlation coefficient have been abstracted prematurely from a larger quantitative study of the Yadgiri region and cannot be reported in detail or given too much credence at this time; nevertheless, the size of the partial correlation

6 Chi square with one degree of freedom equals 6.65, P equals .01.

between public conflict and public cooperation, taken with the previously cited data, provides a reasonably strong indication that there is an association between public conflict and public cooperation which is independent of village size. Assuming that jātras and parties follow the same general pattern as other forms of public cooperation and conflict, there is an implication that a relationship between parties and jātras also exists independently of population size.

This leads to the conclusion that either conflict develops as a result of the presence of jātras in particular villages, or jātras develop as a result of the presence of conflict. In the group of thirty villages, one village appears to have abandoned its annual jātra in recent years, and another appears to have settled a long-term conflict between two parties. In all other villages, the typical response to questions about parties and jātras was, "It has been going on for a long time." Although it is difficult to explain why a particular village chose to perform a jātra, it is evident that the fear of supernatural sanctions and the desire to maintain the reputation of the village make abandonment of the annual performance of a jātra difficult.

Party Conflict

Questions concerning the origins and perpetuation of party conflict are somewhat easier to answer. Although I have discussed this problem elsewhere (Beals, 1961: 27–34), it may be noted that party conflict appears to arise in particular villages whose size or structure inhibits the operation of conflict resolving mechanisms. Specifically, its development appears to be linked with a distribution of castes or lineages which permits the division of the village into two roughly equal parts. For example, party conflict centering about lineages within a particular caste seems to occur most frequently in villages which have a single numerically dominant caste constituting a majority of the population. Party conflict focused between two castes appears to occur when a majority of the village population is more or less equally divided between two castes of roughly equal status. In other villages, where no single caste or pair of castes is dominant numerically, party conflict appears to arise relatively rarely. This leads to the tentative conclusion that the origins of party conflict lie in a condition of cleavage or structural imbalance arising from the arrangement, distribution, and size of particular castes in each village.

Inasmuch as the presence of castes in a village can be attributed in most cases to ecological and historical factors of great duration, it appears reasonable to suppose that the structural arrangement of castes within a village is prior to both the development of party conflict and the performance of annual jātras. Briefly, social segmentation leads to conflict, and conflict leads to a search for means of resolving the conflict or of repairing the damage to the reputation of the village. From a theoretical standpoint, it seems likely that in some cases the presence of tension leads to the introduction of conflict limiting mechanisms before conflict actually breaks out. This is only weakly supported by the data—three villages have jātras without parties; five villages have parties without jātras.

If the jātra is indeed a means of limiting the impact of conflict upon the village and if the conflict actually arises within the social structure, the most effective solution to the problem of conflict would be to rearrange the distribution of castes in villages in such a way as to make the emergence of clearly defined parties more difficult. Such a solution, although realistic in a utopian sense, is not politically realistic.

Hence, the presence of tendencies toward conflict in certain villages represents an insolvable problem. The jātra does not present a solution to this problem in the same sense that a rearrangement of the village social structure would, but the requirements for total village cooperation evident in virtually every aspect of the jātra performance provide a mechanism for suppressing conflict and providing a superordinate goal which lessens the importance of the goals to be achieved through conflict.

Conclusion

The principal outlines of the activity known in the Yadgiri region as "jātra" have been presented and an attempt has been made to identify its contribution to the social organization of the region and of the villages where it is performed. Although the jātra may be presumed to fill many economic, social, and psychological functions, most of these functions can readily be fulfilled by other equally available means. A listing of the general functions of the jātra does not serve to explain why some villages in the region perform them and why some do not, or, why the Yadgiri region possesses interlocal festivals while other regions do not. An approach to this problem requires that the jātra be shown to perform functions which could not otherwise be fulfilled within the contexts of the regional culture and social organization. I have suggested two such functions: it regulates relationships between villages by providing a time, a place, and a set of rules governing conflict and potential conflict, and it serves within the village as a device for compelling a periodic cessation of party conflict and for publicly demonstrating the absence of such conflict. The fact that the jātra appears to accomplish these things without having any impact upon those characteristics of village social structure which appear to be responsible for the development of conflict in particular villages suggests its essentially religious character, for it is the essence of the religious solution that where the desire or the ability to alter circumstances is lacking, circumstances can nevertheless be reinterpreted and redirected in such a way as to make it seem almost as if there had been no problem requiring a solution.

It has not been the purpose of this paper to present a final solution to the problem of the functions and origins of either jātras or interlocal festivals in general. An explanation of the functions of any particular activity or class of activities requires continuous long-term observation and detailed comparative study. Although it cannot be imagined that all interlocal festivals are identical in function, it is hoped that this discussion of the jātra will serve to identify interlocal festivals as a cultural phenomenon worthy of comparative study and to suggest some of the data relevant to such an investigation.

References Cited

Beals, Alan R.
1961 Cleavage and internal conflict: An example from India. The Journal of Conflict Resolution. 5:27–34.
Roy, Sarat Chandru
1915 *The Oraons of Chota Nagpur*. Ranchi.

The Structure of Sinhalese Healing Rituals

NUR YALMAN

As social anthropology has set up new standards for the analysis of social structure, the lag in the study of religious thought and behavior has become increasingly apparent. New departures have been rare in this region and the figures of Freud, Durkheim, and Weber have continued to dominate the scene.

There are three systematic approaches to the study of religious behavior: first, the Freudian approach which seeks to penetrate the unconscious motivations behind religious behavior; second, the social structural approach of Durkheim and Weber which seeks to relate religious phenomena to the fundamental features of the societies under investigation.[1]

A third approach, with which I shall be mainly concerned, was outlined by Radcliffe-Brown (1933) and followed up by Srinivas (1952). This approach seeks to examine the internal consistency of religious thought, symbolism, and behavior. It rests on the assumption that the religious categories of primitive societies form a coherent and internally consistent set of beliefs and symbols (like language) which, given the premises, follow logically. To a greater or lesser extent all anthropologists must utilize this approach when they attempt to understand the religious language of an alien society.

The learning of a religious language for the anthropologist is similar to the learning of any other language: the implications of symbols and the contexts in which their use is appropriate must be understood. But although there are these similarities, much of the work in religion has remained in the realm of ideas and has not been concerned with detailed analysis of the language of religion as a symbolic system. There have been few attempts to examine specific myths or rituals in detail, and although Warner (1958:244ff), Berndt (1951) and others have described the symbol system of certain myths and have noted their connections with ritual, there is no accepted theoretical framework for this kind of analysis.[2]

Recent advances in structural linguistics and communication theory have left their mark on anthropologists.[3] In particular Lévi-Strauss advocates the application of the key concepts of structural linguistics to the study of myths, which are to

---

The author is Assistant Professor of Anthropology at the University of Chicago.

[1] In some cases these two approaches have been brought together in a stimulating fashion (e.g., Fortes 1945; Gough 1959; Leach 1958; Nadel 1946, 1954), but in others they have remained complementary methods whose results may not be mutually compatible (e.g., Gough 1955).

[2] The question of the interconnection between myth and ritual is still wide open: Lévi-Strauss (1956) suggests not a one-to-one consistency but a "'dialectic'" and Nadel (1954:78) throws doubt on any connection between the two realms.

[3] Apart from attempts to adapt mechanical computers which have had great influence on theoretical linguistics (Jakobson 1961:245) for anthropological use, there are suggestions that certain aspects of primitive thought categories are susceptible to linguistic analysis (Conklin 1962; Leach n.d.).

be treated as "communications" in an unknown language (Lévi-Strauss 1955:4.1, 4.2). Communication is made up of "units" (1955:3.0), and each stands in a "context," or as Lévi-Strauss puts it, "will consist in a relation" (1955:3.3). The analysis of these relations will show that they exist in "bundles" (1955:3.4), and that these bundles recur in different stages of the myth. In other words, the "structure of the Myth" will be analogous either to the recurring themes or rhythms of an orchestra score, or to the recurring problems or worries contained in the communication of a patient to his analyst.

Lévi-Strauss' proposals for the analysis of myths have had their earlier exponents like Propp, who advocated a similar strategy for the investigation of the "morphology" of the folk tale (1958),[4] and recently Leach has used Lévi-Strauss' method in the examination of the structure of the Genesis story (1961a). There is no doubt that the method bristles with difficulties. It is by no means sure that two anthropologists will understand it in quite the same way, nor that they will succeed in analyzing the text of the myth in a truly comparable fashion. But even with these very serious reservations, I find Lévi-Strauss' examination of various myths extremely illuminating. Although the application of his principles is by no means unambiguous, he does appear to have placed his finger on certain universal attributes of myths. He also brings a new spark to a subject which has been seriously neglected since Malinowski: after all, to say that a myth is a charter for certain institutions, though no doubt true, does not tell us much about the intricacies of the myth itself.

In this paper I am concerned with ritual rather than myth. Rituals present problems similar to those that we face in the analysis of myths, and much of what Lévi-Strauss has to say concerning the structure of myths also applies to ritual. The differences are, however, important. Myth always tells a story. Ritual may be much more abstract and may simply consist of the handling of particular objects by specialists in a stereotyped way. Still the continuous action of a ritual may be broken down into "ritual acts" and these in turn may be analyzed into "items." In the case of Sinhalese rituals, there is little doubt that a systematic analysis of items (such as limes or saffron) in their particular contexts (e.g., used as anti-pollution agents) gives us a "code" which can be used to understand other communications in that culture. I assume that the ritual acts in which the items occur form part of a logical structure and are never simply meaningless. In fact, there is a logical symbolic structure about the total ritual which brings about the desired effects in the realm of ritual action.

The analysis of the code or the symbolic structure of the ritual is only one level of analysis. We must go deeper into the problems with which the ritual is concerned. Lévi-Strauss states that myths are designed to deal with unwelcome contradictions in human existence, such as life and death, fertility and barrenness (1955:4.10 & 6.2). He treats the Oedipus story as an attempt to answer the riddle of creation: how does one produce human beings from one pair of ancestors without incest? Leach (1961a) thinks that the Book of Genesis is concerned with the same worry. It is my thesis that, in a similar fashion, rituals are also centered around basic con-

[4] I am grateful to Professor T. Sebeok of Indiana University for bringing this work to my notice.

tradictions such as pollution and purity, fortune and misfortune, health and illness, and appear to be attempts to turn one side of an "opposed category" into the other.

We thus have three levels of analysis: the contextual analysis of items to allow the construction of a code; the formal symbolic structure of the action; and, the deeper contradictions and problems the action is concerned with.

I shall attempt to put some order into the great mass of descriptive material we possess about Sinhalese religious ideas and healing rituals.[5] In this paper I shall not try to construct a code, but shall simply provide certain contexts in order to interpret key items.

The Sinhalese, who are culturally similar to the people of South India, are Buddhists. They are divided into castes (Ryan 1953) and also worship the well known Hindu deities called *devaya* (*deva,* male; *devi,* female) such as Vishnu, Pattini, Kataragama, Ganesha. Buddhism in Ceylon is associated with Buddhist temples (*vihara*)[6] and a priesthood (*sangha*) divided into various orders. Hindu deities are seen as the assistants of the Buddha and are generally associated with special temples (*devale*) in charge of ritual practitioners called *kapurala*. In contrast to the Buddhist priests (*bhikku*) who shave their hair, take on a new name, and are vowed to celibacy, the Kapurala wear their hair long, retain their names, marry and have families. In most villages the devale consists of a conspicuous site which is purified and decorated on certain ritual occasions by a kapurala who is invited for this specific purpose. Although the kapurala observe special food taboos, they otherwise lead the same life as ordinary Sinhalese. They are always of the highest Goyigama caste.

The Buddha and the deities do not exhaust the supernatural beings of the Sinhalese. Demons (*yakkuva*) (*yakka,* male; *yakkini,* female) who are believed to inhabit all parts of the earth and sky, are extremely dangerous, and unless propitiated may bring misfortune and illness; *grahayo,* the "planetary deities" who are associated with the individual's horoscope, determine his fate (*karmaya*) and may bring difficult periods in his life; *peretaya* are spirits or "ghosts," who inhabit polluted places like graveyards and bring illness. Altogether these form an hierarchy of supernatural beings, ranging from the all-benevolent Buddha to the impure spirits of the dead. The exuberant proliferation of the supernatural ideology of the Sinhalese can be gathered from a brief perusal of Wirz (1954). I shall attempt to show that in contrast to the manifest content of their rituals, their basic structure is exceedingly simple.

The analysis of the connections between the religious ideology and the social structure of the Sinhalese does not lead very far. Aspects of their social structure have been described. (See Leach, 1960, 1961b; Pieris, 1956; Ryan, 1953, 1958; Tambiah,

[5] Callaway: 1829; Cartman: 1957; Deraniyagala: 1936; Dixon: 1884; Disāve of Vellasa: 1817; de Silva Gooneratne: 1865; Grünwedel: 1893; Gunasekera: 1953; Hocart: 1931; Le Mesurier: 1884; Meerworth-Levina: 1915; Nell: 1881–82; Pertold: 1922, 1925, 1929, 1930; Raghavan: 1951; Sarathachandra: 1953; Wirz: 1940, 1954, to mention a few of the writers on the subject.

[6] I write vihara in shorthand fashion. In fact the temple is a complex around a *pansala* (monastery), consisting of a vihara (shrine with image of the Buddha), a *dagoba* (stupa: memorial tomb), a Bo tree, and a *bana maduva* (preaching hall).

1958; Yalman, 1960.) It is well known that they have named and endogamous castes, and that so far as is known all the castes have a basically bilateral kinship system. Kinship groups take the form of semi-endogamous kindreds (Yalman, 1962c) and although the persons who will attend *rites de passage* or personal health rituals are often members of the kindred, the personnel may change by marriage alliances, and there is no permanent structure of authority in the group. In like manner, none of the supernatural beings of the Sinhalese can be traced to particular social groups—all castes are equally associated with all aspects of Sinhalese religion. Although the castes do have specific duties to perform (Ryan, 1953:95ff.; Hocart, 1931) and the low castes are not allowed into temples, the pattern frequently described for South India in which particular deities are associated with particular castes (e.g., Gough, 1960:43) or with particular lineages (Dumont, 1957) is not to be seen in the dry zone of Ceylon.[7]

The highly individualized nature of kinship ties is reflected in the preoccupation with the personal horoscope and fate (karmaya) (see Fortes, 1959). In religious activities there is much concern with pollution, a concept which is also operative in the caste hierarchy. Elsewhere I have shown that female puberty rites, the general idea of rebirth, and the notions of asceticism, are associated with the caste system (Yalman, 1962c, 1963). But there is little doubt that if we confine ourselves to a discussion of those areas of Sinhalese religion which can be approached only through their social structure, much of the complexity of their religious thought is lost.

Since Sinhalese beliefs about disease are primarily supernatural, beliefs and practices concerning ritual healing are best classfiied according to the specialists who deal with particular types of supernatural beings (Figure 1). The rites usually referred to as "devil dancing" or exorcism, with which I shall be mainly concerned, are those which fall between the double lines in Figure 1. The chanting of pirit (sacred text) by the bhikku does not fit neatly into this scheme, for in this rite, as we shall see, the priest does not deal directly with the Buddha.

Before we describe particular rituals, we should also note that the well-being of the Sinhalese villager is influenced by "good" (*honda*) and "bad" (*naraka*) categories which are also associated with the states of purity (*pirisithu*) and impurity (*killa* or *apirisithu*), illness or good fortune, and danger or protection from danger. These positive and negative states are also related to supernatural beings. Impurity (killa) is associated with *vas* ("supernatural danger" or literally "poison"). The demons (yakkuva) and the deities (devaya) as well as human beings may be dangerous by having vas. With humans it takes the form of evil eyes (*as vaha*), evil mouth (*kata vaha*) or evil thought (*ho vaha*). The patient, in other words, is not directly responsible for vas. It strikes him like a weapon from the outside. On the other hand, vas is also associated with sin (*dos*) which is the consequence of the "mistakes," wrongs, or sinful actions (*varada*) of the patient. The individual is responsible for his sins and this responsibility can be carried over from his earlier lives into his present existence as "fate sin" (*karma dos*). The balance of an individ-

[7] Particular shrines or temples may be owned by a local caste group in one locality (Ryan, 1953:286ff.), but even this is rare.

FIGURE 1.—RITUAL SPECIALISTS AND THEIR RITUALS (Central Ceylon)

Specialist		Supernatural Being	Rite	Principal Object	Main Offering	Activity
	bhikku		*pirit* *bana*	*pirit* book sermon	*dhana* (food)	Chanting Preaching
Rites involving *natanava* (dancing) and the	*kapurala*	*devaya* (deities)	*deviyange sellama** *yatika***	ayuda (weapons)	*adukka* (food)	Possession Dancing Singing
bera (drumming) of tom-tom beaters	*bali adura*	*yakkuva* (demons) *grahayo* (planets)	*bali*	*bali rupaya* (*bali* image)	*dola* (food)	Possession Dancing Singing
i.e. "devil dancing"	*yakkuva adura****	*yakkuva* *grahayo*	*tovil*	*yantaraya* (charm) or *dehi* (limes)	*dola* (food)	Possession Dancing Singing
	**** *sastra kariya* (astrologer)	*grahayo*		*yantaraya* (personal horoscope)		Horoscope interpreting for good and bad times
	vedarala (general practitioner)			*behet* (medicine) *yantaraya* (charms)		Reciting charms etc.

* (Play of the Gods) subsumes all rituals concerning the devaya: i.e., an keliya, gam maduva (see below), maleliya, perahera (Processions)
** Prayers directed to the deities.
*** Also known as: kattandiya, yakku vedarala, dehi vedarala.
**** Also known as nekatrala (time master).

ual's sin (dos) against his good deeds or merits (*pin*), determines his chances for attaining a better or worse state in his next birth. Poison (vas) and sin (dos), impersonal and personal inauspiciousness, are often spoken of as a single category of *vas-dos*. All health rituals with which we shall be concerned are directed towards the elimination of vas-dos and their common source in pollution.

With these preliminaries I turn to the formal analysis of the pirit rituals. After drawing attention to the relatively simple formal structure of the rites and the use of certain items in their contexts, I will discuss the *bali* and *maleliya* (*gam maduva*) types of rituals.

1. Pirit Ritual in Teripehe Village

The occasion for this pirit ritual is the consecration of a new hut for the Rural Development Society. The priests of the Amarapura sect have been invited by the officers of the society. The ritual is to take place inside the new hall. A special cage-like structure, *pirit maduva* (pirit hut) has been constructed for this purpose, and is decorated by clean cloths brought by the washermen. Inside is a table covered with a white cloth (*viyan*) and on it are some water bottles (*pirit pen*) as well as certain charms (*yantaram*) (also horoscope).

The priests arrive from the temple in order of their ordination carrying one of the main ritual objects of the Buddhist temple, the "relic casket" (*karanduwa* or *kota*), made of gold and containing precious stones which symbolize the relics (of bone, tooth, hair, and nails) which remained behind after the cremation of the Buddha (*dhatu*). A brass pitcher full of water which is decorated with coconut flowers (*malwattaya*) is placed on the table.

After the priests enter the enclosure (pirit maduva), the tom-tom beaters start beating the round drum (*davula*). The small oil lamps around the enclosure are lit, and one of the priests sprinkles some rice over the table. A string called the *pirit nula* is attached to the white cloth above the enclosure. It is then passed around the table and held by each priest. The string then goes to the malwattaya and thence to the audience outside the hut.

The pirit itself is a Pali text recorded in a book (*pirit pota*) which tells of the struggle between the Buddha and his rival, Maraya. The tom-toms stop and the priests start chanting the initial prayer. At this point the string is handed around among the audience so that every person can have contact with it.

At the beginning of the ceremony, the seven priests chant together. Later two of them pick up the text, and in this fashion, taking turns, they keep up the chanting the entire night. The audience often goes to sleep; but it is considered important to hold onto the string.

As the priests are chanting, they hold fans in front of their faces. Two explanations are given of this act: The ordinary people say that the priest's chanting is very powerful (*saraya*) and that this may strike (*gahanava*) the audience (an idea which is similar to that of katavaha, mouth poison, see above). Others say that in this fashion the priest cuts himself off from the world around him (see Yalman, 1962a).

In the morning after the book is finished, the priests leave with the tom-tom beaters. The string is cut into small pieces and members of the audience tie portions of it around their wrists or necks for added protection (*arakshava*) from any kind of danger. Some drink the water (pirit pen) on the table; others put it on their faces.

Later in the day there is a dhana offering (mainly food) to the priests. As usual every day the Buddha figure in the temple is given the dhana of rice. The offering is made by the priest; laymen make offerings of flowers (*mal puja*). After the food offering to the Buddha, the priests move into a specially purified place where they are offered food by members of the Goyigama caste. Since the food is offered in a pure place, the priests wash their feet before entering the enclosure. Moreover, the place where the priests consume their food is surrounded on all sides by white cloths (*viyana*) brought by the washerman.

This type of pirit is commonly found in any Sinhalese village. Sometimes, when the pirit takes place on a national scale—such as for the arrival or departure of the Prime Minister at the airport—the numbers of the priests or tom-tom beaters may be much larger, but the ceremony remains much the same.

The essential aspects of the pirit ritual can be brought out by contrasting the above with a simpler example.

2. Pirit Ritual for a New House

A pirit takes place in the house of a newly married couple on the occasion of their completion of a new house. There is only one priest present. He has not brought the relic casket, but only the pirit book. There is no hut, but the chair for the priest is covered with a white cloth. There is another chair beside him on which he has some betel and tea. There is a table covered with a white cloth on which there is the pirit water, some coconut flowers, and the pirit book.

The priest chants the pirit alone in three half days (*varuva*). The string (pirit nula) comes from the book and is held at the other end by the young bride only. The priest holds his fan in front of his face and chants. When the chanting is finished, the pirit nula is tied around the wrist of the woman and the neck of the man. The priest ties the string himself and recites prayers.

The formal symbolic structure of the pirit may be indicated as follows: a. There are one or more bhikku (or sometimes laymen who are empowered to act in their place); b. A pure place is provided (the viyana, pirit maduva, etc.); c. The sacred text (pirit) is chanted by the priests; d. The text is connected by a string to the audience. (The connection may be established in various ways: the priest may hold the end of the string in his hand or, the sending end of the string may simply be tied to the enclosure which contains the sacred area, the relic casket, the water bottle in the middle of the table, or the pirit book); e. At the end of the rite the string which has been activated is tied around some part of the body of those who witness the ceremony.

The core of the ceremony consists of the transmission of the goodness of the sacred text to a recipient or recipients. A pirit chanted by one or more bhikkus, is more effective than are those chanted by lay singers.

The difference of elaboration around the basic pattern (the text, the string, the recipient) suggests that it is useful to distinguish between the primary structure and secondary structures in the rite. Thus, returning to the first version, we may refer to the enclosure, the white cloth covering the table inside the enclosure, and the relic casket as secondary structures of the ritual.

But there are also distinct subsidiary ritual acts connected with the primary structure. Giving of food (dhana) to the Buddha and his priests at the end of the first pirit ritual is one of these and is intended as an elaboration of the primary structure. There are many such special ritual acts which recur in other Sinhalese rituals. In the same ritual, the leaving of the horoscopes and charms in the pirit is a similar subsidiary act: it is expected that the charms (yantaram) will absorb some of the sacredness of the pirit text.

Having described the basic structure of the pirit ritual, I now turn to the *bali* (image) ceremonies. In contrast to the pirit ritual, which is a general palliative utilizing the power of sacred Buddhist texts, the bali ceremony is specifically directed against he-and she-demons (yakkuva) and against the planets (grahayo) and is conducted by members of the tom-tom beater caste (*Beravayo*). The specialist in bali rituals is known as *bali gurunnanse* or as *bali adura*. He usually has helpers of the same caste, some of whom dance while others beat the elongated cigar-shaped drums (bera).[8] Bali rites are distinguished from all others not only because they are the specialty of tom-tom beaters but also because they involve the construction of elaborate painted clay images and figures. These figures (*bali rupaya*), which are often seven feet high, depict the planetary beings or particular demons.

A bali ritual may be held whenever an individual has been consistently unlucky, or weak and ill. A bali is thought to be particularly appropriate when the individual suffers from epilepsy or forms of neurosis and hysteria. Two explanations are often given for the cause of the patient's difficulties. First, it may be said that a yakkuva is "eating flesh and drinking blood" of the patients; for they are known for their partiality to flesh (which is polluting) and blood (which is even more polluting). Second, it may be stated that the particular configuration of the stars under which an individual was born has produced a period of difficulty (*apele*). The apele period can be predicted accurately from the horoscope of the individual by the astrologers. Hence the bali rituals are often recommended by the astrologer.

Whether the difficulties are caused by the planets or the demons, the ritual is intended to get rid of the vas dos of the patient, to get the yakkuva out of the patient's body, and to appease them by the offering of food and flesh. This offering to such creatures is known as *dola*—in contrast to the dhana, offerings of food to the Buddha and the priests and *adukka* food offerings to the devaya. With these explanations we can turn to a description of the bali rituals.

1. Bali Ceremony in Teripehe Village

A bali is held in the tom-tom beaters' hamlet of Teripehe village. A large bali figure has been prepared inside a special enclosure made of plantain trunks which has open sides but the top of which is covered by white cloths. This separates the bali area from the rest of the village. The center is occupied by a large figure referred to as Senasura; who is standing on a cobra. There is another small figure on top of him whom some people call Gini Devi, but others suggest that he is Maha Brahma, "the creator of the earth." These figures are surrounded by the nine planets, the grahayo. (For the association of Giri Devi and the theme of incest, see Wirz, 1954: 129f.)

Opposite this effigy a small cage-like structure has been prepared for the sick person (*leda*) or (*aturuya*) who in this instance is a member of the tom-tom beater caste.

On a narrow ledge in front of the effigy, the offering (dola) is placed. It consists of fried foods (special offering to yakkuva), fried rice, fried oil cakes, fried jack fruit, also manioc, jaggory (sugar) and some grain. Near these foods is the skull of a

---

8 The davula which looks like an ordinary drum is normally used for functions in the vihara or those connected with the Buddha and his priests. The elongated drum mentioned here (bera) is normally used in connection with devale or exorcism rituals. More generally, whenever the ritual practitioners have to "dance" (natanava) the bera will be used.

wild cat; yakkuva food can be cooked in this. There is also a mirror, some hair, a comb, red flowers, betel leaves, sandalwood candles, incense, and plantains. On the floor there are some coins on betel leaves called *pandura* which are a frequent offering to deities and yakkuva and rice in plantains. Also on the floor, apart from the dola, are two large coconuts and a rice pounder. There is a pot of saffron water (*kaha pen*) nearby. The entire dola is covered up with plantain leaves.

There are a considerable number of spectators inside the bali area. The proceedings start with the bali gurunnanse and his son and brother's son dressed in special decorative clothes, singing and dancing to the rhythm of two tom-toms. The patient is isolated in his special little cage (*maduva*) covered with a white cloth.

The string (nula) which has a lime (dehi) attached, comes from the top of the effigy and is held by the bali gurunnanse. After some dancing and singing, the end of the string is passed on to the patient behind his cloth.

Two torches (*pandam*) are brought and lighted. The proceedings now take a new turn. The cloth covering the patient is taken away. The nine grahayo and the yakkuva are separately invoked, and the lighted torches are placed on either side of the effigy.

The "saffron water" is placed beside the patient, and two young girls (ideally virgins) hold arecanut flowers in their hands and with a sweeping gesture move the flowers from the patient's head toward his feet. At the same time they chant *ayu bowan* (long life!—also used as a general greeting in Sinhalese). It is said that with this gesture, dos descends lower (*dos bas venava*) and falls away from the patient.

The covering on the dola is removed. The cobra on which the main figure Senasuru stands receives a lighted candle on his head. The dola is being offered. There is singing and dancing for each of the nine grahayo and the four yakka which takes a long time.

The dancing and singing proceed in this pattern through the night. The patient may get excited and start shrieking and dancing to the tune of the bera drum. He may get violent and fall unconscious.

At the end of the ceremony, the patient throws the lime with the string straight toward the effigy. As the figure is of soft clay, the lime usually sticks to some part of it. The arecanut flowers with which the patient was being given "long life" are also thrown at the effigy. Finally the effigy is covered with the white cloth which originally covered the patient. The patient has some food taboos for three half days, and must eat from specially clean plantain leaves.

The figures of the grahayo and yakka are then taken into the jungle and abandoned. This marks the end of the ceremony.

There is not much agreement on what the figures signify. During the ceremony it was said that the Gini Devi was troubling the patient and that the cobra was her agent. The large figure in the middle was likened to the patient. The mother of the patient, when questioned the day after the ritual, claimed that two planets, Angaharu and Rahu, had been troubling her son.

I obtained no explanation concerning the limes thrown upon the figure except that they "belong to the deities." In view of the great importance attached to limes in many Sinhalese rituals, this is particularly unsatisfactory (see below). Some comments on the contexts of the items used in rituals are called for before we go on to compare this account with other versions of bali ceremonies.

First attention should be drawn to the string, which has a similar function in other Sinhalese rites. It is clear that the string (nula) used in the bali serves the same general purpose as the nula used in the pirit ritual: it connects the ritual objects with a person or persons. But the intention of the string in the bali is the opposite of pirit. In the bali ceremony the illness of the patient is made to travel along the string *back* to the bali effigy, while in the pirit ritual the purity of the text travels *to* the audience (cf. Gunasekera, 1953:73). The bali figure represents the demon in its corporeal form outside the patient. The demon moreover, is presented with an offering of food (dola) to appease its hunger and to induce it to depart from the patient.

Second, the reversal aspect of the ritual is particularly obvious with respect to the white cloth and the string. At the beginning of the bali ceremony, the patient is covered with a white cloth and the string is brought to him. Then the cloth is removed and the patient is left face to face with the terrible yakkuva to which he is connected by the string. At the end of the ceremony, the string is thrown back to the demon and the connection is broken. Moreover, the yakka is now covered with the white cloth. In this sense, the patient and the figure have changed their places. The figure now contains the illness and is therefore taken away to be destroyed.

Third, the dola is offered to the yakkuva in lieu of the patient. Here again is a stream of ideas which associates the yakkuva and the illness with impurity (*killa*). The patient is in an impure state and hence the ritual of long life (ayu bowan) whereby the poison (vas) and sin (dos) are made to leave him. Because the yakkuva are particularly interested in pollution and are always said to hang around polluted places and objects, the dola (offering) contains many items which are considered polluting to the Sinhalese. Thus the food for the yakkuva is cooked in a skull, preferably one found in a graveyard. Hair and a comb are offered. The mirror into which boys and girls are not allowed to look until puberty may perhaps stand for the patient. Fried foods are conspicuous in the offering. According to Sinhalese folk ideology, fried foods are difficult to digest, and they are considered to remain as feces inside the body for a long time and thus to endanger one's health. But the yakkuva love fried things, which are associated with impurity.[9]

Fourth, the lighting of torches (pandam) or lamps (*pahana*) accompanied by the recitation of charmed verses (*mantaram*) is sometimes known as *jivan karanava* (make alive). It signifies that the object of attention is now "alive." The rite of jivan karanava is often said to be applied to objects used in sorcery (*huniyam*), but the lighting of candles on the cobra and torches stuck on the sides of the bali figure imply that the images have been activated.

Fifth, the saffron water is used much like pirit water, as a purifying agent. Saffron water is often used in contexts where killa and/or vas-dos is being counteracted. It is well known that the robes of the Buddhist priests are ritually dyed in saffron.[10]

---

[9] The usual offerings to the yakkuva are five kinds of fried foods (*pulutu pas vagei*) consisting of two kinds of fried flesh (*kili mas:* water flesh, *die mas,* i.e., fish, and land flesh, *goda mas,* i.e., meat), and three kinds of fried grains.

[10] It is relevant to note here that the cloth from which the sacred robe is made should ideally be picked up in graveyards, which are places polluted by corpses (*mini killa*). (See below, and Yalman, 1962a).

Incidentally, we may also note that pollution houses (*killa gedara*), i.e., houses in which a death, a birth, or menstruation has taken place, will be cleansed either by spreading a new coat of cow dung (*goma*) or by the sprinkling of saffron water. The decoration of the pot with coconut and/or arecanut flowers—again like the pot in pirit ceremonies—indicates the association between the flowers and the water; and it is true that the flowers in question are again used as pure decorations with the white cloths (or with betel leaves—also considered very pure) or agents with which to counteract pollution. Hence, again, the receiving end of the pirit string may be tied around a bunch of coconut or arecanut flowers and betel leaves. In the bali ritual in question, the virgins chanting "long life" were in fact sweeping the pollution and vas-dos away with bunches of arecanut flowers.

Sixth, all that has been said about saffron water also applies to limes. They are a specific purifying agent against pollution. One of the main anti-pollution rituals of the Sinhalese consists of the cutting of numerous limes with sweeping gestures over each and every joint of the patient. The patient's end of the string in bali rituals may be tied to a lime. At the end of the funeral ceremonies, the persons who have come into contact with the corpse will cleanse themselves of pollution by rubbing limes onto their hands.

It is useful to compare this account with another bali which I observed near Monaragala in the Wellassa province.

2. Bali Ceremony in Makulle Village

An extremely elaborate structure (*maduva*) has been erected with plantain trunks and decorated with the usual objects used in many of the rituals of the Sinhalese. This bali is referred to as a *kiri maduva* (milk hut; milk signifying purity). At an auspicious time (*honda valava*) specified by the astrologer on the examination of the personal horoscope of the patient, a six-foot pole is erected inside the enclosure. The act, known as *kap hitavinava,* is simply the erection of a milk exuding tree (*kiri gaha*) to mark the beginning of the ceremony at the correct moment. The particular pole in this ritual is painted and decorated at the top.

Two large yakkuva images, referred to as Ririyakku Baliya and Dalakumara Baliya, have been prepared. They both stand on animal figures. The Dalakumara stands on a buffalo and the Ririyakku stands on a cow. Both the yakka have their faces painted black. They have terrible aspects with conspicuous teeth, some of which protrude like tusks. They both have numerous cobras forming a headdress. Dalakumara Baliya is flanked by six smaller figures who are called *pirivel* and are like the grahayo in the first bali. Ririyakku has a fowl in either hand and some rats on two sides of his face.

Near the center of the square is another figure which I had never come across in other bali ceremonies. It consists of an ordinarily dressed female *yakkini* sitting on a stool. She wears blue and white clothes and is referred to as Katina Rupaya. Along the side of the square four *pidaniya* (objects with flowers and limes in them) have been prepared.

The animals upon which the yakka stand are their "vehicles." (The high deities [devaya] also have their vehicles—like Kataragama's peacock—who are at the same time their symbols.)

Facing these figures there is another hut covered with white cloths and intended for the patient. A woman of twenty-five sits in this structure. The reason for the ceremony is that she is "mad" (*pissu*). Her madness, however, is partly the result of sorcery. Someone has made huniyam against her by charming part of a jack fruit and placing it across her path. The act is considered to be a specialty of the Veddah people but no specific accusations are made. She has been subject to fits and trembling. She falls down in her hut and starts wailing. The form of the wailing, which I have heard many times, is long drawn out, blood curdling "Hooo! Hooo!" sounds. The same sound is made when a patient gets possessed in bali ceremonies. The reason for her wailing is again stated to be that yakkuva have entered her and are "eating her flesh and drinking her blood." The bali ceremony is intended to induce the yakkuva to leave her.

The specialists for the ceremony are again the tom-tom beaters from a neighboring village. Two are dancing and singing and two others are beating a rhythm on the bera drums. The specialists are wearing their appropriate costumes.

It is stated that the two yakkuva images want fowls and blood; Katina Rupaya wants meat.

The ceremony commences by covering the patient with a white cloth. After much dancing and singing the string which connects the Katina Rupaya with the yakkuva figures is handed on to the patient. Later the white cloth which hides the patient is taken away. The dola offerings are offered to the yakkuva figures. A fowl is killed and offered to the yakkuva. Parts of it are given to the sitting female demon on skewers which are set all around her. Much incense is burned near the sick woman and she starts trembling. The explanation is that when the bera is played the vision of the yakkuva appears to the woman and that then the woman will simply go mad (*pissu hadanava*). The possessed women throws herself on the ground and shrieks, "Hooo! Hooo!" Saffron water is sprinkled upon her and her excitement subsides. She is carried back to her enclosure in an exhausted state.

The specialist tom-tom beaters resume their dancing. Arecanut flowers are given to them which they hold in their hands instead of the usual bells. They chant "long life" while sweeping the vas-dos away from her toward the sitting yakkini. Later parts of the arecanut flowers are broken off in small pieces and again with sweeping gestures are thrown away from the patient towards the demoness.

The bali ends with the string thrown at Katina Rupaya. The yakkini is then covered with the cloth which covered the patient. There is much singing and dancing before the ceremony is finally concluded.

The bali figures, the pidaniya, the pole are then taken into the jungle to a place where they can no longer "see" the house. They are placed on the ground facing upwards and the tom-tom beaters make some feeble attempt to burn them with kerosene. The act is only symbolic and with the final recitation of mantaram they abandon the figures.

When we compare the two bali rites the main differences between them are as follows: (a) In the second bali ceremony three figures were involved. While the figure stands on a cobra vehicle in Bali 1, the vehicles of the second bali are cattle with cobras on their heads. This is part of the difference in the character of the yakkuva concerned. (b) Bali 1 has no special pidanya offerings, but the dola stand serves the same purpose. (c) Bali 1 did not commence with a pole erection ceremony. (d) Bali 1 is directed against ill health in general whereas Bali 2 is specifically against madness and sorcery. The patient in Bali 2 becomes possessed by the yakkuva. (e) The dola in Bali 2 is a newly killed fowl. In Bali 1 the dola is more complex but exploits the same theme. In both cases the dola contains pollution.

As against the differences listed, the basic symbolic structure of the rites is remarkably similar: (a) The bali area is demarcated and isolated by a hut (maduva). (b) Bali figures are created by the specialist. (c) The patient is covered at the beginning of the ceremony. (d) Bali figures are sacralized. (e) Bali figures are connected with the patient with string and the patient is uncovered. (f) The dola offering of yakkuva delicacies is presented. (g) The vas-dos of the patient is swept away. (h) When the yakkuva is out of the patient, the string is thrown back, the connection is broken and the figure covered. (i) The figures are destroyed or taken away into the wilderness. (j) The patient, still in a heightened state, is told to observe certain food taboos while gradually returning to ordinary life.

The bali ceremonies described in an unsystematic but detailed fashion by Wirz (1954:105ff.) also conform to this symbolic structure.

The description of pirit and bali rites forms an introduction to the sphere of ritual healing among the Sinhalese. The structure of these rituals is meaningful only when placed in the context of rituals directed toward the Hindu deities (devaya) and the rest of the complex of Buddhist concepts and ideology. In this section I provide an analysis of a maleliya rite, intended for the deities. I hope in this fashion to indicate some of the further implications of the category of supernatural beings under the Buddha which the Sinhalese refer to as the devaya and the yakkuva.

Maleliya is an elaborate ceremony undertaken by the kapurala on behalf of a village or a family. The Sinhalese would consider it to be part of the general category of sacred ceremonies referred to as "play of the deities" (*deviyange sellama*); "horn play" (*an keliya*); "village hut" (*gam maduva*); "procession" (*perahera*), or simply "ceremony" (*mangalaya*).

1. Maleliya at Teripehe Village

The ceremony takes place in the Galpitiya hamlet of Teripehe, and is intended for the ill grandson of a neighbor of the Goyigama caste. The main kapurala, Appuhami (my cook), has invited other kapurala to add to the occasion. The kapurala from Ekassa Temple (*kovil,* i.e., small devale) has brought the weapons (ayuda) of the deities in a box. The Ekassa kovil particularly is associated with the deity of the locality (Ekassa deva), but there are also numerous other deities associated with it.

A large hut has been prepared with plantain trunks and has been elaborately decorated with arecanut, coconut flowers, and white cloths brought by the washerman. At one end of the hut a small altar (*masa*) has been constructed about five feet off the ground. The altar is again decorated with white cloths and covered with plantain leaves. The most conspicuous objects upon the altar are the weapons of the deities (ayuda)—arrows, swords, and tridents, which are arranged vertically in an orderly fashion.

Three tom-tom beaters have been invited. Large amounts of pure food have been prepared and these will be offered later to the ritual practitioners who take part in the ceremony.

The maleliya starts with an initial slow dance and song sequence. The kapuralas take turns dancing. At certain points there are no songs but only dancing. Eventually the kapurala become possessed (*amaru* or *mayan*) one by one. They sing epics concerning the birth, life, and deaths of the deities associated with the weapons on the altar. Each weapon stands for a different deity, and as the songs are continued, betel and arecanut flowers are offered to the gods.

After an interval, the Ekassa kapurala becomes possessed. The tom-toms beat out a frenzied rhythm and the kapurala, swinging his hair, dances wildly. He is given some lighted torches which he "eats." After eating fire, the kapurala, still in a state of possession, turns to singing charms. He has a long staff in his hand and touches people gently as he dances. Some persons in the audience offer him money wrapped in betel leaves (*pandura*). He takes this, and standing in front of the person foretells the future. The assumption is that a deity has entered into him and is speaking through him. Some of the audience, particularly some young people, do not believe that the kapurala is really possessed and make fun of him. The audience is uncertain as to which deity has possessed him and different informants give contradictory answers. On the whole, they appear to say that this is the Ekassa deva speaking through his kapurala. There is another interval.

As the night proceeds, the other kapurala become possessed one by one and recite the stories of the deities. The kapurala appear to become possessed, particularly when the dancing and the tom-tom beating reach a certain intensity. The handling of the weapons of the deities or the offering of food-stuffs to them also appears conducive to possession.

The final rite in the morning consists of the Ekassa kapurala doing a dance for a goddess. This dance, known as the *kiri amma natanava* (the dance of the grandmothers), is said to be the offering of pardon for mistakes to those who have provided milk, i.e., the mothers. It is also said that during this dance the kapurala becomes the goddess Pattini. The Ekassa kapurala, in an appropriate fashion, wears a sari over his shoulder. During the dancing, the grandchild who is ill is given to the kapurala, who holds the child in his arms and dances violently near the weapons. Many of the words he utters are incomprehensible; but he is said to be relating his visions (*pehena*).

At the end of the dance of the grandmothers there is a final outburst of dancing by all the kapuralas concerned.

The symbolic structure of the rite is as follows: (a) A hut (maduva) is constructed; (b) Pure food (adukka) is prepared; (c) The symbols of the deities are brought and placed on an altar (mesa); (d) The symbols (ayuda) are sacralized by singing and dancing and beating of tom-toms; (e) Adukka is offered to the deities; (f) Each deity is handled separately and his history from birth to death is recited. The kapurala becomes possessed by the deity and speaks as an oracle (see below); (g) Possession (i.e., *amaru vima*) is repeated with variations for each deity; (h) The ayuda are taken back to the temple.

In fact the most complicated and formal version of the rite is a repetition for each male and female deity of the offering of adukka. Secondary structures may be elaborated around this basic theme. Thus in the preparation of the food, the utensils may be singled out for purification and worship; the men (women are impure) who do the cooking may cover their mouths with clean cloths to prevent saliva (very polluting—bodily excretion) from falling on the food. The purification of ayuda by the blacksmiths with lime and saffron and the washing of Pattini with milk fall into this category. While these ritual acts are of vital significance when we construct the code for the analysis of the contexts in which milk or saffron or limes are used, they may or may not be considered necessary parts of the formal symbolic structure of the rituals.

Up to this point, I have been concerned with the formal structure of Sinhalese healing rituals, and hence have had to translate many of the ritual objects and acts involved in the rite by indicating their contexts in the symbolic code used by the Sinhalese. These are the first two levels of the procedure I previously outlined. I now turn to the third level of analysis. What is the significance of these rites? What problems are they concerned with? The best approach to these questions is to examine certain features of the categories of devaya and yakkuva.

I must point out immediately that I have not discussed here the more elaborate ceremonies intended for the devaya. Some of these are annual rituals and have nation-wide importance. For instance, the mysterious ceremonials in the jungle shrine of Kataragama last a full fortnight, and pilgrims from all over Ceylon and even South India visit the shrine to worship the god Kataragama and his mistress Valli Amma. (Wirz, 1954:145ff.; Yalman, 1962b.) Similar annual ceremonies which culminate in colorful nocturnal processions with elephants, tom-tom beaters, and diverse castes take place in most important temples in Ceylon. (Ryan, 1953:211ff.) But even with the limited material presented, we may proceed with our analysis.

We have noted, first, that both the devaya and the yakkuva are concerned with this life. The sins of an individual in his earlier lives (*karma dos*) may still cling to him in his present existence and may render him more susceptible to misfortune. But the benefits the deities will bring or withhold, and the attacks of the demons, do not affect his future rebirths.

In contrast, the Buddha and his priests are concerned with the next existence and eternity. The priest comes into the life crises of a person only at his funeral. If his merit (pin) outweighs his sins, he will be reborn in a higher state or even reach Nirvana. The teaching of the Buddha expresses the interests in the other world. The way to Nirvana is to minimize the importance of wealth, family, friends, and all things which tie the person down to this existence. The individual is urged to give up everything and turn to good deeds and purity, prayer, and meditation, to reach Buddha-hood in his next existence. On the other hand, immediate disaster and happiness are associated with the devale, the devaya, and the kapurala. They can give health, money, children, good crops, and fertile wives. It is noteworthy therefore that the ritual acts at the vihara consist of "prayer" (*vandanava*) whereas people go to the devale to "beg" (*nyaknya kirima*) or to "request" (*illasitima*) the help of the deities.

The Buddha and his priests are superior to the deities and their kapurala. The latter are seen as the servants of the former. The relationships between the Buddha and the devaya are expressed in a most suggestive fashion by the transfer of merits (pin) from the Buddhist temple (vihara) to the devaya. Thus, the layman can acquire merit by the performance of good deeds and by making offerings (*puja dhana*) to the Buddhist temple. He may then go into a devale or simply turn aside in a private place and offer a share (*pangu* or *kotas*) of his pin to the devaya. In return for giving some of this merit to the devaya, the individual is supposed to receive "protection" which will immediately aid him in this existence.

There are very important category oppositions in the realm of high Buddhism (see Figure II). Thus while the Buddha stands for Eternity, Maraya, his cross-cousin, his rival in all his lives, stands for Death. Yet both Maraya and the Buddha are one; for Maraya is sometimes described as only a thought in the mind of the Buddha. Here again is the polarity between eternal existence and finite death, which Lévi-Strauss notes is a recurring theme in mythologies and religions (1955:59–62).

Such oppositions also exist in the categories of the devaya and yakkuva (Figure II). Let us note immediately that the yakkuva and devaya are similar in many respects. There are males and females in both categories (deva, devi and yakka, yakkini). Both are supernatural beings in human form. Both have vehicles (yantarava) on which they can travel and which they can delegate to act on their behalf. When they are depicted as images, such as the bali effigies, images of the yakkuva, or the pictures of the devaya in Wirz (1954), there are remarkable similarities between their external manifestations. Of course the yakkuva are often distinguished by their black faces or blood-thirsty aspects and long teeth, but their general appearance seems similar to the manifestations of the devaya. Both the devaya and the yakkuva have supernatural power (*balaya, dishtiya,* vas) which can make people mad (pissu). The devaya and the yakkuva are so similar that sometimes the distinctions between them get blurred even for experienced specialists such as the kapurala.[11]

One of the best known kapurala in the Walapane district was my cook Appuhami. While taking down the names of the devaya who were expected to make their appearances for a gam maduva rite, we arrived at a group of Bandara devaya: Vannia Bandara, Alut Deva, Menikbandara Deva, Kumara Bandara Deva. Appuhami claimed that these last were really yakkuva, but yakkuva "who lived in the jungle like elephants" and who were respected in the same way as elephants (see Leach, 1962).

Although the devaya and the yakkuva are similar as a general category, they are diametrically opposed in all their vital aspects. The devaya are considered to be extremely pure (pirisithu), and the devale in which they reside is also an extraordinarily pure place. Persons afflicted with even a minute amount of pollution (killa) must avoid the devale and the devaya. Hence persons from "birth, menstruation, and death houses" (killa gedera) cannot go into the devale. Persons who have eaten killa food (flesh, fried foods, smelly things) would be endangered in the devale for the god would attack them. The nature of the attack is expressed in various ways: there are "white cobras" in the devale that will attack impure persons; the devaya will attack impure persons with vas (*vas gahanava*) and will make them mad or cripple them; the devaya do not have vas, but there are yakkuva in the devale who do have vas, and they will attack and make the impure person mad.[12]

In contrast to the devaya, the yakkuva are extremely impure. They live in filthy places, hang around graveyards, and thus are associated with the most intense

[11] Gooneratne (1865, *passim*) also notes the similarity of the devaya and yakkuva.

[12] This last statement comes from a kapurala who wanted to distinguish between vas and dishtiya.

pollution of all—death pollution (mini killa). One has to take ritual precautions when approaching graveyards because the yakkuva go through graves, and if they happen to go through one's body, all is finished!

The opposition of the devaya and the yakkuva is manifested in the food they like. The devaya will be offered only the purest food. The adukka prepared for them must be specially cooked by men—women menstruate and are not as pure as men. The food must be offered in specially purified places. Hence the cleansing of the house with cow dung or saffron water before preparing adukka and hence the closing up of the mouth with cloths like surgeons in an operating theatre. The boiling of milk (*ḳiri uturanava*) is a special ritual offering to the devaya.

The yakkuva may be offered "five kinds of burned things" or "three kinds of flesh" (*mas tun vage*), i.e., land-pig (*uru malu*); air-peacock (*madara malu*); sea-fish (*magula malu*); all polluted condiments (kili malu).

As noted above, both the devaya and the yakkuva have a similar kind of power which ordinary people refer to as *vas*.[13]

The specialist kapurala is more careful in his distinctions. Appuhami kapurala claimed that the devaya have dishtiya (power, also *deva balaya*) whereas vas, which is mainly negative, belongs only to the yakkuva. The devaya use it for good purposes, whereas the yakkuva use it for bad purposes.

An important aspect of this power is that it "makes madness" (pissu hadanava). It has different manifestations in the case of the yakkuva and the devaya. When the dishtiya falls on the kapurala, who has observed food taboos, has kept himself ritually pure, and is in a pure place, then he is relatively safe. He will start trembling and shaking. He will start swinging his head round and round and will become "possessed" (*mayang venava*) by the deva or devi in question. His progressive entrance into the trance state is explained by saying that he becomes "difficult" (*amaru venava*—also used in the case of serious illness, loss of consciousness) or "mad." It will be said that his blood becomes heavy (*bara le venava*). The kapurala thus becomes an oracle for the particular deity devaya who has possessed him. The people will offer panduru to the deity who is speaking through the kapurala. The kapurala will tell his "vision" (*pehena ḳiyanava:* foretelling the future) and will advise the worshipper. Such possession is always accompanied by frenzied tom-tom beating and much incense. I witnessed no difficulty in the kapurala's getting out of the trance state. Some of these trances were quite genuine, but in many others the specialists showed indications of faking the manifestations.

Just as the devaya enter into the specialist and possess him, the yakkuva enter into ordinary persons and make them mad. The ceremonies for the yakkuva are intended to induce them to leave the patient. The outward manifestations of such madness often appear to follow the same lines as the possession of the kapurala. In fact the kapurala in the trance is spoken of as mad (pissu).[14]

---

[13] It may also be said that the vihara has no vas for the "Buddha is uninterested in such things." And hence women who are polluted may be allowed into the vihara. But these are probably theological points which would stand much disputation, for the Buddha obviously has great power (balaya) but does not make men mad.

[14] The convergence of the cultural manifestations of possession and epileptic fits raises important questions (see Nadel, 1946). The entry into trance states, the simulation of epileptic fits, the tom-tom beating, all seem very similar in Africa, Asia, or Haiti (Metraux, 1959:120ff.).

FIGURE II.

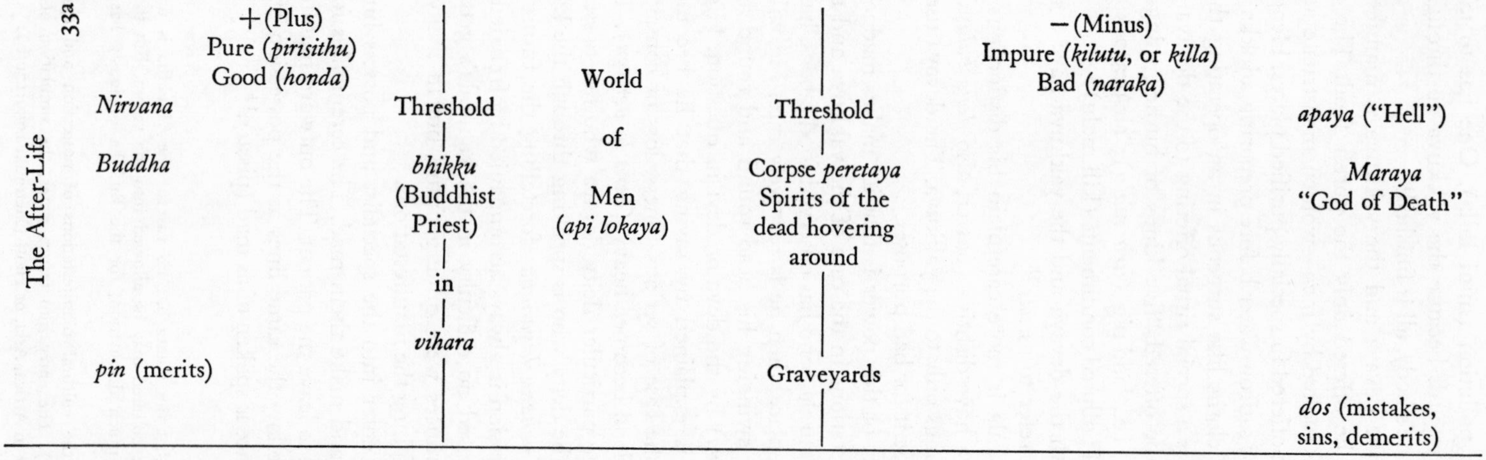

Above: *vihare* Pattern: No dancing (*natanava*) ceremonies; tom-tom beaters use round drum (*davula*); no spirit possession.

Below: Devale Pattern: Dancing, gods' "games" (*deviyange sellama*); tom-tom beaters use elongated drum (*bera*); possession rites; may not be seen by Buddhist priests.

This Life	*deva lokaya* *deva* *devi* (in pure places) *dishtiya* (power of deity) White Cobra Bring *pihita* (luck, fertility, happiness)	*kapurala* in *devale* or *maduva*	(*api lokaya*)	*bali adura* *yakka adura* in charmed enclosures (*maduva*)	*apaya* *yakkuva* *yakkini* (hang around graveyards, polluted places) *vas* (poison, supernatural danger) Black Cobra *polanga* (Russels viper) Bring *leda-duka* (illness, barrenness, misfortune)
Planetary Deities	+ brings: "Good time" (*honda velava*) +		Personal Destiny (*karmaya*) Fate— dependent upon configuration of *grahayo* at moment of birth or conception. Specialist: Astrologers (*nekat rala* or *sastra kariya*) constructs horoscope (*yantaram*)		— brings: "Bad time" (*apele*)—illness, misfortune

There is a similarity between being hit by vas or falling under the power of the deity (*dishtiya vetanava*). The terminology utilized for yakku or devaya possession is identical. The kapurala and the patient start shivering and trembling (*vevulanava* or *kili pelume*); they may lose consciousness (*sihi neti vanava*); the yakkuva will appear (*yakku pehanava*) to the patient in the same way as the kapurala will have visions (*pehenna*). The usual term for the possession of the kapurala is mayang venava, whereas the term for madness is pissu hadanava.

The Buddha or Maraya, on the contrary, are never involved in possession rites. The Buddha or the state of Buddha-hood are approached by meditation and the relinquishment of all desire. The active nature of the devaya and yakkuva compared to the passivity of the Buddha is part of the opposition between their concern with this life and the next.

The devale are said to have white cobras in them, which are sacred or divine. The poison of the cobra is also referred to as vas. The yakkuva are also associated with snakes (e.g., bali, above) and particularly with the black cobra. The two aspects of the snake are also manifested in the mythology concerning the rivalry between the cobra and the Russels Viper which are both among the deadliest creatures on the island.[15]

The polarity between the devaya and the yakkuva is best clarified by what the ceremonies are intended to accomplish. The rites for the devaya if carried out correctly have the following effects: (a.) Happiness and health (*sepa sanipa*) increases in the village; (b.) The fertility of Women, Cattle and Lands (*sampata*) is enhanced; (c.) The village becomes lucky (*vassanava*); (d.) Deaths decrease.

If the rites are forgotten, however, the village gradually relapses into the opposite state:[16] (a.) (Leda duka) Illness and sorrow increase; (b.) Fertility is reduced; paddy yields are lower; (c.) The village becomes unlucky (avasanava); (d.) Deaths increase.

This contrast in the state of the individual or community is summed up in Sinhalese by the expressive words honda (good, auspicious) and naraka (bad, inauspicious). The same words are used to speak of low (naraka) and high (honda) castes, and of impurity and purity.

The essential contrast is that the rites and offerings (adukka) to the devaya are intended to bring about the set of positive effects, and the rites (bali) and offerings (dola) to the yakkuva are intended to oppose the set of negative effects. This simple dichotomy underlies all the complexity of Sinhalese thinking on the subject of the supernatural.[17] All the rites and their minor details are directed towards the contrast between these basic issues:

---

[15] Elephants, who also have divine attributes, have their positive and negative aspects. The white elephant is sacred and fertilized the mother of the Buddha, Maya, in a dream. The elephant of Marea, Nalagiri, however, tried to kill the Buddha.

[16] The negative state can also be induced by sorcery (huniyam): the charms and rites which are directed towards the yakkuva to bring about the death or illness of a particular person (see Gooneratne 1865:68ff.).

[17] Our observations are directly borne out, e.g., by the ritual activities at harvest time. There are elaborate precautions taken on the threshing floor to assure the increase of paddy and keep away the yakkuva who hover around. Thus, the threshing floor is made like a devale and is especially pure. No impurities, even women, are allowed to enter into it. A special language, *kammata bhasava,* is spoken which the yakkuva will not understand. If the precautions are not carefully observed the yakkuva will enter the threshing floor and the paddy will decrease.

Life	—Death
Happiness	—Sorrow
Health	—Illness
Luck	—Misfortune
Fertility	—Infertility

All of these dichotomies are related to the opposition between purity and pollution, an opposition constantly reiterated in all Sinhalese rituals.

We must emphasize again that the logical connection between the positive and negative sides of the equation is so close indeed[18] that it seems as if the positive qualities are the negative qualities turned inside out. The purpose of the ritual is precisely to accomplish this conversion of pollution into purity. The rituals appear to oscillate between all that is impure and all that is pure. There are such oscillations at every level of Sinhalese religious thought. The ideology of pollution, for instance, has associations with life as well as death. Death is polluting, but the corpse, people say, becomes fertilizer (*pohora*) for the fields. The corpse is intensely polluting because "the feces cannot be excreted." But feces and manure pits are also fertilizers. In Buddhist ideology too a death brings about immediate conception in some womb. At the same time, birth is intensely polluting (bodily excretions). Sexual intercourse which results in birth is polluting. The same dichotomy that life and death and purity and pollution are opposed but bring about one another is also embedded in the preoccupation with female puberty, which though it is the sign of female fertility is itself very polluting (Yalman, 1963).

Feces are impure, but the feces of the cow (goma) are very pure and auspicious. The ashes of cow dung, just as the relics of the Buddha's corpse after cremation (see below) are even more intense in their purity and sacredness.

Just as the rituals may be said to oscillate between positive and negative states, it is also noteworthy that the ritual practitioners are themselves "mediators." I discuss the Buddhist priests below, but let me draw attention to the position of the kapurala. The word kapurala carries the meaning of "middleman." The ordinary kapurala in the Sinhalese villages is a "marriage broker" who brings two families together and mediates between them. This type of kapurala has nothing to do with the healing ritualist and may be distinguished from the latter by the qualification "wedding" (magula) kapurala. Interestingly enough, the marriage kapurala is always the object of much joking. The Radcliffe-Brown point regarding the ambivalence of "joking relationships" certainly applies to him (Radcliffe-Brown, 1952:90ff.).

The ritual specialist kapurala, on the other hand, is a mediator between men and the gods and goddesses. During his role as a mediator, he wears special costumes which have the characteristic that his breasts are carefully covered by a red sash. He also has to observe severe sex taboos. I suggest that the costumes and the taboos are intended to disguise or submerge his virility and render him sexless. When, however, he is possessed by a deity he will usually dance with one of the weapons and partakes of the sexualty of the god or goddess that has possessed him. In contrast, when pos-

---

[18] So close that some writers miss the differentiation between devaya and yakkuva completely (e.g., Pertold, 1930:127).

sessed by a god, he uses the weapons which are pointed objects; but when possessed by a goddess, he dances with the symbols of the female deities: round objects which often have holes—necklaces, rings, brass mangos,[19] etc.

We must also note in this context that the kapurala mediates not merely between the deities and men, but also between male and female deities. We have mentioned that the maleliya rituals include the recitation of epic songs concerning the birth and death of the gods. A number of other rituals which are beyond the scope of this paper, however, are directly concerned with sexual intercourse between male and female deities (*ganu-purussiya sambandam*) (Yalman, 1964).

The oscillation between impurity and purity at the level of the devaya and yakkuva is to be noted in the realm of high Buddhism as well. Consider the relics (dhatu) of the Buddha. These are parts of his body (*sarira*)[20] which are supposed to have remained behind after his cremation. They are described as his bones (*hakuru* and *lalata* dhatu), his teeth (*denta dhatu*—in the Temple of the Tooth [Hocart, 1931], his hair (*khesa dhatu*), his nails (*nyepata dhatu*). It is not simply that parts of his corpse become sacred by being purified by fire during the cremation. Quite apart from the bones, some of the relics selected for religious attention are precisely the most polluting parts of the body, e.g., the nails and the hair (cf. Leach, 1958). These relics of the corpse become extra sacred, and extra fertile. Hence the belief is that it always rains when the dhatu are shaken, or when the tooth relic in Kandy is taken on a procession in its relic chamber.

Hair is selected for special attention. The hair of ordinary humans is very polluting (but women's long hair symbolizes fertility). The Buddhist priests must be very pure (and celibate, i.e., infertile) so their entire body is shaven from head to foot. But the Buddha figure has tightly curling black hair in all his representations; and as we suggested, his hair relic is again sacred and fertile (Leach, 1958, *passim*).

Consider the implications of the robe (*siura*) of the Buddhist priest, which should be made from cloths found in graveyards. In the funeral ceremony of the Sinhalese, a piece of cloth is left at the head of the grave with the recitation of the *pansakulaya* prayer. The cloth is thus imbued with death-pollution. But when stitched (in 108 pieces, which is said to be like the 108 sections of *dos* [sin]) and then dyed with saffron, the robe becomes extremely pure, sacred, and auspicious. It is then said to symbolize the ripe paddy fields of the Buddha's father which the Buddha saw during his ascent to Nirvana. Thus just as the bhikku mediates between life and death at funerals, the robe he wears reiterates the same polarity at the symbolic level.[21]

There is an important difference between the bhikku and the Buddha, which is partly brought out by the handling of hair in the case of these sacred persons. The bhikku is extremely sacred and is revered as a holy man. He is, however, still involved in the contradictions of purity and pollution. His hair is shaved to emphasize his purity. But he also has a negative aspect: to meet a bhikku first thing in the morning

---

[19] The mango (*amba*) is the symbol of the goddess Pattini and in popular use stands for vagina.

[20] The Buddha image (rupaya) is a symbol of the Buddha's sarira and contains precious stones as "relics" (dhatu) inside it.

[21] The tapasa bhikku (ascetic monks) who make a point of living in graveyards and who meditate on death wear soiled brown robes which bring them even closer into the polarity between pollution and sacredness. They claim to be the true custodians of Buddha's teaching (Yalman, 1962a).

means death; to go to the paddy fields after having met him is believed to decrease the paddy yield; to dream of a bhikku symbolizes Maraya (i.e., death)

While similar oppositions may exist in the case of the Buddha (like the statement that Maraya is a thought in his mind), they are, as it were, resolved. It is said that the Buddha, though sacred and perfectly pure, does not care about pollution. Hence polluted women may enter his temples. Again, though his priests are shaven, he does retain his hair. In him all such contradictions are ended: life and death, purity and impurity, are no longer opposed but resolved. The main achievement of the Buddha is to move out of the cycle of life and death, happiness and sorrow, into Nirvana, where there is neither: the Buddha *is* Eternal Being.

The resolution of the contradictions between life and death comes through with particular emphasis in the case of the dagoba (also known as *stupa*). The word stands for *dhatu-garbhaya.* My informants give the following associated meanings for dhatu: (a.) relics of the Buddha; (b.) seeds; (c.) semen.[22] For garbhaya they simply say *gaba,* i.e., a pregnant womb. The explanation is that the relics of the Buddha are safe in the womb. When the Buddha died and was cremated, his body (sarira) became like tiny seeds, which were put into a dagoba. Although no direct association is made between the vitality of semen and the fertility of the relics, the dhatu are said to have "life" (*pranaya*) in them. It is also said that the land around a dagoba is particularly fertile. At other times my informants have said, "When the Buddha died his goodness (*gune*) became seeds (*atta*) and went into the earth and created the world." In Buddhist thought it is clear that in the dagoba there is no longer a contraditcion between life and death. The sacred object, which is a memorial tomb built upon the relics of the cremated body of the Buddha, also stands for the creation of the universe. More exactly, it is the perfect statement of Eternal Being.

I have been concerned in this paper with the formal aspects of Sinhalese healing rituals. The analysis proceeded on three levels. First, I noted that the items used in the ritual were part of a consistent code and could be examined in terms of their contexts. Second, I drew attention to certain formal arrangements in the rites (e.g., reversal themes in bali, the use of the string) and noted that they follow a logical procedure and bring about the desired effects in the realm of ritual. I also noted that all the rites and all the objects utilized in the rites either reiterated the opposition between positive-negative, good-bad, pure-impure categories or that they mediated between these binary pairs. I conclude that Lévi-Strauss is correct in calling attention to the orchestra score structure of rituals; as in folk poetry (see Sebeok, 1960:233), certain themes and elements are repeated in different forms through the text. In short, the exuberant complexity of the manifest symbolism of the rites we have been describing covers an underlying conceptual structure of extreme simplicity. But the analysis of the structure can be accomplished only by painstaking attention during field work, to identifying and recording the contexts of the ritual items.

My critics may claim that since I did not lay down completely unambiguous and explicit rules to guide my analytic procedure, the results are simply a set of personal opinions and do not indicate that there is any order in Sinhalese thinking on the

---

[22] As the informants put it, "Very high, good word for semen."

subject. They may also claim that I have analyzed only those items which I found convenient.

The second point is easily answered. A complete elucidation of any one of these rituals would mean the analysis of all aspects of Sinhalese folk religion—an undertaking far beyond the scope of this paper. As to whether the structure exists in the rites or in my own mind, I may draw attention to certain independent observations without going into the metaphysics of the question. I want to mention three points made in the paper: (a) the distinction between the after-life and this life, (b) the devaya-yakkuva binary pair, (c) the position of the peretaya in Figure II.

(a) While working on this paper, I came to the conclusion that there was a division of labor between the Buddha and the devaya-yakkuva. I expressed this as the concern with the after-life and this life respectively and noted that the division was reflected in the use of special drums, and also by the taboo on Buddhist priests watching dancing ceremonies, or coming into contact with auspicious ceremonies of this life—i.e., birth, puberty, and marriage. Towards the end of the writing of this paper, I read Gooneratne, who reflects the same opinions, thus, "Buddhism does not hold out worldly advantages or immediate rewards in this life to its votaries . . . Its task is to obtain salvation for the soul . . . a consummation to be attained only in another state of existence . . . Demonism on the other hand deals with the concerns of this life and of this life alone" (1865:5ff.).

(b) Again, I concluded that the yakkuva and the devaya were the two opposed aspects of one category. The point is directly reflected in Gooneratne (1865), who states, for example:

> [The devaya cult] like [the yakkuva cult] also refers to the interests of this world; but while the object of the latter is to inflict or cure diseases by the agency of demons, the object of the former is to protect men generally against all manner of evil, and from diseases . . .

(Concerning their similarity, he adds:)

> [Neither] Dewo nor Yakseyo are born from the womb of a mother, but suddenly spring into existence full grown . . . Nevertheless the last two classes, viz., Dewo and Yakseyo may have mothers in a peculiar fashion . . . marrying and giving in marriage prevail among them as well as among men . . .

(c) I had found the peretaya, ghosts or spirits of the dead, difficult to place. They were lowly, filthy creatures and could belong with the yakkuva. But they were distinguished by a separate name and did not appear to be so concerned with this life as the yakkuva. I eventually classed them as the category opposite to the Buddhist priests. I have already indicated the close association between the priests and death and I have noted the extreme purity, the sacredness, and the food taboos of the bhikku.

Consider now what Gooneratne says on the subject:

> The PRETAS are entirely a different race of beings from all that have yet been mentioned. They are the most helpless and miserable creatures in existence. They live only to suffer. Their only aliment is spittle . . . They can only look at it with burning desire . . . Their skins hang about them in loose folds . . . The Pretayo are not included in Demon workings . . . They are not possessed of power to injure a man . . . [except] by *looking*

with desire at the food he is about to take; but this is a power, which is attributed to . . . men . . . as well as to Pretayo. (He too concludes, finally) The Pretayo . . . are creations of Buddhism, and not mere popular fancy (i.e., like *devayo* and *yakkuva*). (1865:38ff.)

Although not completely explicit, the peretaya category of supernaturals appears to be close to the negative aspects of the priest (the word bhikku means beggar) who is supposed to beg his food and who wears a loose robe.

Wirz's (1954) observations on the peretayo also underline the opposition:

Thus, not every individual is turned into a preta or preti after life, but only those who, up to and immediately before their death, fostered all kinds of desires, cravings, or passions, whether it was those who directed all their thoughts to money and earthly goods, those who massed treasures through avarice, those who were always planning the building of houses and palaces . . . (p. 184). (And finally, he says:)
. . . a . . . (dane) offered to the bhikshu of a monastery is always a cause to remember the preteo . . . (p. 191).

The psychological implications of the Sinhalese concepts which I have described are beyond the scope of this paper. Obviously, the point that feces, the bad-object *par excellence,* are aggressive and dangerous, and that they are at the root of the pollution complex is frequently met with in psychoanalytic literature. The bad-objects are also part of the self and have good aspects. This close association between the self and polluted but powerful bodily exuviae is also reflected in the sacred relics (hair, nails, bones, teeth, etc.) chosen to represent holy beings in almost all cultures. But these questions, however fundamental, take us into another realm where we cannot wander without expert guidance.[23]

APPENDIX I

Versions of Pirit Ceremonies

Pirit 3

The ceremony takes place in a polyandrous household. An infant is ill, and pirit will restore its health. The pirit starts at about 9:30 p.m. and will continue until midnight. The mother of the child is sitting near the doorway of her hut with the infant in her lap. There are no chairs in this poor house and everyone is sitting on mats.

There is no priest, but a group of lay singers take his place. His permission is asked in a formal manner and the priest gives it by reciting certain verses. Those who sing pirits have to be clean; the fact that this is only a ritual cleanliness is evident from the group assembled.

No rule can be made about the relationship of the singers. Some of them are known for their interest in religious matters, and one in particular who lives mostly in the temple is referred to as an *upasaka* (pious man). One of the "fathers" is singing and there are other neighbors and relations. The minimal importance of kinship

[23] The field work on which this essay is based was carried out in Ceylon in 1954–56 and was generously supported by the University of Cambridge and the Wenner-Aren Foundation. I am grateful also to the director and staff of the Center for Advanced Study in the Behavioral Sciences for providing the admirable circumstances in which the essay was written.

ties is suggested by the fact that one of the singers is of the washerman caste, (see Yalman, 1960:82–83). Since they all sit on the floor, the problem which the presence of the washerman presents in seating arrangements is solved.

The pirit nula is held by the singers and passes to the woman and her children. There is a water pot (pirit hen) near her with some red flowers in it. This is surprising, for they are usually appropriate offerings to the yakka. The flowers associated with the Buddha are normally white flowers (*sapu*) of the temple trees.

Pirit 4

A bamboo structure (pirit maduva) has been prepared and twelve lay persons, friends and relations of the householder, are singing like priests inside it. The hut is inside an ordinary village dwelling. Just outside the structure, which is also referred to as a *pirit ķotuva,* oil lamps (*pahana*) are burning. The tom-tom beaters are seated outside and the washermen who have brought the cloth with which to decorate the structure will return in the morning. The relics (*ķaranduwa*) have not been brought out this time and only the priests are allowed to handle it. On the table around which the singers are seated, there are water pots, coconut flowers, betel, rice.

A string (pirit nula) is attached to the cloth above the structure and descends to the singers who all hold it. Then it goes around to the wife of the householder, who at the receiving end is holding it with an arecanut flower. The pirit is intended to protect (arakshava) the household and to counteract apele, (*apele dura enta*).

The singers hold the book (pirit pota) in their hands and are divided into two groups. (I am unsure as to whether this choral element involved in the singing represents the contest between the forces of evil [Marea] and the forces of good [Buddha].) The next morning all the singers get together and drink *ķanja,* which is some form of milk and rice. They then tie the pirit nula around their wrists or necks and drink the water on the table.

There is another little structure with flowers and a lamp just outside the dwelling. This is known as a *mal palliya* (flower basket) and is of the same category as the *mala bulat tattuva:* an offering to the deities. The householder is unsure as to which particular deity it is intended for and recites the names Vishnu, Kataragama, Saman or "the god of four directions" (*hatara varan deva*). The offering is not a normal part of pirit. The fire is said to be lit to get guidance from the gods.

Pirit 5

A week before a birth is expected, a special pirit called *angulimala pirita* (birth pirit) is held for the pregnant woman. The verses of this pirit are different from the verses that are normally sung. The leda (patient) holds the pirit string. At the end of the ceremony, she has some food taboos imposed on her. She is not allowed to eat any kind of flesh or other dirty things. She may eat betel, which is very clean.* The patient has to avoid heavy fried food which will be difficult to digest.

Pirit 6

The pirit hut has been prepared. There are about nine singers who enter the

* There is a story connected with the betel leaf which describes the way the leaf was brought by a snake. It is thought that the two ends of the leaf contain the vas (poison) of the snake and must therefore be torn off before it is eaten. Here again is the association between extreme purity and vas.

structure at different times. Some are friends and relations, and some are simply the laborers of the owner of the house.

The pirit is being held for an old schoolmaster who owns many fields (Cooray). He has a wound in his hand (*tuwalayak*); it is said that blood is collected in his hand (*le gallanava*) and that he is losing strength (*saraya yanava*).

The sending end of the string comes from the singers and is wrapped around a pot of pirit water. The arecanut flower wrapped in a betel leaf at the end of the string is handed to the patient only after a great deal of singing. The object is being passed back to the singers at intervals. The schoolmaster makes some fuss about the fact that the string has to touch the white cloth (viyana) around the structure. The next morning the string will be tied around the wrist of the patient and he will drink the pirit water.

APPENDIX II

Pulutu Pas Vage
(Five Kinds of Burned Things)

Burned or fried objects are part of the more general offerings of dola made to yakkuva. The rite is also referred to as a *tun mansala araksava maturanava,* i.e., lit three street corner protection charm: the charming of protection at the meeting point of three roads which are inhabited by yakku.

The ceremony consists simply of the recitation of charms and the offering of five kinds of burned things: die mas (water flesh), *goda mas* (land flesh), and three kinds of grains: *abba* (mustard), *vilanda* (fried paddy), and one other grain. There are also red flowers (*ratu mal*) and *le* (blood). The red flowers are specifically intended for the yakkuva and stand in contrast to the white flowers usually offered to the Buddha. These five kinds of burned things are put into small receptacles (*goduva*) made from jack fruit leaves (*kos kola*). The jack tree is one of the category of *kiri gaha* (milk tree), milk-exuding trees like the sacred Bo tree which stand for the Buddha. But branches of the jack tree are used in sorcery.

APPENDIX III

Bali 3

The usual bali hut has been prepared and three effigies have been made which are similar in their general lines to the effigy in Bali 1. The informants suggest that one of the effigies is the figure of Maha Brahma and that the other one is the figure of Valli Amma. They are uncertain about the personality of the third effigy. Other informants would undoubtedly give different interpretations as to what the effigies stand for. What is certain is that two effigies are male and one is female. It is also noteworthy that the names offered by the informant are names of devaya, yakkuva. (This is the double aspect of devaya and yakkuva to which attention has been drawn.) All the effigies are standing upon large cobras. On a ledge in front of the effigies, food offerings (dola) have been placed, again as in Bali 1. The dola is at the moment covered with plantain leaves. Opposite the effigies, again as in Bali 1, there is a hut which is covered up in front with a white cloth. The patient is inside the hut. The ceremony is an extremely elaborate one with six tom-tom beaters (*bera kariya*). The patient is rich and has spent more than 200 rupees on the ceremony.

After much singing and dancing by the tom-tom beaters led by the bali adura, the sick person is revealed. He is holding the string (nula) which connects him with the three figures of the yakkuva opposite him.

The dola is opened up and a mirror and a basket of food—fried rice, fried cakes (*kavum*), plantains, curries, hair—is in evidence. On the opposite side of the dola in front of the patient there is a *molgaha* (paddy pounder) placed on a plantain leaf in front of the sick man and there are pots of water with flower decorations on top (*kaha pen:* saffron water) on either side of the hut in which the patient is sitting.

As the tom-tom beaters proceed with their dancing and singing, a request is made by one of the schoolmasters to sing the *jayamangala sutra*. This is one of the Buddhist texts and is not normally part of a bali ceremony. The tom-tom beaters do sing it. The impression that as long as the singing and the dancing are continued it does not much matter what is actually sung, provided it does have sacred power, is strengthened.*

In the morning, the patient is made to put his feet on the molgaha (pounder). (There is a parallelism here; just as the effigies have their feet on the cobras, so the patient has his feet on the molgaha.) A special ayu bowan takes place in which the tom-tom beaters address the patient and sweep away the vas-dos from him with arecanut flowers. They take some limes and stick these on the effigies. The patient then throws the cloth upon the bali images. He then throws the end of the string with a lime also upon the image.

There are subsidiary rites. Just before the final phase of the ceremony, all the singing and dancing stops. The two younger boys among the tom-tom beaters give their bells back to the older tom-tom beater. They then worship him and he returns the bells. After this, they worship each other. Then the youngest worships the oldest, and after this, the youngest in turn worships the two elder ones without giving the bells back. These ritual salutations are a recognition of the generational hierarchy among the tom-tom beaters. The asymmetry involved is that of kinship status and is not connected with relative age.

The images will stay in the house for three half days (*tun varuva*) and will then be taken into the jungle. The patient has food taboos placed upon him and will eat from pure dishes (plantain leaves).

APPENDIX IV

Versions of the Gam Maduva (Village Hut) Mangalaya (Ceremony) in the Village of Teripehe

(Accounts of Informants)

The leading people in the village will discuss the question of having a gam

* See Gooneratne (1865:52), ". . . much of what now seems . . . gibberish, may at one time have been an intelligible language."

maduva. If there have been many deaths or misfortunes in the village, it is time to make an offering to the deities. Some people will make the rounds of all the houses in the village to collect contributions in paddy or money. A temporary hut (maduva) will be built for the seven kapuralas and the six or seven tom-tom beaters who are necessary for the occasion. The women cannot take part in the ceremonies but may only watch them. The washermen will provide the white cloth, and the men of the high caste will do all the cooking for the day. They will beat the paddy and prepare the food, and the kapurala will make the first offering of the food to the god.

The blacksmiths have to go to the kovil in Ekassa. There are some weapons (ayuda) which belong to the deities in the shrine. These weapons will be brought back to Teripehe with the procession. The tom-tom beaters will lead the procession and the weapons will be carried under a cloth provided by the washermen. The potters do not take part in this procession; but the cooking has to be done in new pots, and these are offered by the potter caste.

There are thirteen deities in Teripehe and the kapurala will dance to them one by one. They may dance about an hour for each god. At the very end of the ceremony there is a *kiri amma* dance. A man dresses up as a grandmother, wearing a sari, with a baby in his hands and becomes possessed.

The last act is called *at bandima* (literally "the tying of elephants"). Ten people dress up as elephants with a piece of cloth hanging in front of them like the trunk of the animal, and another ten persons hold them from behind. At the beginning of the rite, the elephants will be in the front and the tom-tom beaters behind. The elephants will move up and down and dance. There will be some other people who will hold a crossed pair of paddy pounders in front of the elephants like a gate. The elephants will push on the gateway, saying, "We want to go to the god." The persons holding the paddy pounders will object and will demand some plantains. The elephants will return again and again, saying, "Can we go to the god?" Eventually they will hoot and dance and the tom-tom beaters will play the drums, and the elephants, thinking that the god has done this, will lose consciousness and fall down. They will be shouting, "Hoo!" Then the people will carry them into the hut. The elephants will be shivering (*veulanava*). A lot of food (kavum) and plantains remain. These will be given to the kapuralas, the washermen, the blacksmiths and the tom-tom beaters. If anything remains, this will go to the visitors and it will be said, "Hereafter, god, look upon us." The elephants are also a god referred to as *gana deyyo* (i.e., Ganesha).

The Account of the Rite from a Washerman

The ceremony commences with the planting of a large *kiri gaha* (milk-exuding tree) pole (*kanuva*). The act is referred to as *kap hitavima.* Drums will be played, songs will be sung, and a kapurala and some people will be present. This pole is planted near the devale.

Processions will visit the houses of the village collecting rice and money and a date will be fixed for the gam maduva. The planting of the tree is like the foundation stone of a house (*mul gala,* i.e., root stone).

There will be a procession from the village where the paddy pounder (molgaha), the mortar (*van gediya*) and the paddy will be brought in procession under a white cloth with the singing of *kavi* songs and the beating of drums. Only the men will get together and prepare the food. They will cook some special rice called *de bata?* (god rice?). This food is cooked for the washermen, the tom-tom beaters, the kapurala and the other persons with specific duties (*atara kariya*). It is like a dhana to the gods. The food will be eaten then and there. After this, the tom-tom beaters and most of the villagers will go in procession to bring the weapons from Ekassa kovil.

The washermen will be busy in the village making *haluva*. Haluva are made of starched cloth in the shape of a fan, and are something like a deity. Since fourteen will come, fourteen haluva are needed. Furthermore, each deity needs different colors. Thus, (a) Kiritibandara needs a white haluva; (b) Kohombandara, red; (c) Kalukumara, black; (d) Nile bedde deviyo, blue; (e) Devatabandara, again, white, etc. The *kiri amma deviyo* needs two small haluva of white. All sorts of other deities will come too.

In the meantime, a box is made in Ekassa, and with the singing of sacred texts, all the weapons are put into that box and covered with a white cloth. Then the procession with the tom-tom beaters in the front and the weapons under the white cloth will start toward Teripehe. The blacksmiths will cleanse the weapons with limes and saffron at one of the mountain streams.

The haluva are prepared in a private place. The weapons (deva ayuda) are brought to the hut. The haluva will be brought in the same way with singing and dancing to the hut where the weapons have been placed. Both the weapons and the haluva are now outside the gam maduva (village hut) on a masa (altar or table).

The *atara kariyo* will cook fourteen pots of rice, and they will prepare curries. They will also prepare plantains and kavum (fried cakes). At night the washermen, the kapuralas, and the tom-tom beaters will be given food.

The gam maduva ritual starts at ten o'clock at night. Then two weapons for each deity will be taken inside the maduva. They will be placed on a masa (altar). The singing and dancing will last about an hour. The kavis that are sung are known as *nyaknya kirima* (begging). The haluva are also taken into the hut one by one.

Then the food which is cooked is brought in procession to the same hut. All this must be done by men because women cannot touch these things. The food is placed on small table-like objects made of sticks and plantain trunks, called *karakala* (*pideniye*). There will be fourteen of these, one for each deity, and they will be arranged around the altar on which the weapons and the haluva have been placed. The small tables with food will have betel and heaped rice and curries on them.

Then the kapurala will recite the names of the gods one by one (*kannalav kirima*) and after this, the food will be placed in a corner. It is only after this that the *magul bere* (tom-tom beating) and the dancing will commence.

The kapurala will be singing the births and deaths of these deities. The good deeds of these gods will be recited, and if the ritual is well carried out, the fields will be more fertile and there will be not trouble with animals. The village will be lucky again.

Another Version of the Rite from Appuhami Kapurala

The necessary paddy is collected seven days before the intended ceremony. The kapurala will go from house to house in the village with the conch (*hak gediya*) and request food from the people. All the offerings will be placed in a specially prepared hut (maduva). Seven days after this initial collection of food, kap hitavima takes place (see Version 2). This starts the ritual. The tree is tall and has an arecanut flower on the top of it. The next day the hut is built around this tree.

Then the mortar and pestle are brought by men to the site of the ritual under white cloth. Women who have stopped menstruation may help the men to prepare the paddy and the food. The kapurala will start the initial stroke of beating the paddy and then the men will go on. The women are not allowed to take part in this stage of the proceedings. Three days before the ritual, all this is prepared and the kapurala will send letters to other kapurala, requesting them to attend the celebrations. When they arrive, they will be sent to houses to eat and the next day the celebrations will take place.

The cooking is a very special act which is carried out only by some people. These persons will bathe, will be dressed in white, they will close up their mouths with clean cloths and tie them up before touching the food. This preparation of the food is referred to as *adukka uyanava*. Kavum (oil cakes), *kiribat* (milk rice), plantains, and curries will be prepared.

Next the procession will go to the devale with tom-toms to bring the weapons of the deities. The kapurala in the village are in charge of the weapons. They will bring them and put them aside, but will not take them into the huts right away. They will make a masa (altar) on which the food will be placed. Then the kapurala will sing a *yatika* (see below) with the tom-tom beaters playing their drums inside the hut. At the end of the yatika the food is brought out and the people are allowed to eat. Then the kapuralas will dress up and get ready. Then there will be a yatika to the arecanut flowers. After this, each kapurala will take a little of the flowers into his hands.

The kapurala will recite the god's verses and dance. The dance is referred to as *pela paliya* (the parade of weapons—also referred to as ayuda, or *kanu mangalaya:* weapon or staff ceremony). The weapons will have been cleaned by the blacksmiths with limes and saffron.

There will be dancing to the following deities: Nila bedde deva; Kohomba deva; Kiritibandara deva; Menikbandara; Kumarabandara; Abinnana; Alut (new) deva; Kadavara deva; Davatavabandara; Pallya bandara; Alut nuwara bandara (Alut nuwara: A sacred place in the eastern jungles, also referred to as *Mayangene*); Velassa deva. (It appears from the recitation that the number and names of the deities are somewhat immaterial. Kapurala Appuhami had quite a difficult time filling in the names for the twelve deities.) There are seven *kiri ammas* who are the sisters of the gods. They are also referred to as *ammala hatdena* (the seven mothers). These are the mothers who have given milk, and the intention of the ritual is to ask pardon of those who have given milk for any "mistakes" (varada).

After the *ayuda palya,* there is a *haluva palya.* All the haluva will be taken into the hut singly. The only explanation of the haluva is that they belong to the gods (*deviange aiti*).

Appuhami referred to another god (Dummala palya?—incense) as the chief deity. He is also referred to as Palle bedde deva. The kapurala dances for half an hour and tells of his visions (*pehena*). He tells of things which have passed and are to come, and he reads people's minds.

No incense is used for the other deities. For the first dance, there is incense but no weapons. In the next dance, the kapurala dances with his staff (*pol kotuva:*

coconut staff) which is also said to belong to the gods. After this dance, the weapons are handled one by one. Appuhami's account of the kiri amma dance follows version 2 (above).

Appuhami kapurala's account of elephant tying is similar to the earlier versions. Each kapurala holds the elephants from the sides and dances with them. The elephants will eventually become possessed (*mayan*) and will be difficult to manage. Two men will hold the paddy pounders crosswise to form a boundary (*kadavata*) which the elephants cannot pass. These two men will ask the elephants for food. "If you want to go to the deity, you must give kavum, plantains, etc." just to pass the time. Then, as soon as the two men take away the boundary which prevents the elephants from approaching the deity, the elephants will go mad (pissu). They will dance violently and fall on the ground. They will be like dead bodies. Then they will be taken into the maduva and when the kapurala sprinkle some saffron water upon them, they will revive (See Yalman, 1964).

This account of the gam maduva by Appuhami is similar to the maleliya ceremony described in the text. I recall that when the kapurala was preparing the ceremony of maleliya, he did point out that it was going to be "just like" the gam maduva. In fact the maleliya was a much simpler ceremony than the one described here which leads me to believe that some of the ritual acts are dispensable.

The Mangalaya Davasa *(Ceremonial Day) in the Village of Vilava in the Maho District*

(Here is an account of a ceremony from an entirely different part of Ceylon which follows in its outlines the gam maduva of Teripehe.)

A small hut is built outside the local devale, called *multen ge,* i.e., "food for the deities" house. The hut is decorated with white cloths, and new clothes are given to the kapurala. The castes involved is this ceremony are, again, the washermen, the tom-tom beaters, the potters and the blacksmiths (who are expected to cleanse the weapons of the deities).

Before the ceremony takes place, the devale is ritually purified. After the preparation of the hut, new oil is prepared and food is brought by procession, by the various castes. The food is referred to as *deva tovil pasdena,* i.e., five offerings to the deities: rice, plantains, the plantain flower, curries, and coconuts. New pots are used.

Before the food offering is made, the kapurala cleanses the weapons. He takes the ayuda one by one and dances with them. The ayuda in question are a trident, a sword, and arrows, symbols which are normally used. For the goddess Pattini, however, there is a haluva which is a round object looking like a fan (see above). The kapurala washes Pattini with "sandalwood milkwater" (*handum kiripen*).

In this village the kapurala becomes possessed for five deities. They are listed as follows: Gam devatava, Ayya nayaka deva, Kadavara deva, Kambili deva, and Gama bahirava. The third and the fourth deities are known as elder brother, younger brother, or as cross-cousins.

The ritual is described as follows. At the devale the offering is made. After this there is some recitation (*yatika kirima*) by the kapuralas. They then get possessed and start telling the future. The ceremony starts during the day and ends in the middle of the night. It is clearly patterned on the same lines as the gam maduva in Teripehe.

My informants say that during the ceremonies women may be brought into the devale; if there are yakkuva in them they will come out. The women will be possessed and will hoot and may lose consciousness. After the yakkuva come out, the kapurala will chase them away.

APPENDIX V

Offerings to the Devaya

The boiling of milk (kiri uturanava): The ceremony is a simple adukku. It takes place near a devale or any selected pure spot in the village. The people may first come and promise to give the deities some food. When their promises come true, they will prepare seven *mutti* (small pots) of food to the village deity, gam deva. Rice and coconut milk (*pol kiri*) are brought from the various homes and are cooked on the spot. An important part of the ceremony is that the milk must boil over. The mixture is then eaten by the people. (A ceremony of this kind, but much more elaborate, takes place in the annual rituals of the Jaffna Tamils. Huge cauldrons of milk and rice are boiled over in the midst of great crowds of spectators.)

The offering of adukku, or a prayer (yatika): A man from Teripehe has lost his buffaloes and does not know where to find them. He has come to request Appuhami kapurala to ask the gods where the animals have disappeared to.

Appuhami has ordered the hut in which the ceremony is to take place to be cleansed with cow dung earlier in the day as a preparation for this event. Saffron water was sprinkled on the cow dung to make it doubly pure. A small altar (masa) has been prepared and the food is placed on it. Appuhami wears his special kapurala clothes.

The ceremony proceeds as follows. The kapurala begins to recite the epics concerning the birth and adventures of the deity. He takes a small, shallow basket in his hand which contains some food. After a while, his hand begins to tremble. He goes on speaking and suddenly begins to laugh and grunt to himself. The possession takes hold of him very gradually.

The possession lasts about half an hour. Appuhami comes out of it and walks toward me, smiling. It appears that the god who came was Kohomba deviyo.

References Cited

Berndt, Ronald M.
1951 *Kunapipi: A Study of an Australian Aboriginal Religious Cult.* New York: International Universities Press.

Callaway, John (ed.)
1829 *Yakkun Nattanavā:* A Cingalese Poem Descriptive of the Ceylon System of Demonology to which is appended the Practice of a Capua or Devil Priest as described by a Buddhist. London: Printed for the Oriental Translation Fund by A. J. Valpy.

Cartman, James (Rev.)
1957 *Hinduism in Ceylon.* Colombo: M. D. Gunasena and Co. Ltd.

Conklin, Harold C.
1962 Lexicographical treatment of folk taxonomies. In: Supplement to International Journal of American Linguistics, 28, ed. by Fred W. Householder and Sol Saporta.

Deraniyagala, P. E. P.

1936 Some blood games of the Sinhalese. *Man:* 36:46–47.

Dixon, Sir J. F.

1884 Notes illustrative of Buddhism as the daily religion of the Buddhists of Ceylon and some accounts of their ceremonies before and after death. Journal of the Royal Asiatic Society, 8:297–330.

Disāva of Vellase

1817 An account of the Kandy Perahera. Ceylon Government Gazette, Sept. 13, 1817.

Dumont, Louis

1957 Une sous-caste de l'Inde du sud: organization sociale et religion des Pramalai-Kallar. Collection: Le Monde d'Outre-mer, passe et present, 1 serie Etudes, 1. La Haye: Mouton & Co.

Fortes, Meyer

1945 *The Dynamics of Clanship Among the Tallensi.* London: Oxford University Press.

1959 *Oedipus and Job in West African Religion.* Cambridge: University Press.

Gooneratne, Dandris de Silva

1865 On demonology and witchcraft in Ceylon. Journal of the (Ceylon Branch) Royal Asiatic Society, 4:1–117.

Gough, E. Kathleen

1955 Female initiation rites on the Malabar coast. Journal of the Royal Anthropological Institute, 85:45–80.

1959 Cults of the dead among the Nāyars. In: *Traditional India: Structure and Change,* ed. by Milton B. Singer. Philadelphia: Publications of the American Folklore Society, Bibliographical Series, 10:240–272.

1960 Caste in a Tanjore village. In: *Aspects of Caste in South India, Ceylon and North-West Pakistan.* Cambridge Papers in Social Anthropology No. 2, pp. 11–61. London: Cambridge University Press.

Grünwedel, Albert

1893 Singhalesische Masken. International Archives for Ethnography, 7:71–130.

Gunasekera, U. A.

1953 *Puna Maduva* or the Scapegoat Idea in Ceylon. Spolia Zeylanica, 27:63–75.

Hocart, A. M.

1931 The Temple of the Tooth in Kandy. Memoirs of the Archaeological Survey of Ceylon, 4. London: Luzac and Co.

Jakobson, Roman

1961 Linguistics and communication theory. In: *The Structure of Language and its Mathematical Aspects.* American Mathematical Society: Proceedings of Symposia in Applied Mathematics, 12:245–252.

Leach, E. R.

1958 Magical hair. Journal of the Royal Anthropological Institute, 88:147–163.

1960 The Sinhalese of the dry zone of northern Ceylon. In: *Social Structure in Southeast Asia,* pp. 116–126, ed. by George Peter Murdock. Viking Fund Publications in Anthropology, No. 29.

1961a Lévi-Strauss in the Garden of Eden: an examination of some recent developments in the analysis of myth. Transactions of the New York Academy of Sciences, 23:386–396.

1961b *Pul Eliya, a Village in Ceylon: a Study of Land Tenure and Kinship.* Cambridge: University Press.

1962 Pulleyar and the Lord Buddha: an aspect of religious syncretism in Ceylon. Psychoanalysis and the Psychoanalytical Review, 49:81–102.

n.d. A linguistic analysis of rural Sinhalese kinship terminology (Unpublished MS).

Le Mesurier, C. J. R.

1884 *An Keliya* (a Sinhalese national game). Journal of the (Ceylon Branch), Royal Asiatic Society, 8:368–394.

Lévi-Strauss, Claude

1955 The structural study of myth. Journal of American Folklore, 68:428–444.

1956 Structure et dialectique. In: *For Roman Jakobson: Essays on the Occasion of his Sixtieth Birthday, 11 October, 1956,* comp. by Morris Halle *et al.* The Hague: Mouton, pp. 289–294.

Meerworth-Levina, L.

1915 The Hindu goddess Pattini in the Buddhist popular beliefs of Ceylon. Ceylon Antiquary and Literary Register, 1:29–37.

Métraux, Alfred

1959 *Voodoo in Haiti.* Translated by Hugo Charteris. New York: Oxford University Press.

Nadel, S. F.

1946 A Study of shamanism in the Nuba Mountains. Journal of the Royal Anthropological Institute, 76:25–37.

1954 *Nupe Religion.* London: Routledge and Kegan Paul Ltd.

Nell, Louis

1881–82 A Huniyam Image. Journal of the (Ceylon Branch) Royal Asiatic Society, 7.

Pertold, O.

1922 The Pilli charm: a study of Sinhalese magic. Journal of the Anthropological Society of Bombay, 12:594–609.

1925 *Inquiries into the Popular Religions of Ceylon, Part I: Singalese Amulats Talismans and Spells.* Prague: Publication of the Philosophic Faculty of Charles University.

1929 The conception of the soul in the Sinhalese demon-worship. Archiv Orientalni, 1:316–322.

1930 The ceremonial dances of the Sinhalese: an inquiry into the Sinhalese folk-religion. Archiv Orientalni, 2:108–137, 201–254, 385–424.

Pieris, Ralph

1956 *Sinhalese Social Organization: the Kandyan Period.* Colombo: Ceylon University Press Board.

Propp, Vladimir

1958 The morphology of the folk tale. International Journal of American Linguistics, 24:1–134. Publication 10 of the Indiana University Research Center in Anthropology, Folklore and Linguistics.

Radcliffe-Brown, A. B.

1933 *The Andaman Islanders: A Study in Social Anthropology.* New York: Macmillan.

1952 *Structure and Function in Primitive Society.* London: Cohen and West Ltd.

Raghavan, M. D.

1951 The Pattini cult as a socio-religious institution. Spolia Zeylanica, 26:251–261. (Bulletin of the National Museums of Ceylon.)

Ryan, Bryce

1953 *Caste in Modern Ceylon: the Sinhalese System in Transition.* New Brunswick: Rutgers University Press.

1958 In collaboration with L. D. Jayasena and D. C. R. Wickremesinghe. *Sinhalese Village.* Coral Gables, Florida: University of Miami Press.

Sarathachandra, E. R.
1953 *The Sinhalese Folk Play and the Modern Stage.* Colombo: Ceylon University Press Board.

Sebeok, Thomas A.
1960 Decoding a text: levels and aspects in a Cheremis Sonnet. In: *Style and Language,* pp. 221–235, ed. by Thomas A. Sebeok. The Technology Press of Massachusetts Institute of Technology and John Wiley and Sons.

Srinivas, M. N.
1952 *Religion and Society Among the Coorgs of South India.* Oxford: Clarendon Press.

Tambiah, S. J.
1958 The structure of kinship and its relationship to land possession and residence in Pata Dumbara, Central Ceylon. Journal of the Royal Anthropological Institute, 88:21–44.

Warner, W. Lloyd
1958 *A Black Civilization: A Social Study of an Australian Tribe* (rev. edition). New York: Harper and Brothers.

Wirz, Paul
1940 Die kultische Bedeutung der Kokonuss bei den Singhalesen. Verhandlungen der Naturforschenden Gesellschaft, 51.
1954 *Exorcism and the Art of Healing in Ceylon.* Leiden: E. J. Brill.

Yalman, Nur
1960 The flexibility of caste principles in a Kandyan community. In: *Aspects of Caste in South India, Ceylon and North-West Pakistan,* pp. 78–112, ed. by E. R. Leach. Cambridge Papers in Social Anthropology, No. 2, London: Cambridge University Press.
1962a The ascetic Buddhist monks of Ceylon. Ethnology, 1:315–328.
1962b Sinhalese-Tamil intermarriage on the east coast of Ceylon. Sociologus, 12:36–54.
1962c The structure of the Sinhalese kindred: a re-examination of the Dravidian terminology. American Anthropologist, 64:548–575.
1963 On the purity and sexuality of women in the castes of Malabar and Ceylon (Curl Prize Essay). Journal of the Royal Anthropological Institute, 93:25–58.
1964 Dual Organization in Central Ceylon?—or the goddess on the Tree-top (forthcoming).

Ritual Pollution as an Integrator of Caste and Religion

EDWARD B. HARPER

BELIEFS about ritual purity and ritual impurity form some of the most all-pervasive themes in Hindu culture. They are the basis of "orthoprax" Brahmanism in that only a ritually pure individual may approach the higher gods.[1] Brahmanic concepts concerning pollution relate the Indian system of social stratification to the Hindu religious system. These concepts are applied to matters of personal conduct, health, and justice, and are fundamental to such well-known aspects of Indian culture as untouchability, limited access to wells, and the setting apart of a priestly caste. One of the important rationales for caste separatism (their refusal to intermarry, eat with one another, or touch one another) is that some castes are more ritually pure than others, and that impurity may be transmitted from one caste to another through these acts. But on the other hand, castes are also brought together and integrated into a system of ritual interdependence by the belief that they differ in the degree to which they are ritually pure or impure. Some actions are thought to be ritually too defiling for certain castes to perform, and some castes are thought to be too impure to perform certain other activities. These beliefs are basic to the concept of a division of labor by castes and to the ideal that each caste plays a part in a larger mutually interdependent system.

The theoretical model of the system which relates ritual pollution to caste status appears to be:[2]

(1) Gods are superior to men and thus must be worshipped by men; in return, gods bestow benefits on men.

(2) Gods can be directly worshipped only by those mortals of high ritual purity.

(3) In order for an individual to attain and maintain a state of high ritual purity, he needs to have other people perform certain ritually defiling acts for him, or, looked at another way, in order for the community to function, many actions must be performed which cause the actor to become impure, and some of these bring about a greater amount of impurity than do others.

(4) In a general sense, all members of the community derive benefit from the worship given directly to the gods by those who are ritually pure, but in a specific sense they derive benefit by worshipping those religious specialists who directly worship the gods.

(5) Ritual pollution is transmitted through certain kin relationships; an individual can-

Dr. Harper is Associate Professor of Anthropology at the University of Washington.

1 The term "orthoprax" was suggested to me by McKim Marriott to replace "orthodox," which I had used in an earlier draft of this paper. Orthoprax emphasizes ritual aspects of religious behavior rather than its belief content, and more accurately reflects the lay Brahmin's conception of the religious man. I gratefully express my debt to Dr. Marriott for his painstaking analysis of an earlier draft, and for his numerous substantive suggestions, some of which have been incorporated into this paper without further acknowledgment.

2 This model is derived from fieldwork in the Malnad part of Mysore State, but is phrased broadly in the belief that it may be generally applicable to other parts of South India.

not attain a higher state of ritual purity than his kinsmen. If an individual is to attain and maintain a high state of purity, he must marry only with another whose family has an equally high state of ritual purity.

(6) In order for the gods to be worshipped, some castes must assume the pollution which otherwise would accrue to those castes which worship the gods; if the gods are to be pleased, it thus becomes the duty of some castes to help other castes attain sufficient purity to worship them, even at the expense of thereby becoming impure themselves.

(7) In order to perform ritual cleansing actions for relatively more pure individuals or supernaturals, the actor must himself maintain an only slightly less pure status. In order to prevent those with an intermediate amount of purity from becoming less pure (and thus unable themselves to assume the lesser degrees of pollution from the most pure individuals), there must be even less pure individuals to prevent the accrual of too much ritual pollution to these intermediately pure individuals.

(8) Since purity and pollution are transferred through kinship, the total society must be divided into kinship-based ritual status groups (castes) which are ranked along a purity-impurity continuum.

(9) Lower castes worship the higher castes, who in turn worship the gods. This forms the basis for a system of social differentiation in status which is based upon differences in ritual status.

Although this conceptual model is the foundation upon which the system of hierarchically ranked castes rests, it is only crudely and imperfectly implemented in the actual caste hierarchy; or, to state it another way, the "attributional theory of caste ranking" supplies the context for the "interactional theory of caste ranking" (Marriott, 1959).

In this paper I describe the ritual observances and beliefs about pollution as followed by Havik Brahmins, a "dominant caste" in the area around Sagar in the Malnad part of South India.[3] This is an area stratified by over a dozen indigenous castes, which in native thought are grouped into a three-class system: Brahmins, Sudras, and Untouchables (cf. Harper, 1959a). A fourth caste, Lingayats, occupies a position somewhat apart from these three classes.

Ritual Purity—The Three States

Haviks have three terms to denote degrees of purity and impurity. *Maḍi* translates as "ritually pure"; *muṭṭucheṭṭu* as "ritually impure." Under ordinary circumstances, an individual is said to be *mailigē,* a term which has been translated as "normal ritual status" (Srinivas, 1952:106). I have been tempted to translate it as "lack of ritual status," although this is not completely accurate for a person in mailigē is impure relative to a person who is in a state of ritual purity; that is, contact between the two will cause the person in maḍi to become mailigē, and, a person in mailigē is pure relative to a person in a state of ritual impurity; that is, contact between the two will cause the person in mailigē to become muṭṭucheṭṭu.

To make the transition from mailigē to muṭṭucheṭṭu, a Brahmin must perform some ritually defiling act or have contact with a source of pollution. To regain a state of mailigē from one of muṭṭucheṭṭu, he must undergo a ritual cleansing ceremony. In order to attain a state of ritual purity, maḍi, a Brahmin must also engage in a voli-

[3] In this paper I do not cite parallels in previous analyses, the most complete of which are Srinivas, 1952, and Mrs. Sinclair Stevenson, 1920, nor do I cite points at which my analysis differs from the hypothesis of H. N. C. Stevenson, 1954.

tional act of ritually cleansing himself. He may directly make the transition to a state of maḍi from a state of either mailigē or muṭṭucheṭṭu. Within each of these three states there are varying degrees of purity or impurity, relative to other people and supernaturals.

Maḍi, which can be obtained only by ritual bathing, is necessary to perform a religious rite, such as worshipping a god. The transition from maḍi to mailigē automatically occurs when, for example, the ritually pure individual eats, sleeps, or touches another Havik in mailigē. Muṭṭucheṭṭu follows contact with objects of extreme impurity, such as an Untouchable or a menstruating woman. Contact with a source of ritual defilement does not have to be direct—a Brahmin becomes muṭṭucheṭṭu simply by touching a piece of cloth previously in contact with a menstruating woman.

Muṭṭucheṭṭu, or pollution, is removed in various ways, depending upon its severity. As the worst type of pollution cannot be removed, an individual in extreme defilement must be outcaste. Slightly less severe pollution can be removed only by a purificatory ceremony conducted by the caste *guru* or a priest. The more severe types of pollution that an individual ordinarily may contract can be removed by bathing, changing the sacred thread, changing clothes, and eating *panchagavya* (five sacred products of the cow); less severe types of pollution are removed by bathing and changing clothes, or by changing clothes alone.

A daily bath is absolutely essential for a Brahmin, for without it he cannot perform daily worship to his gods. Ideally, Haviks say, they should take three baths a day, one before each meal. But few do this. Again, a cold water bath is, in terms of ritual purity, most desirable, but Haviks usually admit that they are weak of flesh and prefer to bathe in warm water. In practice, all Haviks whom I have known rigorously observe the custom of a daily bath (*snāna*), which is taken before the main meal of the day and before the household gods are worshipped. The woman who cooks this meal, some of which is offered to the house gods and some of which is given to her personal god, that is, her husband, must be in maḍi. In the event that an individual is too ill to take the daily bath, he is ritually cleansed with *mantras* (mantra snāna).

Havik males, who belong to a relatively wealthy caste and who have a fair amount of leisure time during certain seasons, nevertheless do a great deal of the work required to run their arecanut estates. Every attempt is made to finish work that is considered dirty or ritually defiling—for example, carrying manure to the garden or working with an Untouchable servant—before the daily bath that precedes the main meal. If for any reason this work has to be done in the afternoon, another bath should be taken when the man returns home.

To become maḍi a person must have a complete bath, including pouring water over the hair, and the water should be drawn from a pure source by a Brahmin who is not in muṭṭucheṭṭu. If cotton clothing is worn it must have been washed by someone in maḍi, and to remain in a state of maḍi the wearer must not touch any cloth which is not maḍi. To illustrate with a male example: A man bathes in his *panche,* a piece of cloth wrapped around his waist. He then changes to another panche while bathing so that he can remove and wash the one he has been wearing. While wet, both panches are maḍi. He dries himself using the panche he has just washed (to use a dry towel which was not maḍi would remove his own maḍi), rewashes the panche he has just used as a towel, and then leaves the bathing area to go to the clothesline in the attic of the house. Maḍi clothes are generally dried and kept here to insure that no one not in a state of maḍi accidentally touches them. He then changes to the panche he had washed the previous day and hangs up to dry that which he has just washed and is wearing. Actually, this changing of clothes is for comfort, as he would remain in maḍi if he continued to wear his wet panche. According to some informants, the cotton clothes on the line, provided they are not touched by anyone not in maḍi, retain their state of maḍi for three days.

A person who is in dry "cotton maḍi" becomes mailigē as soon as he is touched by anyone else in the house who is not in maḍi (a child is most likely to be involved in such an accident), if he touches a piece of cloth that is not maḍi, or if he steps into the public road in front of his house. For this reason, most Brahmins wear silk while in maḍi as it, like wet cotton, does not readily transmit pollution. Silk does not lose maḍi when the person wearing it eats, whereas dry cotton does. Also, a Brahmin wearing silk (or wet cotton maḍi) does not lose his state of ritual purity when touched by another Brahmin in mailigē, or by touching a piece of cloth in the house, or by stepping into the road. However, he does become mailigē if he touches someone of a different caste or someone in his own caste who is muṭṭucheṭṭu, or eats, sleeps, urinates, or defecates. Silk retains its maḍi, without being washed, for one week. *Nāru* cloth, which is made from a plant fiber and is like silk in its resistance to pollution, was sometimes used by Brahmins several generations ago. Even though considerably cheaper than silk, it is no longer available in the market.[4] Also, new, unwashed cotton or silk is maḍi, and does not lose this quality even if touched by a Sudra, although cotton becomes mailigē if touched by an Untouchable. (Silk which has been washed becomes mailigē if touched by a Sudra.) New cotton retains its maḍi for one day's wearing, whereas silk lasts for a week.

If in order to reach a place where he will do puja a man in cotton maḍi needs to go on the road (where he may inadvertently step on such things as spittle or animal droppings), he should carry a vessel of pure water to protect his ritual purity. If he is very orthoprax, he may purify the ground in front of him by sprinkling it with water.

Maḍi, especially while wearing cotton, can be lost in ways other than by touch. If a man in cotton maḍi speaks to a person of another caste, or to a menstruating woman, he becomes mailigē. All but the most orthoprax agree that he can, however, talk to them through a third person. If he is alone he may pick up a stick and talk to it, and thus, speaking in the third person, indirectly converse. There is a great deal of variation concerning this custom, and few people consistently practice it. Traditional-minded Brahmins will say that talking through an inanimate object is not sufficient to prevent the loss of maḍi, while modern-oriented individuals do not hesitate to speak directly to a Sudra while in maḍi, although some draw the line at talking to an Untouchable. One informant stated that if he talked directly to a Sudra, he would retain sufficient maḍi to do *sandhyā vandana* but not to do *dēvaru* puja. However, another aspect of this same complex is more commonly observed. A man in maḍi going to a temple to do a puja and finding a lower-caste man blocking his way may

[4] I do not know if this was due to the lack of supply or lack of demand, but Brahmins tend to connect its use with a past era when the price of their main crop—arecanuts—was depressed.

first clear his throat to get the other person to move aside; if this is not adequate, he may use the third person and say "He is in my way."

Two Brahmins in maḍi may freely touch each other without affecting their state of maḍi, but a Brahmin loses his maḍi if he touches a Brahmin not in maḍi or any non-Brahmin, irrespective of whether the latter is or is not in a state of maḍi—in relation to a Brahmin, a non-Brahmin cannot become maḍi.

A shirt cannot become maḍi and thus a man in maḍi may not wear it, although he may, and on ceremonial occasions commonly does, wear a maḍi towel around his shoulders. After a meal is over, men put their shirts on. The most orthoprax Havik that we knew had never owned a shirt, but this was an extreme case.[5] The Gazeteer of North Kanara (Government of Bombay, 1883) states that Havik Brahmin women never wore blouses, but present-day informants deny this. However, orthoprax Havik women do not now wear a blouse while cooking.

Being in maḍi is a relative concept. A Brahmin who is in a state of mailigē relative to another Brahmin may warn a Sudra away by saying, "Do not touch me. I am in maḍi." Informants sometimes speak of a "good maḍi" to signify a state in which all taboos are rigorously observed, versus ordinary maḍi, about which there may be more casualness. For annual feasts and for life crisis ceremonies, ordinary maḍi is sufficient, but for doing "gods' works" (dēvaru *ḳēlsa*), such as puja to the house gods or in a temple, and, most particularly, for doing a *shrāddha,* "good maḍi" is essential. Before doing dēvaru puja, a man in maḍi will often not allow his children to come near him, but if he is in maḍi at a large feast, he will freely fondle them. There is nothing particularly defiling about children—in fact, they transmit pollution less easily than do adults; but until they reach an age of reason, they are not expected to be rigorous about maintaining taboos and therefore are seldom considered to be in a state of "good maḍi." However, if they are naked, and thus wearing nothing which can carry pollution, they are in a state of such ritual purity that even the most orthoprax priest will not hesitate to be touched by them.

Food and Eating

Customs concerning food—what types, from whom taken, and how consumed—are, to a large part, associated with beliefs concerning ritual pollution.

For Haviks, only vegetarian food is permissible. Although within the general purity-pollution system meats are graded as to their relative amount of pollution (starting with the least defiling: eggs, fish, chicken, goats and sheep, wild pork, domestic pork and finally water buffalo and beef), Havik Brahmins absolutely avoid all of them. In addition, certain strong (*shaḳti*) foods, for example onions and garlic, are felt to be inappropriate to Brahmanical status, as are foods which resemble meat in color—pumpkins, tomatoes, radishes, and carrots. These distinctions tend now to be disregarded by the less orthoprax. The prohibition of alcohol may be only indirectly related to the pollution concepts through the value of self control, but nevertheless is supported by the fact that alcohol is manufactured and traded in only by members of lower castes. However, the ban against Brahmins' taking alcoholic beverages from other castes is not as strictly observed as is that against their accepting food or water. If a Havik clandestinely drinks alcohol (and very few do), it does not

[5] It is significant to note in this context that shirts are a relatively new piece of wearing apparel for Haviks. The term by which they are referred to is of English derivation: *"shurṭu."*

express the ceremonial equality implied when food or water is accepted from a lower-caste individual.

Havik Brahmins do not accept cooked food (*musare*) from members of any other caste. No distinction is made between "pakka" and "kacca" foods as is made in parts of North India. For a Havik to accept water or fried snacks from a lower casteman is as defiling as to accept a rice meal.

Uncooked foods may be received from or handled by members of any caste—it is commonplace to see an Untouchable woman cleaning grain for a Brahmin employer or a Sudra retainer bearing vegetables as a gift to his patron. Cow's milk is ritually pure and cannot be defiled. In theory, a Brahmin can accept a cup of milk from an Untouchable; but Brahmins to whom I posed this problem replied that should the occasion ever arise, they would refuse for fear that the milk had been diluted with water. Fruits and nuts, as long as they are whole, are not subject to ritual defilement, but once a coconut is broken or a plantain cut, a Havik cannot accept it from a member of another caste. However, although arecanuts are boiled and dyed, no distinction is made concerning the source from which they come, although the lime paste eaten with them is subject to pollution.[6]

The process of eating is potentially polluting, but the manner determines the amount of pollution. Saliva—even one's own—is extremely defiling. If a Brahmin inadvertently touches his fingers to his lips, he should bathe or at the least change his clothes. Also, saliva (*enjalu*) pollution can be transmitted through some material substances. These two beliefs have led to the practice of drinking water by pouring it into the mouth instead of putting the lips on the edge of the cup, and of smoking cigarettes or *bīḍis* (tobacco wrapped in a leaf) through the hand so that they never directly touch the lips. (Hookas are virtually unknown in this part of India.)

There are two types of meals: *ūṭa,* the basis of which is boiled rice, translates as "a meal." This is eaten with the right hand, thus conveying saliva to the body and to the plantain leaf from which it is eaten, and from there to all of the food on the leaf. *Tiṇḍi,* somewhat equivalent to "tiffin" in Hindi, consists of fruits, fried foods, sweets, and dishes cooked in water but made from rice flour or grains other than whole rice. The eating of tiṇḍi is not as ritually defiling as is the eating of ūṭa, as tiṇḍi *can* be tossed into the mouth (in practice, it is put into the mouth in much the same fashion as ūṭa, especially if eaten with curds). When a person eats tiṇḍi, he should break the food to size with the hand, never bite it. Biting food, even fruit, is blatently symbolic of conveying saliva pollution to the body, and should be avoided except when eating ūṭa.

Eating of any food—even drinking coffee—should be preceded by washing the hands and feet. This applies even though the individual is already in maḍi. After eating, the hands are washed and the mouth is rinsed.

The main meal of the day—ūṭa, which is served in the late morning or early afternoon—must be cooked and served by someone in maḍi. Before this meal is eaten, one male member of the household does an elaborate religious ceremony (sandhyā vandana and dēvaru puja) while the other male members perform a less elaborate

[6] The growing, processing, and selling of arecanuts is the main occupation of Havik Brahmins. Arecanuts that are too ripe when harvested are sold without being boiled. Haviks state that these go to Bombay, where there are people who consider processed arecanuts to be unacceptable if touched by lower-castemen.

ritual, and for these all performers must be in maḍi. Part of this meal is served as *naivēdya* (food offering) to the house gods. The cook cannot taste the food that is being prepared, as by touching her fingers to her lips she would become mailigē and thus could not continue to cook. Rice is pinched with the fingers to determine whether or not it is done. Cooking is done mainly in brass, copper, or iron pots—Haviks do not generally use clay pottery cooking utensils because of their porosity. Pottery vessels which become muṭṭucheṭṭu can never be purified; metal vessels can. This has its greatest relevance to *uppinakāyi* (mango or lemon pickles)—a spice that accompanies every meal—and which is so corrosive that it can be only kept in crockery jars. Extreme caution is used to insure that uppinakāyi, which is generally made once or twice a year and stored in the smoke room on the second floor above the kitchen, does not not become defiled.

Food, which Haviks always eat from a freshly cut and washed plantain leaf that is never reused, can be eaten only with the right hand. But at a meal, liquid in a cup—generally water—is drunk with the left hand. The server of the food must remain in maḍi, and thus cannot touch those being served nor allow the utensils to touch food already on the leaf. An awkward situation is sometimes created by the conflict of this rule and those customs concerning gracious hospitality. A server attempts to press a superabundance of food upon a person of honorary status—a husband, father or elder brother, elder kinsman, or most particularly, a guest. The satiated beneficiary of this hospitality attempts to defend his leaf from further additions by waving his hands over it, while the server, sometimes with great perseverance, other times with humor, attempts to add food. It is inevitable that contact sometimes takes place between the guest's hand and the server's utensil. A server touched by the person being served (who is mailigē if he has begun to eat), if extremely orthoprax, will take another bath or at least change clothes before serving any more food. However, in most houses an accident of this type is ignored.

In most families the main ūṭa of the day is the only one that has to be prepared by a person in maḍi. The first meal of the day usually consists of tiṇḍi. The evening meal is either a warmed-over version of the main meal, or tiṇḍi. On special fast days only tiṇḍi is served. Meals other than the main ūṭa can be prepared and consumed by persons in mailigē (never by a person in muṭṭucheṭṭu), although in a few very orthoprax families all food will be prepared by a person in maḍi.

After a meal the leaves are removed, generally by the server, and are fed, along with any leftover food on them, to the cattle, and the floor from which the meal has been eaten is then made ritually pure by washing it with a mixture of cow-dung and water.

Pollution is transmitted by sitting in the same line (*pangti*) at a meal, but this is primarily of importance when a member of another caste, usually another type of Brahmin, is fed in a Havik house. The outsider is generally seated in a separate row. This creates an ambiguous situation which host and guest can interpret in either of two ways: the guest is set apart as it is felt that he may not want to be classed as merely equal to his host—in short, he is being shown due respect and honor; or, the host does not wish to sit in the same line with another species of Brahmin, that is, he does not regard his guest as a complete equal. Two other counter-balancing factors enter into this situation; the guest, by accepting food from the host, indicates that he is, at the best, merely of equal rank to his host; on the other hand, the host indicates that he is of equal or inferior ritual status to the guest by removing the latter's leaf. If, however, the guest is asked to remove his own leaf and purify the spot on which he ate, there is no doubt about the host's conception of the relative rank of his own and his guest's caste. If the host's family feels hesitant about removing the leaf but does not wish to make this fact known, a member of the house will remove it and bathe immediately thereafter or, alternatively, a member of a lower caste may be sought to remove the leaf. However, as few Haviks have permanent higher-caste servants, it may be difficult to find someone willing to do this. Untouchable servants are too defiling to be allowed into the dining area and thus cannot perform this task for their employer.

If a Havik is in a state of ritual impurity that prevents his eating in the same line with other Haviks, he often is sufficiently defiling that he should be fed entirely outside of the house and remove his own leaf. One way in which changes in orthopraxy are taking place is that individuals who one generation ago would have been fed outside, for example, those who are patrilineally related to a man whose wife has just borne a child, are now most often fed in the kitchen or dining room, but in a separate line.

The person serving food remains in maḍi until others have finished eating, and then serves herself. If she is alone, she must serve the amount that she will want, as once she has begun eating she should not again touch the cooking vessels. If there are several adult women in the house, they may wait until the men and children have eaten to fill their leaves with food and eat together.

After her husband has finished eating, a wife is expected to eat her meal on the same leaf from which her husband has just finished eating (this forms part of the "respect pollution" complex discussed below). In almost no other context, except that of parent and small child, will one person eat from the leaf used by another.[7] This practice of eating from a husband's leaf is observed by most Havik wives, whether they are in an orthoprax or liberal family, unless they belong to an extended family in which it is the custom for some of the wives to eat at the same time their husbands do. Although in other contexts it is considered poor etiquette to leave food on a leaf, a husband is expected to leave a small amount of food for his wife as a symbol of his affection.

Menstruation

A potent source of muṭṭucheṭṭu is a menstruating woman, who is said to be *"muttu"* (*literally,* "touch") or *"horage"* ("outside"). Menstruating women are highly visible; talk about menstruation and about who is menstruating is commonplace.

A frequently heard joke is that a woman has a vacation for five days out of every month. As soon as a woman begins her menstrual period, she leaves the house and remains "outside." The back and front verandahs (*jagali*) are considered to be "outside." Muṭṭucheṭṭu derived from a menstruating woman is more defiling than that from an Untouchable. For five days (measured as four nights) the muṭṭu woman does not change her clothes, comb her hair or wear *ḳumḳuma* (a red spot considered

[7] Village Untouchables delight in pointing out their superiority vis-à-vis a (mythical?) caste which they call "Enjalu Holerus" (literally, "Saliva Untouchables"), who are reputed to eat the food left on the leaves of other castes.

a mark of beauty) on her forehead, and for two to three days she does not bathe. During this time she may not enter the house or a temple, draw water from a well, nor come near any supernatural (such as stones in the backyard in which various supernaturals are believed to live). After the third night "outside," the woman regains partial ritual status by taking her first bath since she became muṭṭu, but only after the bath following her fourth night outside does she regain full ritual status. A muṭṭu woman is given a blanket, a cup, and a vessel for water which she must ritually purify at the end of her four days of separation. While menstruating she is fed on the back verandah, removes her own leaf, and with cow-dung purifies her own eating place.

Should even a child accidentally touch a menstruating woman or any of the objects set apart for her exclusive use, and then touch the house god, it is believed that large red ants will come into the house. This is the god's way of stating that it has been made impure and needs to be purified (made *shuddha*).

A woman in her period often spends a good deal of time chatting and gossiping with other women—women who may or may not also be in their periods. She is free to visit other houses, but of course remains in the designated "outside" area. When visiting and talking, it is customary to sit on a blanket or grass mat, but a menstruating woman is not offered this—it would become muṭṭucheṭṭu were she to touch it.

There are certain types of housework that she can do. She may sweep or clean with cow-dung any of the "outside" area around the house. She can clean rice or other grains in a bamboo basket, and bring vegetables from the garden but not cut them. She may go to the garden to bring plantain leaves from which food will be eaten. She may make cups from plantain leaves, which are used to serve liquids at large feasts, and she may make *koṭṭes,* sheaths made from the arecanut fronds and used to cover the young arecanut bunches during the monsoon season. These plant materials are non-conductors of pollution. She may tie or untie the cows and water buffalo when they are sent from the cattle shed in the morning or returned in the evening. Nearly all of these jobs can also be performed for Brahmins by Untouchables.

The milking of the cows and water buffalo (at least one of each is owned by most Havik families) is generally done by women. Ordinarily a woman discontinues this job during her menstrual period, but if no one else is available, or if a beast will give milk only for her, she may milk. In this case, she will milk into a *completely* dry metal vessel which becomes muṭṭucheṭṭu because of her touch. Should a drop of water be in the vessel, the milk also would be made ritually impure. After the milk has been collected, it is then poured from a distance into a vessel which she has not touched, and removed by other members of the family. Milking for a Havik can in theory also be done by Untouchables, but as one informant explained, he would not allow this for fear that the Untouchable, who would "probably never have seen that much milk in his life," would feel envy and thus might make the cow's milk supply dry up by casting the evil eye (*drishṭi*).[8]

The relationship of a menstruating woman and her children—which undoubtedly has implications concerning the psychological development of a child—is eased by the fact that a naked child cannot be ritually defiled nor cause other people to become so;

---

[8] Untouchables, with a few recent exceptions, do not own cows, bullocks, or water buffaloes.

it is the cloth which transmits the pollution. A child under about six months, who is not receiving food to supplement its mother's milk, stays entirely with its mother. The clothing and blankets of both are muṭṭucheṭṭu and are ritually purified by the mother when she bathes at the end of her menstrual cycle. From about six months until the child is two or three years old, it is freely transferred, while naked, from the mother to other members of the family. In this case the child is undressed by one party and left to be picked up by the other party. The clothing worn by the child while with its mother is ritually defiled, but that worn while the child is under the care of other members of the household is not. After a child reaches two to three years of age, it is felt to be old enough to avoid completely its mother during her period, although exceptions are made for special circumstances.

A woman's menstrual vacation compounds work for other members of the family. If there is another woman in the house, most of the work is likely to fall upon her shoulders unless the periods of both women coincide. In many Havik houses, a woman's menstrual period forces her husband reluctantly to play the female role—to clean the rice, cook and serve the meals, care for the children, draw water for cooking and bathing, and tend the livestock. Alternatively, some of the members of the house may eat with neighbors or kinsmen—the menstruating woman being fed "outside" by a neighbor, while other members of her house visit kinsmen, in or away from the village. A more common practice, especially for a small family, is to invite a kinswoman, often the husband's married sister, to visit and run the house while the wife is menstruating. Thus rules concerning menstruation reinforce the already existing patterns of extensive visiting.

After a woman has spent three nights "outside," she is in too great a state of muṭṭucheṭṭu to use the family bathing facilities, and bathes in either the village tank (*ḳere*), an artificial lake found in all Malnad villages and used to irrigate the arecanut garden, or in a deep water hole (*honḍa*) in the irrigation canals inside of the arecanut gardens. During this bath, she must wash her menstrual cloth as well as the cloth that she wore over her genitals during the preceding month. Havik women wear this cloth at all times, to insure that any irregular vaginal discharge does not ritually defile the house. (On this point in particular, non-Brahmins ridicule Haviks as being overly concerned about pollution.) These cloths are purified with cow-dung. After a girl's first menses her menstrual cloth is buried, as it is believed that should a cobra smell it, the girl would be cursed with barrenness.[9] She also uses cow-dung to wash her clothes, blanket, vessels, and body. Glass bangles and beads, and gold and silver jewelry do not become muṭṭucheṭṭu. The *taḷi,* a gold piece worn around the neck which symbolizes marriage, is tied by a string made from a kind of leaf fiber which does not conduct pollution. If cotton string should for any reason be substituted, a new one must be put on after bathing.

After this first bath the woman returns home in a wet sari, with her washed blanket and vessels.[10] The woman does not at this time regain the status of full ritual cleanliness—she is mailigē but cannot become maḍi. For one more day she may not cook for others (except small children), draw water that is used for puja or for cook-

[9] If a woman's barrenness is attributed to this cause, she can make a pilgrimage to a major temple, usually Gokarna, and undergo a purificatory ceremony to remove the curse.

[10] Often, especially in cold weather, she bathes again at home—this time in warm water. This is a luxury bath which has nothing to do with attaining ritual purity.

ing (unless she is only cooking for herself), nor perform any religious activities. After the bath on the morning following four nights "outside," she regains full ritual purity.

Menstrual taboos, which help to legitimate the social inferiority of women, are rigorously observed by all Haviks—in this area of behavior distinctions between families of greater and lesser orthopraxy are small. However, in less orthoprax families, especially those containing only one adult female, a woman will cook for the family after her first bath. Also, in very modern families, a menstruating woman may take her first bath at home rather than going to the village tank or garden honḍa.

Adults invariably avoid all contact with a menstruating woman as well as objects with which she has had contact. Both of the adult Brahmin males with whom I discussed the subject said that since they had gotten their sacred thread, they had never become muṭṭucheṭṭu from contact with a menstruating woman, although they frequently became so from Untouchables.

To remove muṭṭucheṭṭu resulting from contact with a woman in her monthly period, it is necessary to bathe, change clothes, and eat panchagavya. If the defiled person is a male who has undergone his *upanayana* (sacred thread) ceremony, he must also change his sacred thread. This purificatory ceremony causes a good deal of trouble. The panchagavya—made from five sacred products of the cow (dung, urine, milk, curds, and ghee)—generally has to be made fresh by another member of the family. Except for cow-dung and milk, these products are not easily obtainable. The major milk supply of Haviks comes from water buffalo, and it may be difficult to find curds or ghee made from cow's milk. But the real problem is to obtain cow's urine—as one Havik explained, "They tend to pass urine at odd hours of the day." In addition, a *bhaṭṭru* (priest), or at least a learned man, should be obtained to do a puja to the new sacred thread before it is worn.

Pollution gradually loses its force as it is transmitted from one person to another. If a person who is muṭṭucheṭṭu from contact with a menstruating woman touches another Havik, the second need only bathe and change his clothes. If this pollution is transferred to a third person, he need only change his clothes, whereas contact by this person with a fourth results in no special defilement.

Death Pollution—Sūtaka

Sūtaka is the state of ritual impurity that results from a death. Not only is the body of the deceased impure, but so are his kinsmen—sūtaka pollution is transmitted by genealogical linkage, especially through the patriline.

I shall first describe sūtaka observances among agnatically related kinsmen, and then among affines. When discussing agnates, it must be noted that before marriage a woman is regarded, for purposes of sūtaka observances, as a member of her father's descent group, but after marriage she observes sūtaka practices appropriate to her husband's descent group, while her natal kinsmen regard her as an affine.

There are two kinds of sūtaka, varying according to the closeness of the kinship tie between the living and the deceased. *Guru* (heavy) sūtaka is observed by the members of a *manetana* for the death of any of their members. A manetana is composed of a group of adult brothers of whom one or more are living, and their descendants, all of whom ideally should form a single household. *Laghu,* or light sūtaka, is the ritual impurity that results from the death of certain more distantly related kinsmen. Any person in a state of sūtaka is ritually impure, but those who have guru sūtaka are treated similarly to an Untouchable, while the restrictions upon those with laghu sūtaka are less severe.

The greatest amount of ritual pollution falls upon the *kartṛi,* the performer of a deceased's rites, and lasts until the twelfth day *sapiṇḍi* ceremony is completed. The favorite person to be kartṛi is the deceased's eldest living son; but in the event that no son is available, the ceremony may be performed by a father, brother, husband, wife, or mother. Other sons, if living in the same house as the kartṛi, observe twelve nights of sūtaka; but if they are living in separate households, they observe eleven nights, as do certain more distantly related kinsmen.

Those who observe laghu sūtaka are fed "outside," and only their wives and unmarried daughters or sisters may remove their leaves or wash their cups. Contact with a person in guru sūtaka causes another Havik to become muṭṭucheṭṭu, a state of ritual impurity which can be removed only by bathing and changing clothes. A person in sūtaka is too ritually defiled to worship any supernaturals or to participate in any auspicious ceremonies.

As those who are in guru sūtaka defile that which they touch, it is customary to ask a neighbor who does not have sūtaka to enter a death house through the back door (he would see the body if he came through the front door, and become too ritually impure by this sight to perform the task for which he had been asked) and sort over the clothes, bedding, and vessels which will be needed by the family for the duration of the sūtaka period, and put the remainder away so that these will not be touched by members of the house. Also, this person shuts the door to the gods' room to keep them from being defiled by the sight of impure Brahmins. This neighbor, or anyone else who enters the house in which the death has occurred, must bathe upon returning home.

Guru sūtaka lasts for either eleven or twelve days, after which it is removed in a *prāyaschitta* (expiation) ceremony with the participation of a *purohita* (family priest), and by bathing, eating panchagavya, and, for males, by changing their sacred threads. Also, the house gods must be purified by the priest who bathes them in *panchāmrita,* a mixture of cow's milk, curds, ghee, sugar, and honey. Finally, a member of the Maḍivaḷa caste (Washerman, i.e., "one who makes clothes pure") washes all of the clothes, blankets, sheets, or other cloth that may have been touched by members of the death house.

By virtue of contiguity, the restrictions of guru sūtaka apply to all members of a household which contains one guru sūtaka individual. Those who help bear the corpse to the funeral pyre are generally sufficiently closely related to the deceased that they need to observe sūtaka purely on the basis of kinship, but in the event that a nonkinsman participates, he would observe three days of ordinary sūtaka.

Laghu sūtaka applies to a very wide range of agnatic kinsmen (*dāyādru*) and lineage segmentation is ordered through rules concerning variations in sūtaka observances. All individuals who are related (*sambandha*) through agnatic ancestors up to the seventh ascending generation are known as "eleven day dāyādru," and observe eleven days (or ten nights) of sūtaka for the death of any member of this group. The next lineage segmentation, known as "three day dāyādru," is composed of all who are related up to fourteen "heads" (*tale*), that is, those who are descended from a common ancestor more than seven generations back but less than fifteen. The next group of dāyādru, those from the fourteenth through the twenty-first generations, is subdivided into two categories: "one and a half day dāyādru" (fifteenth through eighteenth generation) and "bath (snāna) dāyādru" (nineteenth through twenty-first generations), for which, respectively, one and a half days of sūtaka need be observed, or only a bath need be taken upon receiving news of a death of a member of this group.

Thus, all individuals related through the patriline from an ancestor twenty-one generations in an ascending line are dāyādru and are closely enough related for death pollution to be transmitted agnatically. From the twenty-second generation onward, these individuals are merely *sāgotra* (of the same clan—Havik Brahmins are divided into seven exogamous patriclans called *gōtras;* all dāyādru belong to the same gōtra, but most members of a gōtra are not dāyādru). The number of generations by which two patrilineally related families are removed is measured by the relationship of the eldest male members of each family rather than exact genealogical linkage, i.e., a father never observes eleven days of sūtaka and his son three days for the death of the same kinsman.

No one not in sūtaka can accept food from someone in sūtaka, and a person in sūtaka who eats in a house of someone not in sūtaka is fed outside and removes his own leaf. Should a member of a lower caste ask for food or water from a Havik who has sūtaka, he should be informed and ordinarily will then withdraw his request.

A family in sūtaka, even of a minor degree, cannot perform any pujas (to do so would cause the deity being worshipped to become muṭṭucheṭṭu), or annual life-crisis ceremonies. If sūtaka occurs during most annual ceremonies, they are simply missed. However, a few ceremonies of major importance—worshipping Gaṇapti (Gaṇēsha) or the annual ceremony when all Brahmin males change their sacred thread—are performed after the period of sūtaka is ended. Shrāddhas also must be postponed. If sūtaka occurs at a time when a boy's haircutting ceremony (*chaula*) or upanayana is scheduled, the ceremony is postponed. If guru sūtaka occurs after arrangements for a marriage have been made, and any time before the actual ceremony has been completed, the proposed alliance is permanently broken off, and another marriage to another spouse cannot take place in less than one year after the end of the sūtaka period. For laghu sūtaka, a proposed marriage alliance is always at least postponed, and often permanently cancelled. This is one of the reasons that helps account for the amazing rapidity with which a marriage takes place after an agreement has been reached. Major festivals to village gods are generally not postponed for sūtaka, but there is considerable village variation on this point. In one village, the *Ārdremale habba* and the annual festival for the second most important village-guardian deity (Gāma) are not performed if any family is in sūtaka. This is explained by saying that all families in the village must give the deity an offering (*haṇṇu-ḳāyi*—that is, plantain and coconut), and this can be accomplished only if all families are in a state of ritual purity.

Sūtaka observances are considered to cause great inconvenience—they occur at unexpected times, cause ceremonies to be omitted or postponed, put one in a state of ritual defilement relative to other Haviks, and in many ways interrupt the normal daily routine. This is particularly true considering the large number of dāyādru in the various groupings.

Sūtaka is measured from the time of death, not from the time when the news of death is first received. If an individual hears of the death of an eleven-day dāyādru more than eleven days after it has occurred, he is ritually impure only until he undergoes the purificatory ceremony appropriate to removing either guru or laghu sūtaka. If guru sūtaka occurs while an individual is observing laghu sūtaka, he must observe eleven additional days of sūtaka from the time of the second death. But a sūtaka period is not necessarily compounded by multiple deaths; for example, if a laghu sūtaka-causing kinsman dies while an individual is observing either guru or laghu sūtaka, but before the ninth day of the sūtaka period has arrived, no extra sūtaka is observed; if the death occurs on the ninth or later day of the first sūtaka period, three additional days of sūtaka must be observed for the second death, extending the total period to twelve days or more.

For the death of a child, a lesser amount of sūtaka is observed by a smaller group of kinsmen. If a pregnant woman miscarries in her fourth month or earlier, the event is treated as an ordinary menstrual cycle. If she aborts in the fifth month, the parents only observe five days of *āme* (birth pollution—see below). For an abortion that occurs in the sixth ("when life enters the child") or a later month of pregnancy, or for the death of a child during the first eleven days after its birth, the event is treated as birth pollution or *āme,* not death pollution, or sūtaka, but applies for the full eleven days. Should a male child die after his mother's eleventh day purificatory ceremony which removed the birth pollution but at less than two and a half years of age, the time at which a boy has a right to a chaula ceremony, or a female child after her mother's eleventh day ceremony, but at less than five years, an age set to be "prescribed by the *dharma shāstras,*" the parents alone observe eleven days of sūtaka. For the death of a boy over two and a half but less than eight years, the age at which he may have his thread ceremony performed, or of a girl over five but not yet married, a three day sūtaka period is observed by the deceased's brothers and unmarried sisters and the deceased's father's brothers and their children, while the parents observe the full eleven days. After a girl is married (traditionally shortly before puberty) and a boy has reached his eighth birthday, they are, for purposes of sūtaka, treated as adults —it makes no difference whether the boy has actually had his chaula or upanayana ceremony; the important point is that at these ages he is entitled to have them.

An adopted son (girls are never adopted) observes sūtaka for his adopting parents as if he were born by them, and in addition he observes three days of sūtaka for the death of his biological parents, and they for him.

In theory, with the advent of each new generation, the last ascending generation in each category of dāyādru moves into the next group; that is, those who are related through a common ancestor seven generations removed, and for whom eleven days of sūtaka are observed, become eighth generation dāyādru, for whom three days of sūtaka are observed. According to Haviks, for most other kinds of South Indian Brahmins, each family group itself determines when to change the amount of sūtaka for other family groups. For Haviks, however, it is not so simple.

In order to reduce the number of days of sūtaka observed for kinsmen who have moved into a new category, it is necessary for one male representative of each family in the eleven-day dāyādru group to go to the caste guru and present their case. By Havik standards of solidarity, this undertaking requires heroic cooperation among these kinsmen. The guru charges a fee for this service, ranging from one hundred to five hundred rupees, depending upon the number of families involved and their wealth. One man has to organize and coordinate the expedition; one recalcitrant individual, by either refusing to accompany the party or to pay his share of the fee, can effectively block the proceedings.

In addition, the guru demands proof of the exact genealogy of the families involved. I have been told of several instances in which the guru refused permission because of lack of convincing documentation. A genealogical tree (*vamsha vṛiksha*) of each Havik family is supposedly kept in the *maṭha,* but these records are now in such a state of chaos as to be unusable (there are over two hundred thousand Haviks). Purohitas do not keep genealogies, and Haviks do not employ professional genealogists. It is up to individual families to keep records of their own family trees, and although I have heard of families that have such records, I have never seen them. For the most part, the best evidence that can be assembled is derived from the memories of elders, and the depth of genealogical memory is very short; even in the patriline many elder men can name only their first three ascending generation male ancestors—those whose names they call out at the annual shrāddha ceremony. Despite these difficulties, I have talked to a number of Haviks who have, in their time or their father's time, successfully reduced the sūtaka period for certain kinsmen. In this case, part of the eleven-day dāyādru group becomes, from ego's standpoint, part of his three-day dāyādru. Ego's three-day dāyādru themselves form a corporate eleven-day dāyādru group, which must itself segment before some of its members can fall into ego's one-and-a-half-day dāyādru group, and so on.

What generally happens is that any one man knows the other families for which his father observed sūtaka, and continues to observe the same amount of sūtaka for them as did his father, preferring to complain than to negotiate with his kinsmen and the guru.

Given this arrangement, with any progressive increase in population, any one individual should have a larger number of three-day dāyādru than eleven-day dāyādru, and so on. This is not the case. When asked to name the members of his eleven-day dāyādru group, a man will typically list the heads of from three to twenty families, generally scattered in a number of villages, but will name only a half or a third as many three-day dāyādru, and he will often state that he has no, or only a very few, one-and-a-half-day or bath dāyādru. There appears to have been a continual process of sloughing off of distant kin ties by convenient lapses in memory. Even if family records were kept, it would be difficult to maintain adequate genealogical accounting over twenty-one generations, a time span of at least five hundred years. Given the tools with which they have to work, the more orthoprax Havik Brahmins do an adequate job of maintaining sūtaka relationships for their more distant dāyādru. It seems likely that many families in fact maintain eleven days of sūtaka for the death of the majority of their patrikin who are related up to the eighth or tenth or more ascending generation. That some kinsmen may be overlooked can in part be explained by the fact that Haviks freely change village affiliation when they obtain new lands, by purchase, marriage, or litigation.

Like many other types of orthopraxy, sūtaka observances are decreasing in importance. The majority of Haviks make a stoic attempt to observe the proper amount of sūtaka for the appropriate individuals, but among the younger males, an increasing number are becoming lax. One middle-aged man stated, "When I was a boy, sūtaka was strictly observed. People suffered from sūtaka. We were treated by other members of the caste (*"samāja,"* literally, "society") as Holerus (Untouchables). Nowadays, except for stopping the daily worship to the house gods (*mane* dēvaru) and stopping the performance of ceremonies, sūtaka is not observed in a strict sense. Possibly my son, who has very little regard for the customs (*paddhati*), will completely drop these observances after my death."

For a Havik to regroup his dāyādru kinsmen without the approval of the caste guru is punished, in theory, by excommunication. However, there are no cases in my informants' memories in which action has been taken over this issue, although some have recounted instances of extremely modern individuals who have ignored nearly all sūtaka observances.

Upon marriage, a Havik woman is transferred from one agnatic descent group (dāyādru) and clan (gōtra) to another. When she dies, her husband's manetana observe the same amount of sūtaka for her as they do for the death of her husband, although I am not sure whether this applies to her husband's more distant dāyādru.

When a married woman dies, some of her original agnates have up to three days of sūtaka because, it is said, she still retains some rights in her natal agnatic descent group, mainly, the right to maintenance should she be widowed and choose not to live with her husband's agnates. Precisely which of these kinsmen observe sūtaka and in what amounts, is a subject about which my informants had varying views. I shall present only the information on which there was a fair degree of consistency, but I am not sure of even these limited data.[11]

A married woman has three days of sūtaka for the deaths of her parents, parents' brothers, and their spouses (except that when her father's brother predeceases his wife, she has one and a half days of sūtaka for this widow's death), father's sisters, brothers and their children, and her unmarried sisters. These individuals also observe three days for her death. A husband observes three days of sūtaka for his wife's parents, who may also be his mother's brother and wife in the event he has made a matrilateral cross-cousin marriage (Haviks prohibit patrilateral cross-cousin marriages). However, for some of his affines through his wife, a man does not have as much sūtaka as does his wife, on which occasion he may have to cook for his wife and serve her separately. A man continues to do dēvaru puja if his wife, but not he, has sūtaka. When a wife but not her husband has sūtaka, her children do not have sūtaka.

A man observes sūtaka for his mother's brothers, mother's brothers' sons and unmarried daughters (a bath if the daughters are married), and for his father's sisters

---

[11] Most of my informants seemed as perplexed as I about sūtaka observances among nonagnatic kinsmen. To quote one: "It is a vast subject, and actually nobody, including the bhaṭṭrus know it correctly according to the shāstras." He went on to demonstrate this by telling the following anecdote: "Two years back on the day when Havik males ceremonially change their sacred thread, after I had bathed and performed sandhyā vandana and dēvaru puja and was ready to change my thread, I received the news that my mother's elder sister's son had died the previous day. Nobody was able to tell me if I had three or one-and-a-half days of sūtaka. If it were to be three days I should not change my thread, but if it was one-and-a-half days I would complete the sūtaka in time to attend the ceremony. The village bhaṭṭru said three days, but as I was not convinced I asked the Gokarna bhaṭṭru who was visiting in the village, but he was unable to give me a satisfactory answer. Then the matter was referred to another bhaṭṭru who is well versed in the shāstras who said the deceased was fourth head to me, and besides it was a mother's relation and should be treated as a distant relative. I asked him how it was four heads and he said that my mother was first, her sister second, and because she has married into another gōtra her son was fourth. Therefore the sūtaka did not interfere with my changing my thread, but it was very late in the evening before I could complete the ceremony because of having waited so long for a final decision."

and their children, except for a married woman in this class, but observes no sūtaka for his mother's married sisters and their children. For his father's mother, who is a dāyādru, he observes eleven days; for his father's mother's brother, three days, and for his father's mother's married sister's death, he has no sūtaka. A male also has three days of sūtaka for his married sisters and their children, and for his brother's married daughters (for the deaths of his brother's unmarried daughter, married daughter's sons, and his son's married daughters, he has three days of sūtaka). Thus sūtaka observances tend to decrease in proportion to the number of affinal links through which the relationship is traced.

There are two classes of individuals for whose death no sūtaka is observed. The Havik caste guru (spiritual and political leader of the caste) generally has a dozen or so *shishya,* unmarried Havik boys who are his disciples and from whose ranks the guru will choose his successor. These individuals are usually taken as understudies while in their early teens. To become a shishya, a boy must renounce the material world by vowing not to desire material goods and to break all emotional bonds with his kinsmen. For the death of a shishya, no sūtaka applies to his parents or other dāyādru. In the other example, kin ties are also broken. Should a Havik be outcaste by the guru, the individual's death rites are symbolically performed as part of the outcasting ceremony. Sūtaka is not observed for this symbolic death, and from that time onwards, the outcaste individual has no kinsmen, thus no one to observe sūtaka for his or her actual death. Outcasting is permanent. When the excommunicated person dies, no Havik may help to dispose of the body.

In the event of a death caused by smallpox, cholera, plague, or suicide, forty-eight days of sūtaka are said to be observed by those who have guru sūtaka.

There is one instance in which sūtaka may result without the death of a Havik. If a Brahmin sees a dead cobra, a sacred animal, he may, in order to earn *puṇya* (merit), and to demonstrate his piety, call in a purohita to give it a shrāddha ceremony. In this case he observes three days of sūtaka for the cobra's death.

Birth Pollution—Āme

Āme, the pollution that results from a birth, is in many ways like sūtaka. Occasionally the term sūtaka is used for āme, but this is more characteristic of lower castes than of Havik Brahmins. As one Brahmin informant explained, both sūtaka and āme are forms of muṭṭucheṭṭu, but āme is "happy" pollution, while sūtaka is "unhappy" pollution. Āme is transmitted through kinship like sūtaka but involves a smaller group of kinsmen. A woman's parents have three days of āme because of kinship, but if their daughter gives birth in their house, as is often the case since it is customary for a woman to return to her natal house for delivery, especially her first, they have eleven days. The brothers of a man who becomes a father have no āme because of kinship, but if they all live in a joint family and the father's wife gives birth in the joint family's house, all brothers have eleven days, based upon the principle of pollution to the house. As with sūtaka, an individual or family in a state of āme cannot perform any ceremonies nor conduct religious rites, including daily sandhyā vandana and dēvaru puja.

A woman must give birth "outside" of the house—in essentially the same areas into which she is permitted while menstruating, except that the birth cannot take place in the cattle shed where cows might be defiled. Usually a part of the verandah is screened off for the event. About ten to fifteen percent of Brahmin women now go to the Government hospital in Sagar for delivery.

There is no midwife caste, but a woman of the Maḍivaḷa (Washerman) caste often helps a Havik mother with her delivery; alternatively, a Havik woman, preferably a widow, or an experienced woman of one of the higher Sudra castes acts as midwife. The clothing that the woman wears during delivery and cloths that are used for the birth are washed with cow-dung by the Maḍivaḷa, and then buried. For the first eleven days, the new mother is in a state of ritual pollution greater than that of a menstruating woman. During these eleven days, except on the seventh and ninth, the mother and child are given a bath, generally by a Maḍivaḷa woman, although a Havik woman may do this. However, if a Havik woman assists in the delivery or in bathing the mother and child, she must afterwards bathe, pouring water through cow-dung held in her hand, and drink cow's urine as *tīrtha* (sacred liquid) in order to remove her ritual impurity. On the eleventh day (after "ten nights"), there is a small ceremony in which the mother bathes herself and the child; also, they both consume panchagavya. To remove āme the husband also takes panchagavya and changes his sacred thread. As part of this purification, the Maḍivaḷa washes all of the clothes and other cloths that have been used or touched by members of the āme house. For these services the Maḍivaḷa woman is given a blouse piece and a coconut as an "honorarium" (*maryāde*) as well as payment in rice and cash. If a Havik woman assists in the delivery or in bathing the mother and child she may not accept payment. This is but one of several examples of work that a Brahmin may perform as a friendly gesture for other Haviks, but for which to accept payment is tantamount to following a ritually impure occupation, the penalty for which is caste excommunication.

The eleventh day ceremony does not completely purify a new mother: she is mailigē, no longer muṭṭucheṭṭu, but cannot become maḍi. She can neither cook nor do puja. At the end of three months, she should undergo a second purificatory ceremony, after which she can obtain maḍi. Actually, the full three-month period is seldom observed—the ceremony may be held in as little as sixteen days after the eleven-day āme is removed. The exact length of time between the two ceremonies depends upon the orthopraxy of the family, the number of other women present in the house to do the housework, and the new mother's state of health. Between these two purificatory ceremonies, no life crisis ceremonies can be held in the woman's parents' or husband's house.

A husband is strongly polluted by āme for eleven days (ten nights) after his wife's parturition, during which time he was said to be "like an Untouchable," or, "like a menstruating woman." Even though his wife is often not present (she may be in her parents' house), a husband lives and is fed "outside" of his own house, removes his own leaf, and purifies with cow-dung his eating place. He causes any other Havik who touches him to become muṭṭucheṭṭu. Āme pollution is strongest for the mother, next for the husband, and then for other members of the house. In the present day village scene, only the mother and father can communicate muṭṭucheṭṭu—the other dāyādru remain in a state of mailigē for the āme period.

Āme observances are rapidly decreasing in importance, and, for all but the most orthoprax Haviks, tend to be overlooked in other than religious and ceremonial situations. One male informant, preparing to perform his son's chaula, expressed his modernism by saying that he would not object to the attendance of a neighbor who was in a state of āme, but added that if he were in āme himself he would avoid such a function for fear of being humiliated by having an elder person or a widow[12] ask him why he had come, or request that he eat separately and clean his own place.

Āme also applies to cows and buffaloes. For the first eleven days after a cow calves, its milk cannot be used in puja. Very orthoprax Brahmins will not drink the milk of a water buffalo for the first eleven days after it calves, though they will that of a cow. On the eleventh day, a special type of curds is made from the milk of a cow or buffalo and given as an offering to Mariamma, the village smallpox deity (buffalo milk would never be offered to a god, or dēvaru). A cow who is in a state of āme can transmit pollution only to a god. A Brahmin will retain his maḍi if he touches a cow with āme but lose it if he touches a buffalo in āme. This reflects the rank order in the scale of purity: an āme cow is sufficiently pure relative to a Brahmin that it cannot cause him to lose his most ritually pure state, but gods are sufficiently pure that they are ritually defiled by milk from a cow that is not in its purest possible state. Deities (*dēvates*) are lower in the purity scale than gods, and like Brahmins can partake of a milk product from a pure buffalo, but again, like orthoprax Brahmins, are ritually defiled by milk products from an impure buffalo.

Other Types of Pollution Among Haviḳs

Besides lower-caste persons, saliva, menstrual and birth fluids, and a corpse, there are other sources of ritual defilement. All bodily emissions, even blood or pus from a wound, are sources of impurity. Urine should not splash on an individual; thus there is a prohibition against a male's urinating while standing (the squatting posture is also reinforced by the taboo against exposing one's genitals, even to someone of the same sex; a male by wearing a panche and squatting is able to maintain his privacy). Water, the most common purificatory agent, is used to wash oneself after defecating (the European custom of using paper causes the actor to be in a state of strong impurity), and this act is done only with the left hand; thus, it is said, food may be eaten only with the right hand. After defecating but before washing—for example, while walking from the forest to a source of water—an individual is in a state of muṭṭucheṭṭu.

To step on the feces of a dog, goat, sheep, or chicken causes a Brahmin to become muṭṭucheṭṭu. For this reason Brahmins try to accomplish any business necessitating their presence in the hamlets of nonvegetarian castes who keep these domestic animals in the morning before their daily bath; otherwise they may have to bathe again.

Although the feces of all animals except cows cause defilement to Haviks, crow droppings are particularly defiling—a Brahmin made muṭṭucheṭṭu this way must take a thousand and one baths, which he accomplishes by pouring water over himself through a sieve—the water coming through each hole counts as a separate bath.

Contact with most forms of leather creates impurity; although leather sandals are often worn, they should not be touched with the hands, and the wearer, before entering a temple or a house, removes them and washes his feet.

The worst way that one person can insult another is to defile him ritually by

---

[12] Widows in particular tend to be virtuously orthoprax.

spitting on him or "by beating him with sandals" (the sandals need merely touch the other person). These expressions of aggression are used only with extreme provocation and cause both parties to be in a state of severe impurity: the person who used the sandal because he picked it up in his hand, and the person who spit because it is assumed that if he was close enough to do this act, some of the saliva rebounded onto him. Both parties have to undergo a rigorous purification ceremony. To defile another in these ways is a crime punishable by law.

Sexual relations with a spouse or someone of the same caste cause a person to be in a state of strong mailigē, and a bath should be taken immediately afterwards, or, upon rising in the morning. Most Brahmins do not observe this custom, but instead remove their impurity only when they take their daily bath.

A Brahmin girl who has reached puberty but has not consummated her marriage cannot become sufficiently pure to cook for others. Traditionally Brahmin girls were married before puberty,[13] and the marriage was consummated fifteen days after she reached puberty, but in recent years Government legislation has substantially decreased the number of prepuberty marriages. Also, a widow who has not shaved her head cannot become maḍi and therefore cannot attend ceremonies nor cook for others. Both of these rules encourage individuals and families into conforming to customary behavior.

Shaving and the cutting of hair and nails, when performed by a Barber, cause muṭṭucheṭṭu. Afterwards, the place where the work was done is purified with cowdung, and the individual must immediately bathe, pouring water over a piece of cowdung contained in his hand. For the past thirty to forty years, some Brahmins have been shaving themselves. It is said that about forty years ago the caste guru attempted to outcaste a Havik who defied caste custom by shaving himself, but, so the story goes, the guru's learned advisors discovered passages in the shāstras which convinced him that a Brahmin could perform this task for himself (but not for another) without incurring severe pollution.

After a solar or lunar eclipse, a time of inauspiciousness that causes everyone to become impure, a Brahmin should bathe. Although one informant said that only about fifty percent of the Haviks observe this custom, my own observations indicate a higher percentage.

Many occupations, if performed in the employ of others, are prohibited to Haviks. These center primarily around acts which cause ritual pollution, such as barbering, washing clothes, midwifery, sweeping a public road, or any occupation connected with death, such as working with leather, disposing of dead cattle, or plowing. Older informants report that during their youth these crimes were punishable by outcasting, but the sanctions against breaches are now attenuated. Some jobs that formerly were performed exclusively by Untouchables no longer are: removing dead cattle; cleaning a Brahmin's cattle sheds; cleaning the drainage ditch between houses that carries away bath water and into which children urinate and adults spit betel juice; cutting firewood for a funeral pyre; and sweeping the public road in front of a Brahmin's house (for an analysis of these changes, see Harper, *in press*). In many instances, Brahmins now do these jobs for themselves, but never for others for pay.

[13] To give a gift to a Brahmin is regarded as a meritorious act, and the greatest gift that can be given is a virgin (in marriage). However, that which is given should be pure and unblemished, and a girl who has begun her menstrual periods is not.

Plowing, which inadvertently takes the life of insects in the soil, is sometimes done by poorer Brahmins who cannot afford the luxury of complete orthopraxy. Middle-aged Brahmins remember that when the first Havik plowed his own land—like the man who shaved himself—there was an unsuccessful attempt to outcaste him. Since this "test case," an increasing number of Brahmins have taken to tilling their own fields, but I doubt if even now this involves as much as five percent of the community.

Outcasting

Haviks state that a person can be excommunicated from caste only if he has attained such a severe state of ritual impurity as to prevent his regaining normal ritual status through any purificatory means. Since impurity is transmitted by kinship, the individual's dāyādru cannot attain a state of ritual purity either as long as their defiled patrikinsman is socially "alive." However, it is more realistic to view outcasting as the result of violations of key customs upon which ritual status of the Havik Brahmin caste is claimed, and which are translated into the idiom of ritual impurity.

When Brahmins talk about behavior for which a member of their caste may be excommunicated, they customarily mention only a few acts. For example, for a male to take food from or have sexual relations with an Untouchable leads to permanent outcasting; with a Sudra, to temporary boycotting (*bahiskāra*). Informants do not, however, volunteer that outcasting may result from marrying a member of another caste, from eating meat, or from a Havik woman's having sexual relations with a lower-caste male. However, if directly queried, they readily state that these acts are all punished by outcasting. Apparently the former are regarded as temptations which need to be explicitly condemned, whereas the latter are felt to be almost outside of the range of possibilities.

Actually, outcasting for fornicating or eating with members of lower castes takes place with extreme rarity for several reasons: eating with a member of a lower caste is seldom done; fornication with a person of lower caste almost invariably involves a Havik male rather than a female, a crime of less consequence; direct action concerning such crimes is taken only if they become public knowledge, and then only if there is indisputable proof, for an accusation without constitutes slander and is likely to cause the accuser more trouble than the accused; the most strongly injured individuals are the violator's patrikinsmen who share in his pollution, but who nevertheless have allegiance based upon this kinship tie; and, finally, some individuals believe it to be better to overlook an incident than to make it a public matter, thus casting reflection upon the Havik caste as a whole. Although I have heard several rumors of Haviks in distant places or in the remote past being outcasted for these acts, I have only one abortive case history. This involved a young man whose parents died before he was married, who inherited a large estate, and who was known to have a sexual alliance with the Untouchable woman who daily came to clean his cattle shed. After marriage arrangements to a Havik girl were made for him by his maternal uncle, and on the day the wedding ceremony was to begin, an objection to the marriage was made on the above grounds. A *panchāyiti* (tribunal) was held which for lack of proof exonerated him of the crime but which nevertheless fined him five hundred rupees for having been accused of it.

For a Brahmin widow to have a child by someone other than her deceased husband is the other major sin punished by outcasting. Although there are numerous offenses for which a Havik may in customary law be punished by outcasting, this is about the only one for which it is carried out. There are, relatively speaking, a number of instances of widow bastardy. A widow is outcaste only after the child is born —before that instant there is no conclusive proof, it is said, that she has done anything wrong. After the widow has borne a child, it is up to her husband's family (her dāyādru by marriage), the ones who become ritually defiled by having an incurably impure kinsman, to initiate outcasting, which can be done only by the caste guru, and does not involve the widow's legitimate children. Her illegitimate child is assigned to the Maleru caste, a high-ranking caste composed only of the illegitimate children of Havik widows and their descendants.

In recent years, not all widows bearing illegitimate children have been outcaste, as the outcaste now has recourse to the Government courts. Haviks feel strongly that their caste guru should not be defiled and humiliated by appearing in court. When our neighbor, a Havik widow with an illegitimate child, was put out of caste, she first signed a statement to the effect that she would voluntarily undergo the ceremony.

All instances of actual or potential outcasting contain the element of pollution derived from outside of the caste ("who knows who really fathered a Brahmin widow's illegitimate child"). These instances can be thought of as Haviks' taking on the pollution of non-Haviks, a direction of pollution-flow inconsistent with their high ritual status.

Conductors

There are many sources of impurity (e.g., low-caste persons, menstruating women, the dung of most animals,[14] or cadavers) and there are different ways in which impurities from these sources can be transmitted or conducted to make a more pure being less pure (e.g., direct conversation with an Untouchable may cause a Havik to lose his state of maḍi).

Kinship, like social intercourse, conducts impurities. Those people who are patrilineally related up to certain degrees are all made ritually impure by certain kinds of impurities (for example, birth and death) stemming from one member of their group. If one member of a ritual pollution group becomes so defiled that no amount of purification is sufficient to remove his impurity, all other members are defiled until the impure person is put out of caste. Upon marriage, a woman does not completely break ritual ties with her natal kinsmen, who thus observe a reduced amount of pollution for states of impurity which may apply to her. Pollution transmitted through multiple marriage links rapidly decreases, whereas that transmitted through agnatic descent only gradually diminishes.

Some inanimate objects act as conductors of pollution. When a Havik is assisted by his Untouchable servant with work in his arecanut garden, he and his servant may

[14] However, there is variation in the amount of pollution derived from the feces of different animals. I shall later discuss cow-dung. I have no information about monkey or cobra feces, two other sacred animals. Goat, sheep, chicken, and dog feces are potent sources of muṭṭucheṭṭu for Haviks. Buffalo dung is said to be impure, but I have never heard a Havik voluntarily mention this, nor worry, under ordinary circumstances, about contact with it. I can only explain the difference between the ritual defilement caused by contact with goat, chicken, and dog dung, on the one hand, and buffalo on the other, as stemming from the differential association Haviks have with these animals—goats and chickens are kept only by Sudras or Untouchables, whereas buffaloes yield milk and are necessary to the Havik "life-way."

simultaneously have to touch a rope or long bamboo stick. Although there may be no other contact between these two individuals, the Havik becomes muṭṭucheṭṭu by the conducted pollution. The rope and stick do not become impure for should the Untouchable first use them, and the Havik later pick them up, he does not become muṭṭucheṭṭu. The same is true of fruits, vegetables, and money, which if directly handed to a Brahmin by an Untouchable carry the Untouchable's impurities, but if indirectly transferred do not. However, some substances retain impurity, for if a piece of cotton cloth or a metal cooking vessel is touched by an Untouchable, and should a Havik later touch it without first pouring water over it, he becomes muṭṭucheṭṭu. Cooked food also retains pollution, but unlike a metal vessel, it cannot be purified by washing. A string made of cotton fiber and one of nāru fibers both become impure when in contact with a menstruating woman, but the nāru one can be purified whereas the cotton string cannot.

Some conductors less readily transmit pollution than do others—cotton worn by ritually pure Brahmins can easily become defiled, whereas silk is resistant to mild impurity, but transmits strong impurities.

Some materials cannot become defiled, nor can they transmit pollution to humans —for example, cow's milk. If an Untouchable pours water into a Havik's vessel, the vessel becomes impure, but if he pours cow's milk, the vessel does not. Water itself does not become defiled, but it transmits the Untouchable's impurity into the vessel. The Havik then has no way of getting the water out of the vessel without being made ritually impure.

Ground does not act as a conductor, but straw which covers it does. A Brahmin should not be in the same part of his cattle-shed as his Untouchable servant for fear that they may both step on places connected through overlapping straws on the floor. Even though a Havik and an Untouchable simultaneously bathe in the village pond, the Havik is able to attain a state of maḍi because "the water goes to the ground, and the ground does not transmit mailigē—muṭṭucheṭṭu."

There does not appear to be any physical principle that determines which substances hold impurity and which merely transmit them. (Some plant fibers are easily made impure, whereas others are not, and copper vessels retain impurity whereas copper coins do not.)

Puṇya (merit), as well as mailigē muṭṭucheṭṭu, can be transmitted by touch. Brahmin women, like most non-Brahmins, cannot directly do puja to most of the Sanskritic gods—instead, they do it through their husbands. In a number of ceremonial situations, a wife touches the arm or shoulder of her husband while he does puja, and in this way derives merit through her husband.

Orthopraxy

The maintenance of rules regarding purity and impurity is symbolic of being Hindu, and the rigorousness of the norms and the degree to which they are adhered by a caste are presumed to be roughly symbolic of its status. Hindu orthopraxy is primarily expressed in terms of the degree of ritual purity maintained. Attainment of ritual purity may involve denial, repression, asceticism, and other-worldliness. Those who are the least worldly remain the most pure—they avoid contact with other castes, restrict the foods that they eat, are, ideally, sexually continent, and spend much time worshipping gods while in a state of ritual purity.

On a more practical level, orthopraxy for Haviks causes great inconvenience. Maintenance of ritual purity interferes with making a livelihood: although most Haviks are shrewd and capable farmers, the very orthoprax find it difficult to engage in business transactions which necessitate contact with lower-caste men, travelling to town, or engaging in legal court battles. The time available for making a living is restricted for a really orthoprax person since he should spend a great deal of his time performing ritual activities and removing any impurities which may befall him. Extra labor is required of the orthoprax—for example, such time-consuming activities as making one's own *avalakki* (pounded and fried rice) or coffee powder.

A Havik should be ritually pure because this state is intrinsically good, not because it is enjoyable (but, without a doubt, some members of the community are accorded respect and approval from others and receive some form of "inner satisfaction" from their orthopraxy). Ritual purity involves discomfort and self-denial: a cold water bath better purifies an individual than does one of warm water; a man who does without food or water when he has to visit the market town is more pure than one who indulges himself; a man who fasts regularly is more pure than one who does not. In order to become and to remain ritually pure, an individual should be willing to undergo discomfort. But beliefs about pollution, and the rigorousness with which they are adhered to, vary according to individual orthopraxy. There is no exact Kannada term for orthopraxy, but instead it is generally discussed in terms of behavior, or an orthoprax person is said to be pure (shuddha), to act as an elder (*hiriyaru*), or "to follow the shāstras (or *āchāras*)."

Up to this point, I have been balancing two concepts—ideal and actual practices. I shall now discuss variations around the norms relating to those customs which are felt to be intimately associated with the Brahmanical ritual tradition.

The treatment accorded my wife and me, Americans, by the twenty-four Brahmin families of the village in which we lived exemplifies this range of variation. In the two most orthoprax families, we were never asked to enter the inside portions of the house, but were instead given coffee and tiṇḍi on the front verandah. In one of these houses, we never saw how they solved the problem of removing and washing our leaves and cups—we were not asked to do it but no one touched them before we left. In the other house, a young Brahmin male performed this job. All other houses served us meals (ūṭa). In one house the family ate with us on their back verandah, and apologetically asked us to remove our own leaves and clean with cow-dung our eating place. All other houses fed us in the dining room, and a member of the family removed our leaves. In two families, the person who did this job, a widow, took a bath immediately afterwards. In many houses we were placed in a separate line (pangti), but in some we were fed while sitting alongside the families' members. Most Brahmins' houses have a dining hall separate from the more sacred kitchen area. The kitchen generally contains the house gods, although a few houses have a separate shrine room. It is customary in some houses for the family to eat in the kitchen at breakfast or when all members are not eating at the same time. Of the houses that had a separate kitchen, we were invited for food into two. Finally, in one house, I was fed in the dining room, at the head of the line containing a group of elderly Brahmin males.

Orthopraxy usually varies among members of a single family. When my wife's assistant, a Brahmin but not a Havik, touched avalakki, the widow who ran the house said that although she herself would not eat it, her twenty-year old son would. In an extended family of two brothers, the younger will eat with a family which has āme while the elder will not. In several families, younger men smoke bīḍis through their lips, while their elders draw the smoke through their cupped hand.

Elders are generally more orthoprax than their juniors, women more so than men, and widows and bhaṭṭrus (priests) are most orthoprax of all. For males, wearing the hair in the traditional fashion and shaving the head except for a small tuft at the rear are symbolic of "a man who strictly follows the shāstras." Widows are almost invariably regarded as following ritual taboos and injunctions more strictly than other people; on the other hand, they more readily than other women do certain impure tasks, such as midwifery, because it is said that it is less inconvenient for them to remove severe pollution—as their heads are shaved, they can easily do a "full head bath." Havik women never cut their hair unless widowed, and long hair is difficult to purify; when changing from mailigē to maḍi, a woman need but pour a small amount of water on her head, but when moving to maḍi from a state of muṭṭucheṭṭu, a full head bath is necessary.

A Havik widow is regarded as responsible for her husband's death; she cannot remarry, but should spend much time in meditation and prayer. Widow orthopraxy is explained as "They have no other way to spend their time," or "Their life is so hard that they constantly pray to god asking that in their next life they will be more fortunate," or "They do these pure things to prevent their doing bad things; to keep themselves [their sexual desires] in control."

All Brahmin males wear the sacred thread, do daily puja to the house god, and take a daily bath. The very orthoprax are those who will not take "even a drop of water" when they have to go to the market town, and who bathe immediately upon returning home. Conversely, criticism of the younger generation is frequently heard: "They take coffee and tiṇḍi in town without even removing their shirts! Even though they go to a Brahmin shop, how can they be sure that those who serve them are really Brahmins?" Women are sometimes considered very orthoprax if they pound and fry their own avalakki or roast and grind their own coffee beans. But most often female orthopraxy is expressed in a zealousness to prevent impurities from coming into the house and by removing impurities that others would overlook.

Although water is easily defiled, that which is running in a stream or standing in a reservoir is not made impure by the presence of an Untouchable in it. However, water in a well or vessel is made impure by contact, direct or indirect, with a person of low caste. A very orthoprax Brahmin will allow no one of a different caste to draw water from his well, but, in recent years, many Haviks have become less concerned with this. In some Brahmin families a high-caste Sudra is permitted to draw from the family well in order to water the Brahmin's vegetable garden, but for no other reason; while in less orthoprax families a Sudra servant may also draw water used for bathing, but not water that is used in cooking, and most certainly not that used for dēvaru puja, which has to be drawn by a Havik in maḍi.

Orthopraxy often depends upon circumstances. In one nuclear family household, the male, who prided himself on his strict maintenance of ritual purity, allowed a Sudra (Divaru) woman to draw the family's bathing water after his wife became too ill to do it. In another orthoprax family, the second ceremony to purify a new mother was held only sixteen days after the eleven-day āme period, because the only other woman in the house began her menstrual period, and it was considered too inconvenient to do without the services of either woman. Among men, bhaṭṭrus (priests) are more orthoprax than laymen. They observe more strictly distant sūtaka, are more careful about the source of their food supply, remain in maḍi for longer periods of time, often regularly bathe twice a day, and spend several hours a day doing pujas. Also, there are special rules for bhaṭṭrus—for example, a practicing bhaṭṭru should not follow his trade (doing pujas for others) after the third month of his wife's pregnancy.

Orthopraxy sometimes conflicts with visiting and hospitality norms. A male guest at a meal is generally seated by his host; if there are two guests present, a Brahmin of another caste and an orthoprax Havik, it is up to the host to resolve the seating arrangements, and it is quite possible that one of the guests will have to eat in a pangti that he would not otherwise choose. A more striking situation was revealed by a young but extremely purity-conscious bhaṭṭru who explained to me that a widow (*prāni*—literally, animal) who shaves her head and wears a red sari (the dress symbolic of widowhood) is pure, and that she can cook both ūṭa (food for men) and naivēdya (food for the gods), but if she does not wear the appropriate costume and shave her head, a widow (in this instance, called by Haviks a *vidhave*) could not cook for naivēdya and most people would not take food from her.[15] He was quite adamant that he himself would most certainly never accept food from such a woman, but volunteered that if he were visiting a house where a vidhave did the cooking, he would feel too embarrassed to ask to have someone else cook and would have to accept the food.

Orthopraxy in ritual pollution observances is occasionally phrased in terms of earning puṇya (merit), but more frequently disregard of such observances is phrased as sin (*pāpa*), or loss of merit. When the wife of a very unorthoprax Havik became insane, several informants explained this as the result of the husband's habits of gambling, drinking, and failure to maintain ritual purity. (However, an explanation of witchcraft was also given for this event.)

Although the orthoprax person is respected and looked upon as setting a good example, extreme orthopraxy leads to ridicule (but only behind the back of the individual concerned). Most Brahmins relish telling stories about the overly orthoprax. An oft-repeated statement was that the more a person worries about where he steps, the greater is the likelihood that he will step where betel juice has been spit. I have seen a group of relatively orthoprax Brahmins bent over in gales of laughter while recounting how an extremely orthoprax widow sprinkled a mixture of cow-dung and water on the floor of the house after any Brahmin had entered it, for fear that the visitors had stepped on spittle before coming into the house, and how she even purified the spot where the caste guru had sat when he visited her house; about how a widow ran to take a bath after someone said the word "chapples" (sandals); about the family who would not feed the leaves from which they had eaten their meal to their water buffalo for fear that the saliva would contaminate the milk; or about the widows who always acted as if they were talking through a third person whenever they communicated with any non-Brahmin. A favorite story concerned the most

[15] This situation is not completely hypothetical, but nearly so. In the Havik community in this area only a few of the younger widows do not shave their heads—they are so rare that I have seen only one. But sentiment of the more liberal Haviks is towards relaxing these symbolic restrictions.

orthoprax woman in the village who, when younger, so it was said, required her husband to be in maḍi when he approached her at night, and immediately afterwards took a cold water bath, so that all of the neighbors knew the precise schedule of her sexual life. These stories are sometimes told as jokes, sometimes in a manner of derision or ridicule. It is surprising how many times such stories were followed by a description of the lingering or horrible death these individuals underwent, or by a statement that they eventually became insane (*huchchu*). Although explicitily denied, there appears to be an unconscious association between carrying orthopraxy to an "absurd" extreme and unfortunate consequences.

Haviks, then, have a choice of being lax or strict in their pollution observances and can choose from a wide range of behavioral patterns. Although either extreme tends to be disapproved by the community as a whole, only the lack of orthopraxy can be formally sanctioned.

Haviks, Pollution, and Other Castes

The most important castes connected with the village from which I obtained most of my data, are in order of their ritual rank: Havik Brahmins; Lingayats (priests and agriculturalists); Goldsmiths; Maḍivaḷas (Washermen); Okkaligas (land-poor agriculturalists and arecanut tree climbers); Divarus (relatively well-off agriculturalists); Potters (of equal ritual status with Divarus); Barbers; Hasalurus (arecanut climbers, marginal farmers, toddy tappers, agricultural laborers, and indentured servants); and, two castes of Untouchables (agricultural laborers and indentured servants). Haviks class as Sudras all of these castes except themselves and Untouchables; only an occasional Lingayat objects.

Havik Brahmins make behavioral discriminations between the relative purity of other castes; the interactional patterns between Haviks and other castes are of major importance in the making of a clear-cut hierarchy, into which all of the indigenous local castes fit.

This is most clearly brought out at a large ceremony, such as a marriage, when performed in a wealthy Havik family. Members of a number of the castes contribute their ritual services to the celebration. Maḍivaḷas wash the clothes of the participants and, at one point in the ceremony, hold a cloth between the bride and the groom (upon its removal, the couple symbolically see one another for the first time). The Sonagar (Goldsmith) who makes the wedding jewelry is given an invitation to the ceremony. Okkaligas and Divarus, both agricultural castes, or occasionally Potters, may furnish and drive the bullock carts upon which the bride and groom travel between their villages or which transport Brahmin guests to and from the ceremony. Women of a high Sudra caste (Okkaliga or Goldsmith) may be hired to wash the vessels in which the feast is cooked. The Barber must shave the groom before the ceremony. Hasalurus jealously guard their caste prerogative of constructing the canopy (*pandal*) under which the marriage takes place and of putting up mango leaves, which indicate an auspicious ceremony, outside the marriage house. An Untouchable servant family, who is either attached to the marriage house or especially hired, runs errands and delivers the initial wedding invitations. In short, all indigenous local castes, with the exception of Lingayats, may play a ritual role in a large Brahmin wedding, although the manner in which these roles are played appears to differ from that in the *jajmani* system.

All of these people (not generally their caste hamlets, but just those individuals and sometimes their families who have some function in the ceremony or who have other close ties with the marriage family) are invited to the feast. They are fed separately after the Brahmin guests. If the Goldsmith has attended, he is fed separately from the members of any other caste and before any other non-Brahmins. After this, the higher Sudras, Okkaligas, Maḍivaḷas, and Divarus are fed, generally on the back verandah in separate pangtis; the order in which they are served indicates their relative caste rank. After this, Hasalurus and the Barber are fed, on plantain leaves, in the back yard at a place more remote from the house than the previous group. Finally, the Untouchables bring arecanut sheaths, some of which are formed into a watertight vessel for liquids, and are given the remainder of the food which they must take away from the marriage house to eat. If it is a small amount, they will eat it along the side of the road or in the arecanut garden; if large, it may be taken back to their caste hamlet and shared. Sometimes the Untouchables are given their food in metal vessels, which they later wash and return, but this is not done by the most orthoprax families.

In some villages, Hasalurus and Barbers are not served on a leaf (as are all higher castes) but instead are requested to take the food, in fiber vessels, away from the marriage house for consumption. In the village in which my wife and I lived, Hasalurus had until a few years previous to our entry, been required to do this. After a long period of objecting, they finally were granted their request to be fed on a leaf, arguing that they were not Untouchables and therefore should not be treated as Untouchables. The new rule is now tacitly agreed among Haviks to be the "village rule," even though a few of the most orthoprax families will not observe it—a few of the less orthoprax Brahmin families had served Hasalurus on plantain leaves before the practice became the "official" village custom. There are other instances in which Haviks in one village treat a given caste differently from the way they are treated in another village. One village has no Okkaligas, Maḍivaḷas or Sonagars, and few Divarus, but a large Hasaluru hamlet, and Brahmins in this village, for reasons of convenience, hire Hasalurus to drive their marriage carts. These differing customs, which the lower castes view with gravity, sometimes are in conflict when Brahmin marriages take place between villages having different customs. In both instances of such conflict about which I have information, the village having the policy which expressed the greatest ritual distance eventually gave way, for the particular occasion, to the more egalitarian policy of the other village.

Haviks, although generally hardworking and given to doing much of the labor required to run their small arecanut estates and their large houses, are frequently employers of other castes. Many Havik families have Untouchable retainers; the male servant works in the arecanut garden while his wife often works as a domestic helping the Havik wife. Untouchables are never allowed inside a Havik house—they may not even come onto the verandah area except when their work so requires. Work inside of the house may, in most Havik families, be performed by higher Sudra employees. An Untouchable may sweep and clean with cow-dung the outside area, including the verandah, but a higher-caste woman is needed to do this inside of the house. For domestic work inside of the house, Haviks prefer Sonagar, Maḍivaḷa, or Okkaliga women, in that order, an order which corresponds to their relative caste rank. These castes, if employed in this capacity by anyone other than the more orthoprax, are allowed to enter any part of the house except the kitchen and gods' room (*dēvaru mane*). Women of the Divaru caste are not allowed to go through the house of a Havik but may work in it.[16] In respect to entering the house most families treat Hasalurus like Untouchables; some Havik families permit them the same house privileges as Divarus and a very few of the least pollution-conscious Haviks accord Hasalurus the same treatment that the mildly orthoprax accord to the higher-caste Sudras.

Milking domestic animals and washing cooking vessels are similar to drawing water from a well; that is, the degree of orthopraxy and need of the Havik family determine whether or not members of a Sudra caste are hired to perform these duties and, if so, what castes. If a Sudra milks a cow, the same procedure is followed to maintain the purity of the milk as if this were done by a menstruating Havik woman. If vessels are washed by a Sudra, they are left upside down. Afterwards a Brahmin woman pours water over them to purify them and enable her to pick them up. If, however, she finds even one particle of food left on them, orthoprax Haviks say they are still impure, and the woman, after cleaning them, should bathe to remove the inadvertently contracted impurity.

The left side is always less pure than the right side. The lowest indigenous caste is sometimes referred to as "Left-Handed Untouchable" to distinguish it from the higher "Right-Handed Untouchable" caste.[17] A Brahmin's right ear, into which the bhaṭṭru whispers the *gāyatri mantra* at the time a boy undergoes his upanayana, is more ritually pure than his left. The sacred wooden post (*vāstupurusha*) used in construction of a Brahmin house is always on the right side. Occasionally a Brahmin's guest of stature will be honored at a meal by being seated to the right of his host. Male guests sit with their host on the right hand side (facing out) of the verandah. Havik males spread a woolen blanket on the floor, and all sit on this. If the guest is a different species of Brahmin, or a Lingayat or a Havik in āme, he is seated on a separate blanket, as wool is a transmitter of pollution. Occasionally Havik women sit on the front verandah when doing domestic work, when listening to a male conversation,[18] or when menstruating, but always on the left side. High-caste Sudras will sometimes be allowed to sit, without being offered a blanket, on the left side of the verandah, while negotiating for work or gossiping with the Brahmins on the right side. Lower-caste Sudras will sit on the left side of the verandah, but on the edge so that their legs dangle over the side. Untouchables will be required to stand in the courtyard or road in front of the verandah, but in this instance no distinction is made between the right and left-hand sides.

Untouchables are not permitted inside temples (either *dēvasthāna,* those containing gods, or *guḍi,* those for deities) whereas Sudras can enter them but may not touch (thus may not directly do puja to) the supernaturals. In the larger dēvasthānas, lay Brahmins may not do puja to the gods, but instead must have it done for them by the temple priest. In recent years, with the Harijan uplift movement and the Temple Entry Acts, there have been instances in the general region in which an outside re-

16 Actually, they are seldom employed as domestic servants as most Divaru families have sufficient paddy land to permit their women to refuse this job.

17 This concept of right- and left-handed castes, so prevalent in the older literature on South India, is not, in this region, applied to any other castes.

18 More characteristically, a woman stands in the doorway if listening, but if she is older she may sit on the left side of the front verandah.

former, usually a civil servant or Congress Party Worker, led a group of Untouchables into one of several Government-run "Sanskritic" temples (dēvasthāna).[19] As a consequence, a higher-caste mythology has begun to grow, warning of the supernatural consequences which may be precipitated by such action. A typical story runs as follows: A group of Untouchables organized themselves to enter a temple. At the door they were stopped by the temple priest, who stated that in light of the new Government legislation, he must permit them to enter, but first would request them the kindness of bathing in the river to purify themselves. While bathing, so the story goes, they were swept away and drowned. In other variants of this theme, they were eaten by crocodiles, attacked by bees, or had their way into the temple blocked by a militant cobra.

Untouchability (*asprishta*) is in this region of India taken literally, and almost no Brahmin will intentionally touch an Untouchable without good reason (for example, when working together in an arecanut garden).[20] When giving arecanuts, money, or bīḍis to an Untouchable, a Brahmin will either toss them on the ground or drop them into outstretched hands. If an Untouchable gives an object to a Brahmin, an event for which there are fewer occasions, he places it on the verandah (or ground), from where the Brahmin picks it up. However, for the less orthoprax Haviks, this pattern is held to only while in a village. Several informants have candidly admitted that while in Sagar, the market town, they will hand a bīḍi to an Untouchable, whereas in the village they throw it on the ground.

Sudra employees are frequently given water, and sometimes coffee, by their employers. The cup is filled, generally by the woman of the house, and then washed by the Sudra. A few Brahmin women will pour water over the dirty cup before picking it up, but most will pick it up to wash it again. A distinction is made as to how the liquid is drunk—whether it is poured from the cup into the mouth without touching the lips, or drunk with the lips touching the vessel. If the latter, the cup is made more impure because of contact with saliva. Haviks generally prefer not to serve coffee to Sudras, because they say it is hot and thus cannot be drunk by pouring from a distance, a belief not unrelated to the expensiveness of coffee. Havik houses also generally have a tin cup (but sometimes half of a coconut shell) on the back verandah for use by Untouchable employees. The Untouchable washes and brings the cup to the Havik who pours the liquid from a distance. The Untouchable washes and replaces the cup, which is never touched by members of the Havik family.

Although Brahmins will go to lengths to avoid being made muṭṭucheṭṭu by an Untouchable, I have yet to talk to one who admitted that he felt any sense of revulsion or dirtiness, or any strong negative emotion, while ritually impure. (But I have never really been convinced that I was asking the question in the right way.) One of the most liberal Brahmins stated, while discussing Untouchability, that he personally saw no reason not to touch an Holeru, but would not want to do so because

[19] Guḍis, as they tend to be privately owned or controlled by the dominant caste in a village, have not been targets for these reformers.

[20] I have not been told of any exceptions to this rule in the village, and in a year and a half of residence in the Malnad, I saw but one deviation: a young unmarried boy, a member of a marginal and completely deviant Havik family, once put his arm around an Untouchable to whom I was talking and removed a bīḍi from the Untouchable's shirt pocket. This was one of the few obvious instances of rebellion against rules concerning pollution that I knew of. In few other cases, did it seem to me, was the lack of orthopraxy a direct expression of rebellion against norms concerning pollution.

"they only take a bath once a month." When talking about his own Untouchable servant (*mane āḷu*), of whom he was quite fond, he stated that he would be quite willing to touch the man from the standpoint of his own conscience, but would worry about what the "society" (samāja) would say.

Lingayats present a rather special case. In some villages in this region they are the dominant caste, own arecanut gardens, and in many ways are the functional equivalent of Brahmins. Lingayats are vegetarians and act as priests for other castes.[21] Officially they claim ritual caste rank equal to Haviks; unofficially they admit to, and are accorded by other castes, a position in the caste hierarchy just below Brahmins. However, they do not follow most of the ritual pollution taboos which are adhered to by *all* other castes—for instance, a menstruating Lingayat woman can be touched by other Lingayats and may cook in the kitchen. Sūtaka and āme practices are not observed, and, in theory and to a limited degree in practice, they do not consider themselves ritually defiled by contact with an Untouchable.[22]

An anomalous situation arises. Brahmins use the respectful form of speech when addressing Lingayats (but not Sudras), and regard them as near equals. But on the other hand, Lingayats are considered to be potentially more ritually defiling than Sudras. For example, one Havik queried: "How do I know that the Lingayat I was with was not muṭṭucheṭṭu from contact with his menstruating wife?" Less orthoprax Haviks freely interact with Lingayats, even in some instances covertly drinking coffee with them—either accepting it from a Lingayat, or serving it to a Lingayat and then washing the Lingayat's cup. On the other hand, the more orthoprax Haviks will assiduously avoid touching a Lingayat, saying they would prefer contact with a lesser-ranking Sudra.

Respect-Pollution

I have so far described pollution concepts from the aspect of ritual defilement and the ways by which ritual impurities are removed. However, behavior that usually results in pollution is sometimes intentional in order to show deference and respect; by doing that which under other circumstances would be defiling, an individual expresses his inferior position. For example, the theme of a wife's subordination towards her husband finds ritual expression in her act of eating from his leaf after he has finished. Havik women are said to be "like Sudras"—they may not know mantras, may not do sandhyā vandana and dēvaru puja or pujas to gods (dēvarus). A woman worships these supernaturals through her husband. It is commonly stated that a husband is a god to a wife.

The theme of respect-pollution is made even clearer in the one other instance I have where adult Brahmins take food from the leaf of another individual. Religious *sādhus* (infrequently encountered in this region of India) may be either male or female, although I have met only one woman sādhu—a Havik. A woman can become a sādhu (only after she has reached menopause) by becoming a disciple of a personal

21 Havik priests, who generally are also owners of arecanut gardens and for whom priestcraft is a secondary occupation, act as purohitas only for other Haviks. Higher Sudra castes are served by Karnataka Brahmins, a sect which in this region is few in number, and generally make their living from their religious trade. Karnataka Brahmins refuse their priestly services to Hasalurus, Barbers, and Untouchables—these groups are served by Lingayat priests, who also serve lay Lingayats.

22 The high status of Lingayats can best be explained historically and/or by an interactional rather than attributional theory (see Marriott, 1959).

guru (not to be confused with the Havik caste guru). She is taught mantras, does sandhyā vandana and dēvaru puja and may be treated with immense respect by both men and women. The Havik woman sādhu whom I knew was, when she visited our village, given a "*pāda* puja," in which her feet were bathed in a mixture of panchāmrita and water. The solution was then passed around to those present, in a special silver vessel used only for worshipping, and poured into the right palm to be drunk as tīrtha (sacred liquid), indicating that she was being accorded the status of a god rather than a mortal. This sādhu, herself a widow, was accompanied by several disciples, all widows. It was reported that these disciples "stole" and ate the food left on the sādhu's leaf "in order to absorb her qualities."

Pāda puja, worship of the feet, is a fairly common practice.[23] In many ceremonies a wife washes the feet of her husband, or a boy who has not yet had his upanayana washes the feet of his father. When a daughter is married, as one part of the ceremony she is "thought of as Lakshmi" and her parents wash her feet. In a shrāddha ceremony, the performer washes the bhaṭṭru's feet, who is at this time an incarnation of the ancestral spirit. When the caste guru visits a Havik house, his feet are washed in water which is then distributed as tīrtha. A very orthoprax man may even have a pair of silver feet, representing those of his guru, which he piously washes so that he may daily drink his guru's tīrtha.

In the pāda puja ritual, different degrees of rank can be indicated, according to whether the feet are merely touched, washed, or whether they are washed and the liquid is drunk as tīrtha.

Touching the feet is also symbolic of status distance across caste lines. An indentured servant (mane āḷu) once a year ceremonially renews his vows of fidelity by touching his master's feet. This obeisance ritual takes place on the master's verandah at a time when the master is in mailigē or muṭṭucheṭṭu; as most indentured servants are Untouchables by caste, this is done just before the Brahmin master takes his daily bath.

The most striking and frequently encountered expression of respect-pollution is in the use of cow-dung as a cleansing agent. A cow is worshipped daily by Havik women and, on certain ceremonial occasions, by Havik men. It is, next to a Brahmin virgin, the greatest gift that can be bestowed upon a Brahmin male. Cows are sometimes said to be gods; alternatively, to have more than a thousand gods residing in them. Simple types of pollution are removed by water, greater degrees of pollution are removed by cow-dung and water, while a greater amount is removed by panchagavya, taken internally. Gods and human incarnations of gods are purified with a mixture of cow's milk, curds, ghee, honey and sugar (panchāmrita), never with panchagavya.

Since the feces and urine of any animal are impure, how do we account for their use as purifying agents? Are the feces of a cow an exception to this statement? I do not think so. Cow-dung, like the dung of any other animal, is intrinsically impure and can cause defilement—in fact, it will defile a god; but it is pure relative to a mortal.

---

[23] The body below the navel is less pure than that above, but of the lower extremity the feet are the least pure. If one Havik accidentally touches another with his foot, the resulting mild defilement is removed when both persons touch, with their right hands, the other person and then touch their right hand to both of their own eyes. This gesture, initiated by the person whose foot was involved, is automatic with most Haviks.

The differential ritual status between a living god (a cow) and a human is expressed as: the cow's most impure part is sufficiently pure relative to even a Brahmin priest to remove the latter's impurities. This, then, is the common theme of respect-pollution which we find expressed in other situations. For instance, a guru's feet are intrinsically impure, but in relation to a lay Brahmin they do not cause pollution because of the great ritual gulf separating the two individuals. Or, by eating from the leaf of her husband, a wife symbolically expresses her deification of her husband. The theme implied by this last act is: "My husband is so high, relative to my subordinate position, that to me even his saliva is sacred." Although she would be defiled by the saliva of any other Brahmin, she is not made impure in this instance because "to a woman her husband is her God."

The ritually pure can be defiled by the ritually impure. If two beings (natural or supernatural) are of approximately equal status, the more impure aspects of each can defile the other; if they differ considerably in ritual status, the higher cannot in any way defile the lower. As gods are somewhat equal in status, the feces of one (a cow) can defile another, but, because a Brahmin is less pure, the same feces can to him become an actively purifying agent. Or, again, a muṭṭucheṭṭu Brahmin can defile another Brahmin but cannot cause ritual impurity to an Untouchable, who, by nature, is believed to be already ritually defiled as compared to the Brahmin. Hence, we can conceive of a caste's lowness in the ritual purity-impurity scale as legitimate pollution, while pollution of an individual within a caste might be thought of as illegitimate lowness.

Pollution and the Supernatural

Havik theories of disease causation are mostly supernatural. Supernaturals are believed to cause harm (*kashṭa*) to humans or their domestic animals. Some supernaturals, *devvas* (spirits), do this capriciously. But other supernaturals, dēvarus (gods) and dēvates (deities) are believed to cause trouble (kashṭa) in order to make their desires known to humans and thus to attain them.[24] A supernatural generally causes human difficulties because it is hungry, or because it has been made ritually impure.

"Sanskritic" gods or dēvarus have few occasions in which pollution may come to them, as they are generally approached only by Brahmins in maḍi and are physically separated from non-Brahmins. Also if they are made muṭṭucheṭṭu, this fact is generally known, and they are immediately purified. Although there is a great sense of urgency in purifying an impure dēvaru, this is not reinforced by a strong fear of supernatural punishment.

House gods (mane dēvarus) can have sūtaka under only one circumstance: if a death occurs in the house while dēvaru puja is being done to them, or if the news of a death of a dāyādru of the man performing the puja is received while the puja is in process. Also, house gods are likely to be inadvertently defiled, especially by children in the house. In both of these instances, the house gods signify their state of pollution by causing red ants to enter the house—certainly a mild enough sanction.

This is not true for Sudra mane dēvarus, which involve a different concept. Sudras "follow" one or another of several gods that live in some of the local regional temples.

---

24 For a more detailed discussion of these categories of supernaturals, see Harper 1959b.

In some Sudra castes, each family has an inherited mane dēvaru to whom it owes allegiance and to whom it may take vows, which are often fulfilled by pilgrimages to the mane dēvaru's temple. In some instances, the followers must give an annual cash payment (to help maintain the temple and its priest). These mane dēvarus may be, if ritually defiled, extremely harmful, and they are defiled when their follower's house is made impure.[25]

In the Keladi Temple *jātre* (religious fair), the images of the major temple gods and their priest are drawn around the village in an immense wooden cart, pulled by several hundred men. In about 1950 a Sudra who was helping to pull the cart was caught under a wheel and crushed to death. The gods and priest inside the cart were consequently in an extreme state of muṭṭucheṭṭu and immediately underwent an elaborate purificatory ceremony in which the gods were cleansed by mantras and panchāmrita and the Brahmin priest with mantras and panchagavya.

Gods may also be made impure when a menstruating woman enters their temple compound. As it is almost inconceivable that a Brahmin woman would do this, and extremely unlikely that a Sudra woman would do so, stories about this type of pollution to a god generally involve Lingayat women. There are several lesser temples in the area in which bees live and they are believed to sting any menstruating woman who enters their dwelling. Stories about these events are frequently told.

Occasionally a Havik will earn extra merit (puṇya) or fulfill a vow (*haraḳe*) by holding in his house a puja to the god Sathyanarayana. For this ceremony, which may last two days, the Sathyanarayana dēvaru is installed in an image to which a puja is done by especially hired priests who also read the Sathyanarayana story. The house is purified before the ceremony by being sprinkled with a mixture of water and cow-dung. While the god is in residence, strict maḍi must be maintained by all attendees. Those involved in doing puja must again bathe if they leave the ceremony to relieve themselves. Male and female guests who spend the night are separated to insure that no sexual acts take place in the house, as this would cause ritual pollution to befall Sathyanarayana. These observances, however, are viewed in the light of customary ways of showing respect, and no Brahmin with whom I have talked has indicated any fear that if the god were inadvertently defiled, malevolent consequences would necessarily follow. Fear of severe supernatural retribution for defiling the supernatural is not generally part of the religious complex associated with these more pure gods.

A dēvate (deity) is generally associated with a social group (household, caste, hamlet, village, or geographical area around which members of the same or different castes have land) which has responsibility for its welfare (the dēvate is, at the minimum, periodically bathed and fed, and is protected from ritual defilement). In return, the dēvate protects this group of individuals. Should it be made impure, either by a member of the group with whom it has a contract or by an outsider, it makes its plight known by notifying (by causing trouble to) a member of the group from whom it can expect rectification. In addition, it may cause immediate harm to the

[25] When we first began field work, my wife carried her sandals through a Divaru's house. For this offense, we had to pay a fine of Rs 50 to the priest at the temple of the Divaru's mane dēvaru. The priest furnished the Divaru family with tīrtha to sprinkle through the house to purify it. We were told that we would be responsible for any accident or illness that befell any member of the family between the time the house was defiled and the time it was purified, a period which, because it fell in the thirteenth month of the Hindu calendar, was nearly a month. During this time the family showed a considerable amount of apprehension.

individual who is responsible for its ritual defilement, but this is done more in the spirit of retaliation than in the expectation of being ritually cleansed.

Below the "village guarding" dēvates, the two most important types of dēvates are those associated with a hamlet or field (generally a *bhūta*) and those associated with a household (generally a *chauḍi*). The closer the dēvate's residence to the general area where its followers' day-to-day activities take place, the greater the chance that it will be inadvertently defiled, and thus ritual purity practices should be most rigorously observed.

The threat of supernatural sanctions constantly reinforces concepts of ritual purity. This is especially true of household dēvates: many Brahmin and some Sudra households have a chauḍi living in or immediately outside their house; as expressed by one informant, "members of these houses have to be very strict about things maḍi." This has relevance to those who feel ambivalent about the degree to which they should be orthoprax. If they lean towards the orthoprax side, but need reinforcement, they can create deities associated with their house or property that sternly force them to maintain practices which keep them, their family, and their deity, in a relatively pure state.

Some dēvates are given animal sacrifices or their symbolic equivalent, while others, generally those associated with a Brahmin household or hamlet, are vegetarian. The blood-demanding dēvates tend to be more quickly angered than are the vegetarian ones and more violently take offense over ritual infractions. Stories about these dēvates are frequently recounted to explain an illness or an accident: when a Sudra lost an eye by getting a paddy husk in it, a *jōyisa* (astrologer) diagnosed the injury as having been caused by a chauḍi in a stone in the Sudra's field who was ritually defiled because the Sudra spit near her (stone); when a Brahmin's female water buffalo suddenly died, the explanation was that a woman in the house had approached the house chauḍi's (mane chauḍi) stone while menstruating; when a worker fell out of the tree from which he was sawing a branch, it was because he had urinated while on the tree and ritually polluted the bhūta who resided therein. Many stories concern Mariamma, the "village guarding" smallpox goddess. One of the most characteristic of these tells of Sudras (infrequently, Brahmins) who get too near her cart while she is being carried in procession while they are wearing leather sandals and as a consequence are punished by being caused to immediately vomit blood and fall unconscious.

Such stories, common in everyday talk, more often involve Sudras than Brahmins. This is in part because Sudras are more likely than Brahmins to work in the fields and forests, the area most frequently inhabited by blood-demanding dēvates; in part because Brahmins are believed less likely to commit acts which defile; in part because Brahmins are more likely to be associated with vegetarian dēvates who are believed to be less violent; and in part because that aspect of Hinduism involving violence from supernaturals constitutes a layer of Hinduism more strongly participated and believed in by Sudras.

Sudras, like Brahmins, value orthopraxy, but have a lesser ability to practice it, and thus may need to create dēvates who more severely sanction ritual infractions. On the other hand, Brahmins support the view that when violence follows pollution to a dēvate, Sudras are more frequently offenders, as this obliquely points to their own superiority.

Case history evidence shows that dēvates are believed to cause much greater harm when ritually defiled than are dēvarus. Both must leave their residence (*sthala*) if it becomes sufficiently impure. It appears possible, although I am unsure of my data on this point, that a dēvaru's residence is more likely to be made mailigē, whereas a dēvate's is more in danger of becoming muṭṭucheṭṭu, and that the supernatural is forced from its residence only if it is made muṭṭucheṭṭu, not if it is merely mailigē. These assumptions, if true, would help to account for the differential responses of dēvarus and dēvates to ritual infractions.

Fields of Purity

A third category of supernaturals are devvas, which I translate as "spirits." Devvas, unlike gods and deities, do not have a locus of residence, do not have any protective functions, nor do they grant boons. Vows (harakes) are never taken to them. They are believed to be malicious and capricious, and frequently to "strike" people and cause illness. They may be exorcised directly, by using superior power to force them to go, or by using a "spirit repellent."

Devvas are most likely to cause harm to the following, in this order: children and cattle; women; Sudra men; and lastly, Brahmin males who have had their upanayana. Adult Brahmin males are seldom harmed by devvas, and also are resistant to harm from dēvates, because they have strength (shakti) obtained from their knowledge of mantras. As stated by one informant:

> Brahmins are not harmed by devvas because they have the right to chant mantras from the Vedas and they give gāyatri *upadēsha.* At the thread ceremony, a boy is invested by the bhaṭṭru with the right to perform gāyatri *japa,* the most important part of daily sandhyā vandana. But even Brahmin women have devvas "come on" them because they do not have the rights of the Vedas—they are just like Sudras.

In many other instances, mantras are used to control spirits, to compel them to act in desired ways, or to force a supernatural to possess an individual. Very infrequently an adult male Brahmin's illness or accident will be attributed to the actions of a devva; more frequently to those of a dēvate. It is said that if a Brahmin feels fear and believes he may be "struck" by a dēvate, he need merely recite certain mantras, and this will prevent the deity from harming him.

There are certain "spirit repellents" that can be used to ward off a disease-causing agent, primarily devvas. These are used to protect women of all castes, adult Sudra males, and most importantly, children of any caste. Rarely are they used by Brahmin males who have had their upanayana—indeed, they appear to be the functional equivalent of the adult Brahmin male's knowledge of mantras.

The simplest "spirit repellent" is *vibhūti,* or sacred ash, made from a burned mixture of cow-dung and urine, over which mantras have been said and which is kept in the mane dēvaru, the most pure area of a Brahmin's house.[26] This is used as a spirit

---

[26] Vibhūti, sometimes called *bhasma,* is made by women. Small balls of cow-dung are soaked overnight in cow's urine, and allowed to dry in the day. This is done for twenty-one days. Then the balls are burned into an ash, which is soaked in cow's urine for forty-eight days, then formed into small balls which are dried upon a plantain leaf in the sun. A sufficient quantity will be made at one time to last a house for five or ten years.

Vidhūti is smeared on parts of the body of most adult Brahmins when they are in maḍi in order to attend a ceremony, and daily by the orthoprax.

repellent, mainly for infants and children, and is generally applied as a household remedy, or at the most, by a conveniently located religious specialist. The vibhūti is merely applied to the forehead of the crying child, and is reported to be an effective pacifier.

The most commonly used method by which the attack of a devva is prevented or repelled is for an individual to wear a *yantra*—a small sheet of metal upon which mantras are written or drawn. This is put into a metal tube (*tāṭi*) which is generally tied around the wearer's upper arm or neck. There are various types of metal sheets that may be used. Copper is the most common, and the effect of a yantra on this material lasts for one year. Sometimes silver sheets are used: these are effective for three years. Gold may also be used, although I have seen but one such yantra. The properties of a yantra made on gold sheet are said to last for a lifetime. One knowledgeable Brahmin said that the most powerful substances of which a yantra could be made were a plate hammered from a bullet which had killed a tiger, or from a copper coin burnt with a body, both of which would superficially appear to be sources of pollution but which I believe are not.

Yantras are a familiar sight—over fifty percent of the children of all castes can be seen wearing them. There are numerous religious specialists, belonging to various castes, who can make them. The writing or drawing is done with an iron nail. Brahmins tend to make yantras by writing mantras consisting of a few characters in Sanskrit, while Sudras more characteristically draw diagrams. Yantras are also made to protect cattle from supernatural harm—the copper sheet is fastened onto a dried coconut shell with iron nails and hung in the cattle shed.

For small children's minor complaints, mantras may be written or drawn on paper and put inside of the tāṭi. These are called *chīṭu* rather than yantras, and their protective power is ephemeral, lasting but a day. After a chīṭu is written, vibhūti is put on it to activate its shakti, or effectiveness.

A yantra has an incense puja done to it. The religious specialist need not be in maḍi when making a yantra but must be when he afterwards purifies and activates it with an incense puja. To be efficacious, a yantra must remain ritually pure. On every new moon (*amāvasye*) and full moon (*huṇṇame*) day, the yantra should be removed from the tāṭi and sprinkled with cow's urine. If worn by a child who is touched by a menstruating woman, the yantra becomes muṭṭucheṭṭu,[27] as is the case when one is worn by a menstruating woman. In both instances, the yantra must be purified by an appropriate religious specialist, who soaks it one to three nights in cow's urine and again performs one to three incense pujas to it.

One informant likened a yantra to "carrying a big stick to frighten away a spirit." Although vibhūti, chīṭus, and yantras are often stated to be effective in preventing or repelling an attack from a supernatural, the real spirit repellent substance is the mantras which they contain. Mantras are equated with strength (shakti), and vibhūti or a yantra are their vehicles. These vehicles must be kept in a state of ritual purity, for the power potentially possessed by the mantras can be activated only by ritual purity.

Dēvates (deities) and devvas (spirits) are conceived of as reacting differently

---

[27] When the subject of yantras is discussed, informants invariably bring up the possibility that they may be made muṭṭucheṭṭu by menstruating women, but, so far as I remember, never mentioned the possibility of their being defiled by contact with an Untouchable.

when ritually defiled. As most dēvates are more pure than most humans, they must be approached by those who have made a special effort to become ritually pure. Dēvates are honored by being given offerings by those who are ritually pure, but if defiled, they retaliate by causing injury, usually in the form of illness, to the offender, to his cattle, or to members of his family. Devvas are never given regular pujas. I have never heard of a devva who caused harm to a person because it was ritually defiled—devvas do not need a reason to attack, only an opportunity, as they are malevolent by nature. Devvas retreat when faced with force (mantras); dēvates are attracted towards ritual purity, but attack when ritually defiled.

Man's major source of control over the supernatural's malevolent aspects comes from mantras. But mantras work only when contained within a "field of purity." Fields of purity exist within space. Whereas pollution can flow and be transferred, purity cannot. But purity can radiate to form a protective shield. Mantras in a field of purity can prevent supernaturals, in their malevolent aspects, from entering it to cause harm to an individual contained within it. Mantras in yantras create such fields, as do mantras uttered by a qualified religious specialist when in a high state of purity. In like manner, temples can be conceived of as fields of purity, into which even a Brahmin cannot enter unless he is in a ritually pure state.

New and Full Moons

New moon (amāvasye) and full moon (huṇṇame) days are of great significance. On these days auspicious ceremonies (*ḳāryas*) for people may not be performed, no trip should be begun, and a girl's father may not search for a son-in-law. Brahmins take special precautions to keep from being defiled on these days of the month, and orthoprax individuals "fast" (by eating only tiṇḍi they remain more pure than if they eat ūṭa). Indentured servants, who are of low caste, do not work on these days.

But new and full moon days are also times when great puṇya can be earned by performing auspicious ceremonies (dharma kāryas) for dēvarus (gods). Major pujas for dēvates (deities) also often take place on these days—dēvates are believed to have more shakti, but also to be more dangerous, at these phases of the moon. Spirits also are stronger, and more likely to cause illness (*ḳāṭa*) or accidents. For this reason, stated an informant, "on amāvasye and huṇṇame we need to pay great attention to matters concerning maḍi."

Dēvates and spirits are not only stronger on these days, but more active and prone to cause harm. At these times bhūtas and chauḍis leave their "place" (sthala), the area over which they have control. Some informants say that on amāvasye and huṇṇame "bhūtas visit chauḍis for sexual purposes"; others say that "these are days on which chauḍis menstruate"; while still other informants state that "on these days chauḍis go to the honḍa to bathe (to remove menstrual pollution)." Also, a shaman's familiar spirit (a type of dēvate) often possesses the shaman on these days, and is believed to have greater accuracy in foreseeing the future or prescribing remedies for already existing problems. Mantras for yantras written on these days are believed to be extra powerful.

New and full moon days appear to be associated with a time when supernaturals are in a state of ritual pollution. While in this state they are more powerful, thus more capable of helping man, but also are potentially more dangerous. My data suggest that when humans worship dēvarus on these occasions, i.e., ritually purify them, they earn merit. Also, by purifying dēvates men play upon their benevolent qualities and prevent them from expressing their malevolent qualities. Devvas also are more powerful during new and full moon times. But in order for men to protect themselves from devvas and from the malevolent qualities of dēvates, they need to maintain themselves in a high state of purity. Since Untouchables cannot attain a high degree of purity, they should not on new and full moon days work in the fields and forests where they are more likely to encounter these spirits.

Possession

Both dēvates and devvas are believed capable of possessing individuals and speaking through them. Shaman are possessed only after they have ritually purified themselves and requested the deity to "come on" them.

One Sudra shaman began his shamanistic sessions by pouring a bucket of live coals over his head and body. The fact that he was not burned was interpreted as proof that his dēvate, a chauḍi, was protecting him. On one occasion he was badly burned: this was said to have resulted because he used the wrong vessel of water for taking the bath that immediately preceded this ceremony. The water he bathed in should have been drawn by his assistant while in maḍi, but on this occasion the shaman confused it with a vessel of water drawn previously by his wife. The fact that the shaman was thus not ritually pure angered his chauḍi, who then punished him for his mistake.

In another instance, a Havik shaman was reported to have been involuntarily possessed by his chauḍi, who protested that she had been made muṭṭucheṭṭu by an Untouchable who came too close to her. She (the stone in which she resided when not possessing the shaman) was purified with panchāmrita; the shaman with panchagavya.

Involuntary nonshamanistic possession is fairly common among Sudras and Brahmin women, less so among Sudra males, and extremely infrequent among adult Brahmin males. Ordinarily, these supernaturals speak through the person being possessed. Sometimes it is difficult to determine if the possessing agent is a devva or a dēvate. It is commonly believed that a devva will attempt to pass for a dēvate in order to obtain a puja (i.e., a meal in the form of the sacrifice of an animal). One test that a shaman can use to determine whether a woman is being possessed by a dēvate or a devva is to ask her to bathe, then to throw a ritually pure substance over which mantras have been said, such as vibhūti or tīrtha, over her. If the supernatural is a dēvate, it is believed that it will obey and the woman will go into a state of trance; if it is a devva, the woman will be so pure that it cannot "come on" her; i.e., it will be repelled by the mantras contained in a field of purity.

Naḳedness, Purity, and the Supernatural

Another example of the relationship between purity and the supernatural involves nakedness. In everyday life no one except children ever appears nude. Clothes are changed semi-publicly, generally during the bath, and in such a way that the genitals are never exposed. Clothing is worn while bathing, while defecating, and while sleeping. Husband and wife do not see each other nude.

The problem of whether or not a nude adult is also ritually pure is too hypothetical for informants to discuss directly. (I have created great confusion and hilarity by asking this question.) Indirect evidence indicates, however, that a nude individual is *ipso facto* in maḍi.

There are religious circumstances under which Sudras may appear nude. Some dēvates who reside in temples grant boons when vows are taken promising them an offering while the devotee is naked. I have only seen small Sudra children presented while nude to Mariamma, but a deity in one temple in the region is noted for her desire for this type of puja. It is reported that at the yearly fair (jātre) honoring this female deity sometimes several dozen Sudras will fulfill their vows to her by bathing in the stream below the hill on which her temple is situated, and then run, while wet and naked, to the temple, and there prostrate themselves before this deity. I would assume that the lack of Brahmin participation in this custom is congruent to their ability to attain a high state of purity, vis-à-vis the gods, while wearing clothes.

In another example, a *mantravādi,* a type of Brahmin religious specialist (but most often not Havik) given to working with aspects of religion that border on the immoral, attempted to gain control over Mahākāli. Mahākāli is, strictly speaking, a dēvaru, but in function resembles much more closely a dēvate. Dēvates, in their vicious aspect, can be made impotent in the face of purity, whereas in their benevolent aspects, they are honored by purity and made malevolent by impurity. To accomplish his purpose, the mantravādi while naked recited parts of the Yajur Vēda in the cremation grounds at exactly midnight on a new moon night. This ritual was fraught with danger, for Mahākāli was being forced to submit, to do something she did not wish to do, and was seeking to harm the mantravādi. Even a single mistake in the ritual would afford her such an opportunity. In order to protect himself, the mantravādi needed to be in the maximum obtainable state of ritual purity, which was in part accomplished by removing his clothes.

Among Haviks, as I have already said, a nude child does not cause a Brahmin to lose maḍi. Also, a naked child will not defile a dēvaru. I once commented on an image in a Havik's dēvaru mane, and my host asked if I would like a better view of it. When I said I would, he pointed out that as he was not in maḍi, he could not get it for me. He then slipped the dress from his prepuberty sister, who went to the dēvaru mane, removed the image, and brought it close to me for my inspection.

In stories of spirit attacks told by Haviks, there are two frequently expressed motifs. The first involves stories of Havik women, who, when possessed by devvas, "take off all of their clothes and run into the street" in an effort to rid themselves of the spirit. I have never witnessed one of these scenes, unfortunately. Another type of story involves Havik males who are out alone at night, usually on a new or full moon day, and pass a place thought to be inhabited by a dangerous dēvate (usually a bhūta). In these stories the male will characteristically see the bhūta, become frightened and realize that he is about to be "struck" by it. One way in which he may handle this situation is to remove every stitch of clothing and run home as quickly as possible. By doing this, "the man appears to the bhūta as a bhūta ordinarily appears to a man." The bhūta, when faced with purity, becomes impotent.

Finally, although mantras themselves can act as spirit repellents, they are effective only when contained within a sphere of ritual purity. Male adult Brahmins know mantras, therefore do not need to have them written down to be carried about on their persons. It would appear that adult Brahmin males are ordinarily in a state of sufficient purity to have their knowledge of mantras act to repel devvas. Dēvates are a different matter. If a powerful dēvate, such as a bhūta, is attempting to harm a Brahmin the protective mantras that he needs can be made effective only if he is in maḍi—hence, as he has no time to attain this state by the usual purificatory methods, he may immediately attain it by quickly removing his clothes.

Purity Aspects of the Caste Hierarchy

In this area of South India, it is difficult hierarchically to rank non-Brahmin castes according to the amount of pollution taboos they observe. I have already discussed the position of Lingayats, close to the top of the hierarchy, but who reject most aspects of the purity-impurity complex to which Haviks are so strongly attached.[28] Untouchable castes and Sudra castes historically can be distinguished from each other by their eating habits; in the past Untouchables ate beef and domestic pork, which they have now given up, whereas Sudras ate, and now eat, only eggs, fish, chickens, goats, and sheep. Except for the fact that Untouchables secretly eat monkeys, and despite the fact that meats are graded according to the amount of defilement caused by their consumption, all non-vegetarian castes in the area now eat approximately the same meats.

Some Sudras or Untouchables, as individuals, are vegetarians or eschew the less pure meats, but these are for idiosyncratic reasons, not because they are forbidden by caste rules. One member of a non-Brahmin household may refuse a non-vegetarian dish relished by all other members of his household.

If another example is used, menstruation taboos, my observations would indicate that Untouchables in general more strictly observe them than do members of many of the Sudra castes. This may be related to the fact that Untouchables are intimately linked to Brahmins through a system of indentureship, and thus have greater knowledge of and contact with Brahmanical customs and values than do Sudras, and because Untouchables are, in the present scene, the castes which most militantly strive for upward social mobility. Again, non-Brahmin castes are not distinguished by the amount of sūtaka they observe. (Lingayats do not utilize the concept.) For Sudra and Untouchable castes, sūtaka involves only a small group of patrilineally related kinsmen, and the length of sūtaka observation is set for them by a Brahmin acting as an astrologer, and varies according to the position of the stars at the time of the death.

---

[28] In fact, Lingayats are informally indoctrinated into parts of this complex, especially as they relate to the "lower levels" of religion—dēvates and devvas. For example, the following instance took place at the Gāma habba, a Sudra festival to the second most powerful village deity, in which goats are sacrificed. The only Brahmins that give offerings, and these vegetarian, are those who own land near the site of the stone in which Gāma resides throughout the year. A Lingayat family also gives a vegetarian offering for this festival. These high-caste offerings are given during the early part of the puja, before the animal sacrifice. At one yearly feast, the following interaction was observed: one rather liberal Brahmin omitted giving his customary offering because he had āme—his parallel cousin's wife had given birth. He and his wife, however, watched part of the ceremony. Gāma was in a temporary enclosure, into which only Sudra priests and members of higher castes were admitted. The Brahmin's wife was asked by a Sudra priest if she wanted to see Gāma, who was then residing in several brass figures inside of the enclosure. After she was taken in, the Lingayat discovered that she had āme and became quite agitated, saying to the Brahmin, in a frightened voice, "Then your wife has āme! But look, she has entered the enclosure. They (such people) should not go inside." The Brahmin replied, "It is not sūtaka—people who have āme can go into the temple—it is just that they cannot do puja. It does not matter here if the woman goes inside." The Lingayat replied, "This god is very powerful. If there is the slightest mistake the goat given in the name of the village (*haṭṭara kuri*) cannot be killed in one stroke (that is, cannot be decapitated with one stroke of the sickle). If the haṭṭara kuri is not killed in one stroke then it is definite that there will be trouble for the village."

Higher Sudra castes are thought of as more pure (shuddha) than lower Sudra castes, which in turn are thought of as more pure than Untouchable castes, by members of the local community. Statements made by Brahmins and by higher-caste Sudras imply that castes are arranged into a hierarchy according to the degree to which they adhere to "Hindu" standards of purity and avoid behavior regarded as impure. Although this is by no means always true, it nevertheless forms one rationale for justifying rules regarding social distance between castes—for example, the amount of defilement that results from physical contact with a member of another caste, or, what parts of a Brahmin's house a member of another caste will be permitted to enter.

Castes are difficult to rank even by occupational criteria. Although Goldsmiths are placed above Blacksmiths because it is said gold is more pure than iron, several Sudra castes which follow the same occupation—paddy farming—are ranked differently, in part according to the type of ceremonial relations they have with Haviks. Also, castes can be differentially ranked by occupation depending upon which side of the coin is viewed. Barbers are low Sudras "because they follow a dirty occupation" whereas Maḍivaḷas, who wash dirty clothes (even menstrual clothes), are high Sudras "because they make things clean." (This contrasts to some other parts of India, where Barbers outrank Washermen.)

For this region of South India, it is safe to generalize that castes are ranked into a hierarchy by the type of ritual interaction they have with other castes—especially with Havik Brahmins—rather than by the relative degree to which they approximate Brahmanical standards of purity. Although an "interactional theory" seems most satisfactory in explaining the details of this caste hierarchy, an "attributional theory" nevertheless seems to form the basic belief structure within which these details are worked out.

Purity and Control Over the Supernaturals

Supernaturals are like humans in that they may be kind, helpful, concerned, obliging, rational, and good-natured; or, they may be mean, petty, jealous, irrational, and easily angered. However, some supernaturals are consistently either benevolent or malevolent, and this is related to concepts of ritual purity. Dēvarus and dēvates have the capacity to help or to harm man, but their benevolent aspects are activated when they are ritually pure, and their malevolent aspects when they are ritually impure.

Dēvarus, I have pointed out, are nearly always maintained in a high state of purity. They are generally worshipped by Brahmins, but only when in a state of ritual purity. If they are ritually defiled, it is generally by a minor and quickly rectified impurity, for which they are almost never strongly malevolent. But when they are benevolent, they tend to use their power for otherworldly (merit) or general (keeping the world in good order) ends rather than for this worldly (disease-protection) or specific (granting individual boons) ends.

Devvas, at the other extreme, cannot become pure and are only malevolent. As they cannot attain a pure state, they cannot be utilized by men to help attain human ends. Devvas, like Untouchables, are innately, and thus legitimately, impure—neither can attain a pure state of being. They are always malevolent in intent, but, again like Untouchables, are repelled by a pure field; devvas cannot enter the field of purity surrounding mantras in a yantra, or into a field of purity surrounding a Brahmin made pure by his knowledge of mantras, as an Untouchable cannot enter a field of purity (a temple) surrounding a dēvaru or surrounding an initiated Brahmin. Devvas are justifiably dissatisfied—though impure, they, like other supernaturals, need food and shelter, but they are never voluntarily fed by man nor given a residence. Their only means of obtaining their desires is to harm men, and man's main protection from devvas is through mantras which are active only within a field of ritual purity.

Dēvates, only the most powerful of which are specially secluded in a temple, and even then they may be periodically brought out to be worshipped and fed nonvegetarian food by non-Brahmins, do not exist in as pure a field of purity as do dēvarus, nor are they so consistently protected from impurity. They thus have more opportunity to express the malevolent side of their personalities. Fields of purity exist like islands in a sea of impurity—they must be artificially created and specially maintained. But the walls surrounding the dēvates' islands are neither as strong nor as tall as those surrounding a dēvaru's. If dēvates are maintained in a field of purity, they can be quite useful to man—particularly in granting a worshipper's (i.e., the person who feeds them) desires, such as preventing or curing illness, either by desisting from causing trouble, or by preventing devvas and less powerful dēvates from harming an actual or potential worshipper (i.e., someone who takes a vow to feed them if his request is granted). But impurity activates their malevolent aspects. However, like devvas, dēvates in their malevolent aspects cannot enter fields of purity, but as they are more powerful than devvas, the fields of purity and the mantras contained therein have to be more pure and powerful to repel a dēvate than a devva. The more pure a supernatural, the more benevolent it will be; the more impure, the more likelihood that it will attempt to harm a human. The less pure an individual is, the more likelihood that a malevolent supernatural can harm him; the more pure he is the more capable he is of resisting harm from a supernatural.

The wall of purity keeps out less powerful impure beings, but can be broken down by impure beings of superior force. If this happens, the field of purity no longer exists. It then becomes a field of pollution from which a dēvaru or dēvate must depart until it and its abode are ritually purified. Devvas, like Untouchables, are always impure. An Untouchable must remain completely outside the field of purity (e.g., a temple) surrounding a dēvaru or most dēvates, whereas a Sudra or a Brahmin who is not in a specially purified state may enter the periphery of this field. The inner port of the temple can be entered only by a Brahmin in a state of full ritual purity. No matter how many such purificatory rituals an Untouchable goes through, he may never become sufficiently pure to approach a dēvaru or most dēvates. In large temples to dēvarus, dēvates guard the entrances to prevent devvas from coming in.

Dēvates can be of potential benefit to men. There appear to be two patterns by which man may interact with dēvates to receive the latters' help. Customarily, a dēvate is fed, bathed, honored, and kept within a field of purity, and in return helps those who have helped it. In short, there exists a symbiotic contractual relationship between man and deity. When man fails to fulfill his end of the bargain, the dēvate causes him harm. In the second pattern the dēvate is forced to use its power to benefit a human who becomes its master. By using the correct mantras a knowledgeable man can command a dēvate and force it to submit to his will. This is of course dangerous, as any ritual mistake will break the spell and unleash the infuriated deity. To protect himself from such an eventuality, the human agent will make himself ritually pure, by, for example, being nude. But, when gaining control over the dēvate, the mantra-user attempts ritually to defile the dēvate, e.g., by forcing it to come into an area of impurity such as the cremation grounds on a new moon night. I suggest that this act of intentionally causing the dēvate to enter a ritually impure arena is related to the fact that those who attempt to force a supernatural to bend to their desires do so in order to attain selfish, antisocial, and immoral ends (self-aggrandizement, wealth, and the ability to harm others supernaturally), and thus the collaboration of a ritually pure and thus benevolent being is not desired; instead, the malevolent aspects of the dēvate, those which are activated by impurity, are those over which control is being obtained.

Conclusions

I should now like to discuss tentatively some of the relationships between caste, pollution, and religion as they relate to the underlying principles which give them unity. I am acutely aware that some of these "underlying principles" are not in accord with all of the ethnographic facts; but these discrepancies do not necessarily reflect on the validity of these principles—it is probable that these discrepancies may be explained on other levels of analysis. I am also aware that the ideas I formulate here are only partial and imperfect facets of a larger system which at this point I have not been able to work out with any degree of elaboration or integration.

Purity is a relative, not an absolute, state. Gods are more pure than deities. Vegetarian deities are more pure than nonvegetarian deities. Gods are more pure than Brahmins, and Brahmins are more pure than Sudras. Some Sudra castes are more pure than others, but all Sudras are pure relative to Untouchables. Within a caste, any member may be more or less pure than others, but from the standpoint of members of other castes all members of one caste are equal in ritual status. There are, then, many degrees of purity.

Purity is the ritual state of a being when it is not impure (the term "being" will be used to include both men and supernaturals). But purity and impurity are not simply opposites. Only some beings can become pure; devvas and Untouchables cannot; for them, impurity is an absolute, permanent, and inherent ritual status. There is no contrasting category of "inherently pure"; instead, beings have the inherent capability of becoming more or less pure; but purity is a temporary state. Or, phrased another way, although all beings are impure unless ritually purified, and only some beings (e.g., Brahmins and dēvarus) have within their nature the ability to achieve the higher degrees of ritual purity. An Untouchable cannot become a Brahmin, but a Brahmin can become an Untouchable. Within a caste purity is a state to be attained, achieved, worked for.

Pollution can flow, directly or through a conductor, from one being to another. Purity cannot flow—it is an impermanent state which can be lost but not transferred. A Brahmin cannot transmit his high state of purity to a kinsman, but he can transmit strong impurity. An impure being cannot be purified by contact with a pure being, but a pure being is defiled by contact with an impure being.

In relation to ritual pollution, members of lower castes perform three distinct types of services for Brahmins:

(1) Those which protect Brahmins from impurities. Other castes plow the fields (which results in the inadvertent taking of life), give animal sacrifices to certain blood-demanding deities, sweep the public roads and dispose of the Brahmin's dead cattle.

Within this society, all of these services must be performed by someone, but they bring one degree or another of impurity to the performer. By protecting the purity of Brahmins, these castes divert its flow upon themselves; thus, they cannot become as pure as those to whom these impurities do not flow.

(2) Those which cause Brahmins to become ritually impure. For instance, a Brahmin must ritually purify himself after using the services of a Barber, or after having worked alongside of his Untouchable servant in his arecanut garden.

(3) Those which do not affect the state of a Brahmin's purity. A Washerman may play a prominent role in a Brahmin wedding ceremony, or a Divaru may drive a Brahmin wedding cart, or an Okkaliga may work inside of a Brahmin's house. But in order for these castes to perform these duties without causing ritual defilement to the Brahmin, they must occupy an intermediate position in the ritual purity scale. In order to attain such a position, they too must be protected from the more severe sources of ritual impurity by other castes who perform the most ritually defiling jobs, such as sweeping the public roads, removing dead cattle for pay, or working with leather.

Dēvarus and Brahmins are legitimately high and pure, but the dēvaru hierarchy begins above the Brahmin hierarchy, at a point where the highest state of purity of the latter overlaps the lesser state of purity of the former. At the other end of this natural-supernatural continuum, devvas and Untouchables appear to occupy approximately equivalent positions of absolute lowness and impurity, both of which are legitimate. Dēvates and Sudras, which exist between these extremes, present more complexities. Sudras are never as pure as Brahmins, as dēvates are never as pure as dēvarus. But there is a wide range of degrees of purity-impurity within both categories. The highest aspects of most dēvates are more pure than are the highest of some Brahmins. Other aspects of these dēvates are too impure to be worshipped by Brahmins.

The higher states of purity, then, are dependent upon a division of labor among castes which are arranged according to a hierarchy of purity. Purity does not come automatically—it cannot be attained solely by a man's own efforts. For a Brahmin to remain sufficiently ritually pure so that through his own efforts (i.e., by undergoing a ceremony of ritual cleansing) he can attain his maximum purity potential, he needs the assistance of other castes.

The relationship of men to gods is slightly different from that of caste to caste. Dēvarus need to be protected from sources of impurity. This is in part done by secluding them—by building a temple around them into which lower castes are not allowed, or keeping them in a shrine in the most pure part of a Brahmin's house. Dēvarus also must be fed, their temples must be swept, and their bodies and feet must be bathed. By performing these services, the Brahmin absorbs the god's impurities. In this instance the priest directly removes the pollution from the god, rather than merely preventing the flow of impurities to it. In order to perform these functions at all, the Brahmin must be in his highest obtainable state of ritual purity, in order not to cause rather than remove pollution. It would seem that the lowest state of purity of a god is slightly higher than the highest state of purity of a Brahmin. By performing these acts, Brahmins are prevented from attaining a higher state of purity than the lowest state of purity of the god. This society is organized around the task of caring for its gods, and a division of labor among the castes is necessary to attain this end.

Deities must also be fed, but many of them are nonvegetarian. To satisfy the desires of dēvates, the services of lower-caste priests who can make the meat offerings are needed. If Brahmins were to do this, they would become too ritually impure then directly to worship the gods (dēvarus). In order to cater to the desires of both dēvarus and dēvates, priests belonging to both Brahmin and non-Brahmin castes are needed. This hierarchy of relative purity is basic to the system of caste stratification and is fundamental to the system whereby men and supernaturals are brought into a relationship.

For a lower being to prevent impurity from flowing to a higher, the relative purity difference must not be too great—otherwise pollution will flow from the lower to the higher. The relationships between castes requires that an occupational differentiation be maintained so that other castes may be more pure, so that these in turn can help still another caste to attain sufficient purity to purify the gods. The lowest castes cannot attain purity as they have no one to assist them—they only indirectly assist others.

The fact that in this part of South India there are three states of ritual purity, that castes are grouped into a three-class system, and that there are three grades of supernaturals, is more than coincidental. Brahmins are potentially pure—they can attain the highest state (unless compared with gods) of purity (maḍi). Untouchables remain in an absolute state of impurity (muṭṭucheṭṭu). Sudras correspond to mailigē, a state that is pure relative to Untouchables, neutral towards Brahmins in mailigē and impure to Brahmins in maḍi. Dēvarus can attain a state of absolute purity, devvas cannot be otherwise than impure, and dēvates fluctuate between the two extremes, in much the same manner as do the hierarchically graded Sudra castes.

References Cited

Government of Bombay

1883 Gazetteer of the Bombay Presidency, Vol. XV, Parts I and II (Kanara). Bombay: Government Central Press.

Harper, Edward B.

1959a Two systems of economic exchange in village India. American Anthropologist, 61:760–778.

1959b A Hindu village pantheon. Southwestern Journal of Anthropology, 15:227–234.

In press 'Slavery' and indentureship in South India. In: *Social Mobility in the Caste System in India,* ed. by James Silverberg.

Marriott, McKim

1959 Interactional and attributional theories of caste ranking. Man in India, 39: 92–107.

Srinivas, M. N.

1952 *Religion and Society Among the Coorgs of South India.* Oxford: at the Clarendon Press.

Stevenson, H. N. C.

1954 Status evaluation in the Hindu caste system. The Journal of the Royal Anthropological Institute, 84:45–65.

Stevenson, Mrs. Sinclair

1920 *The Rites of the Twice-Born.* Oxford University Press.

Index

of supernaturals associated with different degrees of pollution, 33, 122, 183-89; related to *vas-dos,* 118; leads to supernatural retaliation, 124, 130, 159, 183-96 *passim;* saffron, limes, and cow dung as purifying agents, 125; death, 125, 161-67; menstrual, 125, 137, 158-61, 191; birth, 125, 167-69; opposition between purity and pollution as a theme in all Sinhalese rituals, 135; related to caste hierarchy, 151-52; the three states of purity and impurity, 152-55; purity of milk, 156; from saliva, 156, 180-81; from feces of various animals, 169, 172n; beating with leather sandals as a source of ritual defilement, 170; does not result from performing impure activities for oneself, 170; sexual, 170; status of an unmarried postpuberty girl, 170; through illegitimacy, 172; conductors of, 172-73, 194; from an Untouchable, 173; differences in purity of right and left sides, 179; among Lingayats, 181; wife eats from husband's leaf, 181-82; impurity of cow dung, 182-83; impurity overcomes purity, 183; defilement of gods and deities, 183-85; legitimate and illegitimate impurity, 183, 195; purity repells spirits but honors deities and gods, 186-88; "fields of purity," 186-88, 192-93; nakedness equated with purity, 189-91; benevolent and malevolent aspects of gods and deities related to, 192-94; purity as an artificial state, 194; related to caste and religion, 194-96; lower castes prevent impurity from flowing to Brahmins, 195; purity of Brahmins compared to gods, 195-96. *See also Āme;* Caste; Caste hierarchy; Cow dung; Diseases theories, supernatural; Feces; *Maḍi; Mailigē; Muṭṭucheṭṭu;* Orthopraxy; *Panchagavaya; Panchāmrita; Sūtaka;* Temple entry; Untouchability

Possession, spirit: monk possessed by a goblin, 40-41; mentioned, 128, 189

Pragmatic complex. *See* Transcendental complex

Precepts in Buddhism: for laymen and monks, 29; hierarchy of, 29

Predestination. *See Karma*

Priests: compared to shaman, 8-9, 53-68 *passim;* in Buddhism, 33; duties of and services rendered by, 54-55; in *jajmani* system, 55, 62-63; distinguished from other types of religious practitioners, 56; how recruited, 60; as religious technicians, 60, 66; as maintainers of traditional religion and as social innovators, 62-66; as competitors to shamans, 64; in conflict with *purohits,* 64; drawn from many castes, 104; two types in Buddhism, 117. *See also Kapurāla;* Shaman

Pūjava. See Offerings

Purity. *See* Pollution, ritual

Religion: differences in, related to caste affiliation, 9-11, 177-96; examined as an internally consistent set of beliefs and symbols, 115-39 *passim. See also* Buddhism; Hinduism; Pollution, ritual; Priests; Salvation

Respect-pollution, 17, 158, 181-83

Ritual pollution. *See* Pollution, ritual

Rituals, centered around basic contradictions, 116-17

Sacred, opposed to profane, 23, 28, 36, 39

Salvation: unobtainability of in Buddhism, 14, 25-26, 46-47; why desired, 23; how obtained, 24-26, 31, 129; through meditation, 26, 30, 33, 72; venerated but seldom pursued ideal, 27; contrasted with merit-making to obtain different ends, 29-31, 41; obtained in stages ("meaning-raising"), 31, 35-36; bypassed for immediate consolation, 32, 129; *mokṣha* not a serious goal for Hindu peasants, 71, 79. *See also Karma;* Merit

Sanskritization, cultural factors against, 64

Sathyanarayana puja, 184

Shaman: compared to priests, 8-9; types of problems requiring services of, 57; distinguished from *pujaris,* 58; power over clients, 59-60; how recruited, 61; as maintainers and innovators of religion, 62-66; possessed only when ritually pure, 189. *See Kapurāla;* Priests

Social nuclei, 92

Spirit possession. *See* Possession, spirit

Spirit repellents, 186-88, 190-91

Steed, Gitel P., 72

String. *See Nula*

Supernaturals: hierarchy of in Buddhism, 35; hierarchy of in Hinduism, 183-96

Sūtaka: kinds of, 162; groupings among agnatic kinsmen, 162-63; for children, 164; in adoption, 164; breaking of agnatic ties, 165-66; for married women, 166-67; not observed for outcaste persons, 167; to gods, 183-84

Temple entry: prohibitions against, 118, 151, 179-80; menstruating women allowed, 137

Temple estate and state system in Ceylon, 42-46

Temples in Ceylon, castes attached to, 44

Transcendental and pragmatic complexes, 10-20. *See also* Great and little traditions

Universalization and parochialization, 11

Untouchability, 151, 173, 179-81

Van Gennep, Arnold, 86-87

Weber, Max, 22, 75

Widows: outcaste if pregnant, 171; categories of, 176

Wrestling, as expression of intervillage rivalry, 106-7

Yakkura. See Devaya-yakkuva

Yalman, Nur, article discussed, 6, 11, 12-15

Yantras. See Spirit repellents